THE
DEBATE
ON THE
AMERICAN
REVOLUTION
1761-1783

Also by Max Beloff

*BRITAIN'S LIBERAL EMPIRE, 1897–1921
    (Volume 1 of IMPERIAL SUNSET)

*DREAM OF COMMONWEALTH, 1921–1942
    (Volume 2 of IMPERIAL SUNSET)

PUBLIC ORDER AND POPULAR DISTURBANCES, 1660–1714

THE FOREIGN POLICY OF SOVIET RUSSIA
    (2 Volumes)

THOMAS JEFFERSON AND AMERICAN DEMOCRACY

SOVIET POLICY IN THE FAR EAST, 1944–1951

THE AGE OF ABSOLUTISM, 1660–1815

FOREIGN POLICY AND THE DEMOCRATIC PROCESS

EUROPE AND THE EUROPEANS

THE GREAT POWERS

THE AMERICAN FEDERAL GOVERNMENT

NEW DIMENSIONS IN FOREIGN POLICY

THE UNITED STATES AND THE UNITY OF EUROPE

THE BALANCE OF POWER

THE FUTURE OF BRITISH FOREIGN POLICY

THE INTELLECTUAL IN POLITICS

THE GOVERNMENT OF THE UNITED KINGDOM
    (*with G.R. Peele*)

WARS AND WELFARE, 1914–1945

Edited by Max Beloff

THE FEDERALIST

MANKIND AND HIS STORY

ON THE TRACK OF TYRANNY

L'EUROPE DU XIXe ET DU XXe SIECLE
    (*with P. Renovin, F. Schnabel and F. Valsecchi*)

AMERICAN POLITICAL INSTITUTIONS IN THE 1970's
    (*with V. Vale*)

*Also published by Sheridan House

THE
DEBATE
ON THE
AMERICAN
REVOLUTION
1761-1783

Edited by
MAX BELOFF

Max Beloff (Lord Beloff) is emeritus professor
of government and public administration in the
University of Oxford (England)

Third Edition

SHERIDAN HOUSE

First published 1949
Second Edition 1960
Third Edition 1989

© 1960 A. and C. Black Limited

© 1989 by Sheridan House Inc.

This edition first published 1989
by Sheridan House Inc., Dobbs Ferry, NY 10522

Library of Congress Cataloging-in-Publication Data
The Debate on the American Revolution, 1761-1783 / edited by Max
    Beloff.—3rd ed.
        p. cm.
    Bibliography: p.
    Includes index.
    ISBN 0-911378-94-4
    1. United States—Politics and government—Revolution, 1775-1783—
Sources. 2. United States—Politics and government—Colonial
period, ca. 1600-1775—Sources. I. Beloff, Max, 1913–
E211.D33   1989
973.3—dc20   89-10301
                                                         CIP

Cover design and illustration by Jeremiah B. Lighter

Printed in the United States of America

PREFACE

IT is sometimes said that political theory—the general principles by which men claim to act in public affairs—is a diminishing and perhaps out-dated element in "political science". Yet this is clearly not the case since we have seen the vast outpouring of literature sparked off by the anniversary years of the American Revolution and the founding of the constitutional system of the American nation. To understand the course of events and the attitudes of the different leaders and their followers to the problems of the time, we clearly need to enter into their minds and to see what it was they thought they were doing and what they thought their justification to be. Since the documents of the time have still to be quoted in the courts and in political debate, it is obviously important to know what the authors understood them to mean.

The phenomenon is not confined to the United States. Recent decades have seen major changes on the world scene one of which has been the emergence of new nations and new states previously part of European empires, and their struggles to achieve independence and to establish new institutions have also been accompanied by debates arising from conflicting political principles. In even more recent years, European peoples whose independence has been absorbed within the Soviet Empire or limited by its control over them have proclaimed through unofficial leaders a renewed claim to national self-determination.

The final period of the history of the American colonies as parts of a wider British Empire has thus a double significance. Its understanding is essential to appreciating why the Americans, once independent, found particular models of government appealing and hit upon a federal structure with both traditional and innovative aspects. It also represents the classic instance of the parting of the ways between peoples hitherto under a single sovereign and closely linked together through economic, religious and cultural ties. Because the argument from both the British and the American side was carried on by men with similar education and a common cultural heritage, they could address each other and counter each other's arguments in a more sustained and rigorous fashion than has been possible where the colonial power and the indigenous people have been separated by a wide racial, religious and linguistic gulf.

Much political theory is of course to be found in formal treatises and both British statesmen and some of the American leaders were familiar with the classical writers and with the major English contribution to the subject such as the writings of Hobbes and Locke. The literature which forms the basis of the present volume of extracts is of a different kind. It consists of ephemera, documents thrown up by the political conflict itself and often soon superseded as events took a new turn. Two things made this possible. In the United Kingdom Parliament and in the colonial assemblies, possibilities existed for public explanations and justifications of what was on foot. In some notable instances the courts of law—the product of a single common law tradition—also provided opportunities for arguments looking to first principles. The other possibility was provided by the development of newspapers, and above all the common recourse to pamphleteering.

Some of the speeches and pamphlets are banal in expression and merely set out the position of the speaker or writer on the issues that he was presenting; in some cases the writers rose to height of eloquence which has given them a permanent place in the history of thought. A volume which gives a place to Burke and Jefferson is bound to offer enrichment to the mind. One must not pretend that nothing is lost by it being possible only to include extracts from much longer speeches or other writings. It was a more slow moving era than our own, and people took their time over making their case. But the extracts should stand on their own and act as an inducement to students to penetrate further into the works from which they are drawn. Where parliamentary speeches are concerned it should perhaps be pointed out that we are before the days of modern verbatim reporting—indeed in Britain, parliament was not supposed to be reported at all. But the matter is not of the first importance from the present point of view. We may take it that the speeches as reported did represent what was in the minds of the speakers, and that it was the published version which was likely to have the greatest effect. It should perhaps not need stressing that there were physical obstacles to a debate spanning the Atlantic in the days before the steamship, the cable or radio. What was said in London today was not known in Boston tomorrow.

This fact matters less than might at first sight appear to be the case. By the time we get to the Declaration of Independence the debate is indeed one between Britain and the Colonies, even though there were loyalists in the colonies and those in Britain who continued to sympathize with the Americans. But in 1761 when the strains upon the imperial structure were first felt, no one saw the matter in that light. It was a question of trying to find solutions to the financial and administrative problems that had arisen, and of differences within the British ruling elite as to the tactics by which an American contribution to the needs of empire could be made. The nature and degree of rigour to be exerted was thus a matter of dispute within the English ruling elite itself, and as the Americans resisted the demands of the imperial government, the debate became one as to the point at which coercion became essential.

In the colonies themselves there were two debates; first between the colonial governors, the representatives of the imperial authority, and the spokesmen for the colonial elites; and second between divergent groups within the colonial elites as to the point at which to abandon attempts to find a solution through a recasting of the imperial relationship and those who increasingly saw no alternative to total independence.

The development of these different debates and the way in which they generated the particular documents here presented is dealt with at length in the introduction. The important thing to note before embarking upon the volume is that in the course of the arguments, many perhaps most of the main issues in political theory come to the fore—why do men obey government? what are the limitations to such obedience? can sovereignty be divided? is self-determination compatible with a wider allegiance? These are questions we are still asking.

London, March 1989   MAX BELOFF

TABLE OF CONTENTS

PAGE

INTRODUCTION

PART I

IN the second half of the eighteenth century, the development of political thought in Britain was profoundly affected by the two great political revolutions of the age—the American and the French. These two movements which had many points of contact were accompanied, in the whole of the western world, by the most prolonged and far-reaching examination of the basis of society and government which had been attempted since the age of Plato and Aristotle. Many of the leading figures in this intellectual adventure were so placed as to be affected by both the American and the French Revolutions. Some who had been united by the former were separated by the latter—like John Adams and Thomas Jefferson. For some, the development seemed a straightforward one—the Thomas Paine of *Common Sense* is also the Thomas Paine of the *Rights of Man*. In other cases the effect was a more striking one—the Burke of the speeches on conciliation with America is also the Burke of *Reflections on the French Revolution*.

In the present volume we are concerned only with the impact of the former of these great events—we are dealing only with the impact upon political ideas of the troubles between Great Britain and her American colonies, which, within less than two decades after their first real rumblings at the close of the Seven Years' War, were to lead to the establishment as an independent power of the separate American nation of the United States. Since this was the most striking outcome of the struggle, it has been treated for the most part as the prelude to American history rather than as a part of the history of Great Britain. Yet this approach tends to falsify the picture in some material respects. The people concerned were all born, and many of them died, as subjects of the King of Great Britain. The problem, as it originally presented itself was not the problem of laying the foundations of a new state—that part of the American story lies beyond our horizon—but the problem of imperial organization, of seeking for the existing British Empire a constitutional framework more in accordance with the political realities of the age.[1] And it was in this context that the more general problems of political obligation and the nature of political rights were discussed. Furthermore, however inevitable the movement towards American independence may look in the light of later events, independence was not the result generally expected, far less generally desired, throughout most of the period with which we are concerned. This applies to the leading figures on both sides of the Atlantic. Many Americans remained attached to the British connection even after independence had become a fact, and chose exile rather than submission to the new order of things. Many people in England, certainly in the early part of the period, sympathized with a good deal of the colonists' case, and the debate had important repercussions in home politics.

---

[1] This point is admirably brought out in R. G. Adams, *Political Ideas of the American Revolution* (Durham, N.C., 1922). Cf., C. H. McIlwain, *The American Revolution: A Constitutional Interpretation* (New York, 1924), and the criticism of this book by R. L. Schuyler in *Parliament and the British Empire* (Colombia, U.P., 1929). Cf. V. T. Harlow, *The Founding of the Second British Empire*, Vol. I (London, 1952).

For this reason any study of the political thought of the period, just as any study of the period generally, must concern itself both with Great Britain and with the colonies. The documents and extracts in this book are therefore drawn from the works of writers and speakers on both sides of the ocean.

In conformity with the general plan and object of the present series, the aim has been to present, not those documents which are historically of most importance, but rather those which best help to illustrate the general assumptions about politics underlying the thinking of the two sides in the conflict.[1] For the same reason we cannot enter here into the involved history of the dispute between Great Britain, or attempt to indicate its many contributory factors, economic and psychological.[2] Nevertheless it must be emphasized that the political thinkers of the period were not concerned with the development of abstract questions about the nature of the state but with the direct issues confronting them, and that the shifting of the grounds of the discussion as it proceeded was primarily a response to the successive situations produced by action on either side. For the same reason the arguments on both sides kept well within the institutional framework of the English-speaking world with its already long-standing traditions of representation and of the rule of law. There are no ventures in the direction of the absolutism still powerful in continental Europe nor into utopian imaginings of social upheaval. For all

[1] The major documents are usefully assembled in S. E. Morison (ed.), *Sources and Documents illustrating the American Revolution* (2nd ed., 1929). Cf. D. Douglas, *English Historical Documents*, Vol. IX, ed. Merrill Jensen (1955); Vol. X, ed. D. B. Horn and M. Ransome (1957).

[2] The most useful historical studies of the period are C. H. Van Tyne, *The Causes of the War of Independence* (1922), John C. Miller, *Origins of the American Revolution* (1945), and J. R. Alden, *The American Revolution, 1775-1783* (1954).

3

the appeals to Nature—as omnipresent in the eighteenth century as appeals to the Divine Word in the previous one, the thinkers with whom we are concerned were all hard-headed, practical, earthbound men. Nearly all had experience of practical affairs—there was hardly a single closet philosopher among them.

But it would be a mistake to proceed to argue from this fact that the discussions of the period lack interest for the student of political theory, and still more foolish to dismiss the political argument as a mere superstructure concealing some supposedly more fundamental economic motives for the actions of groups or classes. The modern tendency to denigrate the study of political theory and political institutions has not spared the age of the American Revolution. But to give way to it, here or elsewhere, is to be guilty of serious intellectual confusion. Certainly the incompatibility of the economic interests of certain elements in the colonies with those of certain groups in Britain was an important source of friction—although less important we may think than the growing sense of a separate American nationality and of a consequent impatience with all signs of discrimination. But these problems were probably no greater than those which arose later in British imperial history and which received a different and peaceful, if not necessarily permanent, solution, in the transformation of the Empire into the modern British Commonwealth of Nations. What was lacking in the eighteenth century was the ability to conceive a solution for these problems within the accepted limits of British political thought.

Since the heart of the historical problem of the American Revolution is thus a matter of political

4

thought, it can hardly be said that the study of the general assumptions about politics held by the participants in the conflict is irrelevant to the main issue. Indeed, for the non-historian it may well be argued that this is by far the most important and interesting aspect of the whole period. For although the precise circumstances have not repeated themselves, and cannot repeat themselves, the central argument must in one form or another continue to confront statesmen as long as the problem of linking together free peoples, of maintaining unity in diversity, remains an actual one. Not only in the imperial sphere, but as time goes on, in the international sphere as well, this problem is likely to be more rather than less important. And since in both spheres we have to deal, in the twentieth century, with additional complications arising out of the differences of race, language and cultural tradition, it is useful to be able to look at the question in its simplest form, that of a dispute between men speaking a common tongue, and products of a single common cultural tradition. Nor, finally, is its interest confined to the comparatively narrow world within which conscious ratiocination takes place. The more or less unconscious political allergies which form the stuff of the American political mind—the echoes set up by words such as *monarchy, empire, discrimination*—are a direct result of the experiences—and myths—of the age of the American Revolution. To understand the American mind, we must understand its beginnings, and as has been said, these beginnings are an essential part of British history as well.[1]

---

[1] It is difficult to accept the statement of an eminent historian " that the constitutional and political formulæ of the problem were exceedingly simple, and the contemporary discussions of it very trite." (L. B. Namier's preface to his *The Structure of Politics at the Accession of George III* 2 v., 1929).

The simplest way of expressing the nature of the constitutional conflict between Great Britain and her colonies is to say that it was the result of the discovery of the divergence between their interpretations of political ideas which they had once held in common. There was a single political tradition of opposition to arbitrary government which went back to the political struggles of the seventeenth century. In Great Britain it had come to serve as the foundation for a theory of parliamentary sovereignty, in America as the basis of a theory of limited government.

The principal British colonies in the region which was to become the United States had been directly founded (or, in the case of New York, conquered) either in the period of constitutional conflict at home under the first two Stuart kings, or in the less eventful but not less important period between the Restoration and the Revolution of 1688–89. Seventeenth century ideas of government were thus common to both Britain and her colonies; but the period after 1688–89 had seen changes in Britain which in spite of the formal continuity of her institutions were expressive of new and important, if still unformulated, theories and attitudes.

The dominating problem of the seventeenth century had been one of the relationship between the executive and policy-forming branch of government—the monarchy—and the representative branch—the parliament—upon which the monarchy depended for the supplies which made policy effective, and intermittently for legislation as well. The issues were confused—and the confusion was never resolved by the most erudite modern historian of the period, S. R. Gardiner—by the assumption on either side that the

6

particular solution which it advocated represented not an innovation but a return to the true spirit of the constitution as it had flourished in the Middle Ages. For a short time during the reign of James I the opposition leadership had sought to make a battleground of the courts and to circumscribe the actions of the Crown by assuming the existence of a fundamental law, or set of constitutional limitations, by which, it was alleged, the executive—and rather more hesitantly and obscurely—the legislature likewise was bound. But the emergence of new and more dramatic issues and the unwillingness of the bulk of the judiciary to dissociate itself from the Crown, brought about a direct conflict between part of Parliament on the one side and the Crown on the other—a conflict soluble only, as it proved, by force of arms. Yet for a time, the solution seemed likely to prove a temporary one, for in the course of destroying the monarchy, the Parliament all but destroyed itself. Between the defeat of Charles I and the restoration of his son, the English people found itself in the unprecedented situation of having no clearly legitimate government. For those who believed in divine right, there was the king—but he had legitimacy only, without authority. For those who believed in authority there was the victorious army of Cromwell—but for its rule there was clearly no legitimate sanction. For the politically enfranchised there was the prospect of establishing representative institutions upon a basis of consent—but, for the common man, these had neither legitimacy nor authority. The result was much experiment and much confusion. For the student of political institutions, the attempts to solve the problem by providing the country with a written constitution setting bounds upon the authority of the new executive—Cromwell, embodying the will of the army—and upon that of Parliament, have an abiding interest. And even greater interest attaches to the far-reaching theoretical discussions of the period, notably within the ranks of the Army. But the permanent effect of both was surprisingly small. Only in so far as Harrington's *Oceana* (published in 1656) was read, can the political thought of the Interregnum be said to have played a part in preparing the American Revolution.[1]

The English Restoration in 1660 outwardly renewed the ancient forms and principles of English monarchical government. But a decisive shift towards participation in the affairs of state by a proper-tied minority, drawn from the landed and merchant classes, had in fact already taken place. And the Revolution of 1688–89 with its sequel in the Act of Settlement of 1701 and the accession of the Hanoverian dynasty had established a new equilibrium.[2]

The England which, under the leadership of the elder Pitt, triumphed over its secular rival in the Seven Years' War believed then that it was governed under the terms of the " Revolution Settlement " as expounded by that Revolution's principal theorist, the Whig philosopher, John Locke. Recent historians have tended to discount the once popular view that there was a second and alternative Tory theory propounded by Lord Bolingbroke and held and practised by the young George III and his chosen minister, Lord Bute.[3] As Bolingbroke's own career had amply

---

[1] See H. F. Russell Smith, *Harrington and His* Oceana (Cambridge, 1914).

[2] The most important constitutional documents are in C. Grant Robertson, *Select Statutes, Cases and Documents* (6th ed., 1931).

[3] On the political structure of England, see L. B. Namier, *The Structure of Politics at the Accession of George III* (2 v., 1929) and the same author's *England in the Age of the American Revolution* (1930).

shown, the only real alternative to being a Whig was being a Jacobite, and after 1745 Jacobitism could never be anything but the sentimental aberration of a dwindling minority. The non-Jacobite Tory had little to express except the peevishness of a squirearchy which, after its rise in the first half of the seventeenth century, had failed to maintain its ground before the growing estates and growing authority of the Whig magnates—Disraeli's " Venetian Oligarchy ".[1]

For the student of political theory, Locke is of course primarily the exponent of a particular form of the social contract theory of the state. As Professor Barker has recently pointed out, however, " he thought in terms of a contract of society, followed by the creation of a fiduciary sovereign under and by a trust deed ".[2] In other words, the essence of the doctrine lies in the belief that political power is something created by the act of a community, already organized, the members of which possess rights whose origin is antecedent to its creation. This power entrusted to the sovereign can be withdrawn if abused—as power had been withdrawn from James II—and the trust deed can be framed in such a way as to limit the exercise of power. Such limitations had indeed been imposed upon the sovereign in England by the legislation of William III's reign—notably by the Declaration of Rights and the Act of Settlement. But since the rather peculiar circumstances which had made possible the personal rule of Charles II and James II were unlikely to recur, the limitations upon the power of the Crown

[1] What can be said for the Eighteenth Century Tories is said in K. G. Feiling, *The Second Tory Party, 1714–1832* (1938).
[2] Introduction to the volume entitled *Social Contract* (World's Classics, 1947) which includes a reprint of Locke's *Second Treatise on Civil Government* (first published in 1690).

may be said to have been codified after the real need
for such limitations had passed.

What had indeed happened was that the Crown
and Parliament had become associated in the formula-
tion and execution of policy through the device of a
responsible ministry. This development was not of
course complete by 1760. The first responsibility of
ministers was still to the monarch who had chosen
them, and Parliament itself, under the electoral system
of the age, was likely to be the creation of the ministry
and the Crown—acting through official and aristo-
cratic patronage—rather than a direct emanation of
the popular will. This aspect of the situation—the un-
representative nature of the representative institutions
of the country which grew more obvious as population
shifted with no corresponding redrawing of the electoral map, figured prominently in the political discussions of the period with which we are to deal. But,
from the present point of view, it is not the most important aspect. What really mattered was the fact
that in English minds Locke's sanction for rebellion
remained very much in the background. Why indeed
contemplate denying the authority of a government
which the Whigs themselves effectively controlled.
Instead, emphasis was placed upon the idea of representation, of the embodiment of the sovereign will
of the community in Parliament, or more simply,
upon Parliamentary sovereignty. By the middle of
the eighteenth century much of English constitutional
law was already statute law laid down by Parliament.
This made it possible to overlook the vitality of an
earlier tradition according to which fundamental
rights were thought of as embodied in the common law
of England—customary law—and the old tendency of

common lawyers to equate this in some measure with natural law. The exponent of legal and political theory most regarded by Englishmen in the age of the American Revolution was not Coke, nor Locke, but Sir William Blackstone, the first volume of whose *Commentaries on the Laws of England* appeared in the fatal year, 1765, the year of the Stamp Act. And although Blackstone declared that all law, including statute law, owed its validity to its conformity to natural law, this conformity was assumed in the case of the British Parliament, or at least, no method was suggested by which the contrary could be asserted in any particular case. Indeed Coke, whom Americans were quoting as an exponent of the idea of limited government, appeared to Blackstone as an upholder of the untrammelled sovereignty of Parliament. (No. 8.)[1] For Blackstone and his followers "there is and must be in every state a supreme, irresistible, absolute and uncontrolled authority, in which the *jura summa imperii*, or rights of sovereignty, reside " and " this supreme power is by the constitution of Great Britain vested in the King, Lords and Commons ".[2]

For the Englishman of the reign of George III, this simple dictum—a legal-historical rather than philosophical judgment—represented all one knew or needed to know about political theory. Nor, hitherto, had anything occurred to cause its validity to be questioned. The Parliament of Ireland—itself the organ of a minority caste—had been subject, formally since Poynings Law in 1495, and in fact previously, to the limitation that all initiative was in the hands of the King in Council, which by the Eighteenth Century meant of course the English ministry of the day. In

[1] Numbers in brackets refer to the documents.
[2] Blackstone, *Commentaries*, IV.

11

Scotland, the situation was a little more complicated. Under the Act of Union of 1706, Scotland had given up its separate Parliament and accepted instead representation in the Parliament at Westminster. As a part of the bargain which brought this about, the English Parliament accepted in the Act of Union certain limitations upon the full sovereignty of the Parliament of Great Britain which it now became—" that no alteration be made in Laws which concern private right except for evident Utility of the Subjects within Scotland ", that the " Presbyterian Government shall be the only Government of the Church within the Kingdom of Scotland ", and certain others. By these means the abolition in Scotland of its separate judicial system, its own code of private law, and a separate ecclesiastical establishment were formally placed beyond the competence of Parliament. Nor has Parliament in fact overstepped this general limitation, although some of the limiting clauses have been ignored in subsequent general legislation. The reasons for Parliament's forbearance have always been recognized as being political rather than constitutional, and the existence of these clauses in the Act of Settlement does not seem to have been regarded in the Eighteenth Century as conflicting with the dogma of Parliamentary sovereignty.

The assumption that Parliamentary sovereignty applied equally to the overseas colonies of the British Crown was a natural one. The Empire at the accession of George III contained thirty-one subordinate governments of which twenty-one possessed some form of representative institutions—the thirteen mainland colonies in North America and eight island colonies in the Western Atlantic and the Caribbean. It was natural that Parliament as it felt its powers grow should wish to extend them in full to the overseas possessions of the Crown. The age of international conflict which set in with the accession of William III caused all the Colonial Powers to seek to make the best of the resources which their empires contained. Under the mercantilist economic doctrines prevailing at the time, this meant a fairly complete control over the production and trade of the colonies. This could only effectively be done if administration were centralized and the Eighteenth Century Board of Trade with its nucleus of quasi-permanent civil servants was an efficient instrument of this centralizing impulse where the British Empire was concerned. It seemed likely to be aided after 1763 by the fact that the newly acquired colonies of Canada and Florida had no traditions of self-government in any sphere.

The original colonizing impulse in Britain had sprung much more from the people and much less from the State than had been the case with the other major empires. The form it took was influenced by the great chartered trading companies whose members played leading parts in the American enterprises. Some of these took corporate form: the Virginia Company, the Council for New England, the Massachusetts Company. Furthermore the individual character of British colonization was enhanced by the element of religious opposition at the heart of some, though by no means all, of its ventures. The colonies of the Restoration period also included, in Pennsylvania, another nucleus of religious non-conformity.

Much discussion has been devoted to the question of the origins of representative institutions on American soil. Tudor and early Stuart England had been peculiarly rich in free associations—companies, Inns of Court, colleges—while county and parish organization had relied mainly upon the ability of the Monarchy to command for public duties the natural leaders of society at every level. Associations possessing powers of self-government were not always chartered, but the chartered company was a familiar instrument of government, and it provided a working model for some of the early forms of colonial organization under charter. In New England, the concept of free association was transferred to the ecclesiastical sphere as well, and Massachusetts enjoyed a virtual theocracy until its original charter was cancelled and replaced by the more liberal one of 1691.

But the original charter—that of 1629—had done its historic work. For the fact that it did not provide for the headquarters of the Company remaining in London enabled the gap between chartered company and chartered colony to be bridged for the first time. The scheme of an elected assembly dealing with local law-making and with finance, and of a governor and assistants (or council) as executive and chief judicial body simply reproduced the familiar pattern in a political instead of a commercial setting.

Outside New England, the failure of the Virginia Company caused the abandonment of the company as a colonizing device. Virginia early acquired the characteristic institutions of the royal colony—its assembly locally elected, but its governor and council nominated by the Crown. The proprietary colonies, of which Maryland was the prototype, were based essentially upon the ideas of feudalism, but their institutions came to resemble those of the royal group of colonies, except for the fact that their governors

14

were nominated by the proprietor instead of by the Crown.

To appreciate the history of these institutions, it is necessary to take into account the increasing complexities of colonial society and its problems, and the divisions of interest which emerged between various groups and sections within them. But, from the constitutional point of view, the most significant development was a repetition of the main lines of constitutional conflict, as England had known them in the early seventeenth century. That is to say, in most of the colonies there was an independent executive standing over against an elected body which strove to use its financial powers as a means of increasing its political control. The difference was that, whereas the Stuart kings had only the support of the nobility and the aura of divine right to rely on, the colonial governors had behind them the whole weight of the Imperial Government. The Imperial Government from the middle of the Seventeenth Century developed a conscious and fully-worked out policy, of which the essential point was a series of economic regulations— Navigation Laws and tariffs—which were calculated to encourage the production of those commodities thought most valuable for the Empire as a whole and to discourage all others, as well as to see that as much as possible of the trade and shipping of the colonies was retained in British hands.

The ideal of Great Britain, as of the rival empires of Spain and France, was the closed economic system, favoured by mercantilist theory. The mainland colonies with their food, timber and draught animals should act as a complement to the sugar islands with their slave-plantation economy. The importance of the sugar-islands and the wealth of the interests connected with them gave the "West India interest" a definite role in politics and made Parliament inclined to pass legislation favouring the interests of the British West Indies against their competitors even when this could only be done at the expense of the other British colonies in America. External regulation alone was insufficient and the British Government began to intervene to the extent of prohibiting certain branches of manufacture and of interfering with colonial attempts to solve their currency problems by the deliberately inflationary tactics of the printing press. And external regulation itself, since it ran counter to the interests of important groups in the British and in other colonies had to be enforced, if at all, through Imperial rather than local machinery. The comparative neglect of the colonies in the earlier stages of their growth gave way to the careful bureaucratic control of the Board of Trade and the other departments concerned with American affairs. The recurrent wars with the French, the Spaniards and the Indians, and the inability of the colonies to combine in their own defence led the home Government to create military and naval establishments and to intervene in questions such as the permissible speed of westward expansion where the policies of the colonists themselves were likely to provoke Indian warfare.

The machinery of Imperial control was as complicated as the objects it sought to achieve. A Committee of the Privy Council in most cases nominated both the governors of the colonies and their councils. Where the proprietors had the right of nomination, it was exercised under the supervision of the Crown. In Massachusetts, the governor only, not the council was nominated; only in the two small colonies of Connecticut and Rhode Island were both governor and council locally elected. The governor, whose policy was determined by instructions drawn up in England, was commander-in-chief of the colony's forces, could summon, adjourn and dissolve the assemblies, and act with the council as a final court of appeal. He had also certain direct responsibilities apart from his general executive functions. Only his lack of an independent revenue made continuous co-operation between governor and assembly essential for effective government.

The powers of the assemblies where legislation was concerned were also not without their limitations. The validity of colonial laws alleged to clash with Imperial legislation could be challenged on that ground by appeal to the Privy Council in London and, in all but three of the colonies, the Crown could exercise a direct veto in addition.

The Imperial customs system was extended to the colonies by an Act of 1673 and subsequent legislation; cases arising under it were tried by the Vice-Admiralty courts set up in the colonies from 1697 onwards.

The formal authority, the Committee of Council, was advised on colonial matters by the Board of Trade, and its President was the political personage most constantly involved in colonial business, at least until the establishment in 1768 of a separate Secretaryship of State for the American colonies. But really important political decisions, nominations for major appointments, questions of military, naval, and Indian policy and questions of finance all went through the office of the Secretary of State.

The Treasury had direct contact with colonial

affairs through the Surveyor and Auditor General of the colonies, and through the Commissioners of Customs. The work of the office of the Secretary-at-War and of the Admiralty also touched colonial affairs at every turn, and there were finally certain specialized officials such as the Surveyor-General of the King's Woods.

The necessity of following any matter which concerned a colony's fortunes through this maze of authorities led to the appointment by the colonies of agents in London for this special purpose: Franklin represented the Assembly of Pennsylvania in London between 1757 and 1762, and during his second stay in London (1764–75) represented not only his own state but also Massachusetts, New Jersey and Georgia. The post was not always held by native Americans; in 1771 we find Burke acting as agent for New York.

The activities of the colonial agents in the Eighteenth century reflect the major development of the period in colonial matters, the increasing attention paid to them by Parliament. In the first place, the political heads of the departments concerned were now members of ministries based upon parliamentary combinations and seeking parliamentary approval for their policies. In the second place, the large field of patronage in the colonies and the overlapping of the departments concerned made them a peculiarly happy hunting ground for those out to secure places for needy relatives or clients.

This system, then, was a purely empirical one, built up not upon any set of principles of Imperial Government, but to meet the needs of specific policies and their enforcement. All efforts to bring about an institutional connection between the separate colonies had hitherto failed. The link was the common allegiance to the Crown and, in British eyes, the common subordination to Parliament. Whereas the colonies looked to their assemblies as the source of authority, for Parliament these were simply examples of the subordinate law-making bodies of which so many examples existed on the British scene. The fact that the weight of British influence was thrown against movements to make the assemblies more genuinely representative of the expanding colonial society as a whole; the fact that the increased complexity of the colonial economy made the Imperial regulation of trade often appear as a deliberate barrier against the most profitable employment of colonial resources, the fact that the limitation of settlement (the Proclamation of 1763) coming alongside the raising of the Crown's quit-rents suggested that colonial interests were being sacrificed for the benefit of fur-traders and land-speculators; the revival of the dormant anti-popery feeling caused by the apparent favour shown to the Crown's newly acquired French-Canadian subjects; above all, the growth of a sense of American nationality as something common to the colonies and distinguishing their inhabitants from those of Great Britain—these and many other developments of the middle decades of the Eighteenth Century placed a strain upon the constitutional system such as it had not had to endure hitherto. A single failure to deal successfully with some strongly felt grievance, an innovation which seemed to neglect colonial susceptibilities or threaten the very large measure of real independence which the colonies had hitherto enjoyed—any such development was bound to lead to the whole set of assumptions upon which the system rested coming for the first time into the fore-front of discussion. And such discussion was bound to reveal how far apart these assumptions now were![1]

PART II

In order to follow the ensuing debate, it is necessary to remember the complex political situation in England which followed the accession of George III. As has been seen, the dominant Whig philosophy had shifted its emphasis; it has been well said that "the reluctant revolutionaries of 1689 became the complacent conservatives of 1750, and to them Whiggism stood less for the principles which had produced the Glorious Revolution than for the society which it had inaugurated ".[2] The political basis of this society—the sovereignty of a Parliament dominated by the connections and clients of the great Whig houses now received a two-fold challenge.

The accession of George III produced a situation which had not existed under his grandfather and great-grandfather. For the first time under the House of Hanover, there was no adult heir to the throne around whom an opposition could group itself and attack the royal ministers without fearing that the charges of faction so incurred would permanently debar it from office.[3] The result was that the tactical position of the

[1] This rapid summary of the position of the American colonies on the eve of the Revolution is necessarily incomplete. For a one-volume introduction to the whole subject, and to its voluminious literature, it would be hard to improve upon C. P. Nettels, *The Roots of American Civilization* (1939). For greater detail there are the works of three pre-eminent scholars in this field: H. L. Osgood, *The American Colonies in the Seventeenth Century* (3 v., 1904–07); *The American Colonies in the Eighteenth Century* (4 v., 1924); C. M. Andrews, *The Colonial Period of American History* (4 v., 1934–38); L. H. Gipson, *The British Empire before the American Revolution*. (The first volume of this work was published in 1936; nine have so far appeared.)

[2] G. H. Guttridge, *English Whiggism and the American Revolution*.

[3] The classical view of George III's aims as set out for instance in the works of Sir George Trevelyan is challenged in the works by Professor Namier already alluded to and more particularly in the introduction by Romney Sedgwick to his *Letters from George III to Lord Bute* (London, 1939).

monarch was much strengthened and the parliamentary patronage which he controlled could be used with less deference than hitherto to the rival claims of Whig grandees. On the other hand the use made of this power by the ministers of George's choice, and especially their attempts to suppress criticism as manifested in the affair of the " general warrants " and other episodes in the career of that unsavoury popular hero, John Wilkes, went far towards producing an opposition capable of questioning in a fundamental fashion the relation to the country of a Sovereign Parliament whose claim to a representative character became more and more tenuous as the century progressed. The liberty of the Press, and particularly of parliamentary reporting, the right of Parliament to control its own membership by expelling a duly elected member and seating a defeated rival in his place—these questions were the forerunners of a movement for radical reform which was to be stimulated and brought forward by the dispute with the American Colonies— only to see its hopes blasted for a generation by the reaction against the Revolution in France.

In the 1760's and 1770's, the radicals of England and those of America believed that they had a common interest in sustaining each other's demands. But it must not be overlooked that their opposition to the acts of Britain's unreformed Parliament arose from fundamentally different reasons; the English radicals opposed Parliament because it was not representative —the Americans because it was a foreign body, and, however reformed, would not represent them.[1]

Although for most of the period with which we are

[1] Cf., D. M. Clark, *British Opinion and the American Revolution* (Harvard, U.P., 1930). Cf. C. Ritcheson, *British Politics and the American Revolution* (1954).

concerned, the demands of the radicals were moderate enough—the instruction of members, more frequent elections and the exclusion of Government servants from Parliament—they were dangerous allies for the Whig opposition, since the Whig leaders looked for a revival of their fortunes to a preservation of the same parliamentary system of which George III was making such effective use. For bringing about this revival they placed their hopes upon developing a properly led political party out of the heterogeneous personal groups of which the Whig body in Parliament was made up. If they could act together, they could force the King to accept them as his ministers, and wield the sovereignty of Parliament as effectively as anyone else.

This was a long way from the original tenets of Whiggism. But the original doctrines of limited government, of unity within the framework of a constitution based on a system of rights, were not altogether without their spokesmen. Of these, the elder Pitt was the foremost; and his opposition to the idea of organized party, and to that of unfettered Parliamentary supremacy helped to prevent that union with Rockingham and co-operation with Burke which might have brought victory to the Whigs. In the end Pitt's ideas, combined with the natural country opposition to the Whig magnates, produced a new Toryism rather than a revived Whiggism—but these developments lie outside the framework of the dispute with America and beyond the chronological bounds of the present volume. Meanwhile the confusion of doctrines and the blurring of party lines were partly responsible for the uncertainty of the British reply to colonial claims. In answering the specific problems which the American resistance to Parliamentary edicts raised, the leading British statesmen were forced to consider the abstract foundations of their policy in a way rarely demanded by the humdrum domestic politics of mid-Eighteenth-Century Britain.[1]

One other element in the English scene deserves mention. The Church, which with the Crown had given the original Tory creed both its object and its strength, had been the major sufferer when the Whigs triumphed. Whiggism was the ally of Dissent. But the Eighteenth Century transformation of Whiggism had made the Church a much less alien body, while Dissent found a new outlet for its energies in the radical cause. In the struggle with America, the Whigs had an ally in the Church whose jurisdiction over the Anglican colonies could not survive a political breach, and which had no cause to love the Puritan polities of New England or the tolerant Quakerism of Pennsylvania.

Such then were the main ingredients of English political thought. On the American side it was faced by an equally unsettled amalgam of British constitutional thought, traditions of local self-government, musings upon the common law, and a growing contribution from the natural law doctrines of contemporary Europe. While on the whole the American argument broadened in the course of the struggle, from a legalistic concern with charters to the bold universalism of the Declaration of Independence, it is almost equally true to say that there is hardly any element in their thought which cannot be found from the very beginning of the dispute.[2]

---

[1] The above paragraphs are based on the very valuable essay, *English Whiggism and the American Revolution*, by G. H. Guttridge (University of California, 1942).

[2] The literature on the American side is described and analysed in much detail by M. C. Tyler in his *Literary History of the American Revolution* (2 v., New York, 1897).

Indeed the issues involved had, as it were, a preliminary run during the abortive attempt by James II to merge the northern group of colonies (except for Connecticut and Rhode Island) into a single autocratic Dominion of New England.[1] The opposition to this move quoted in its support, not only the colonial charters which they claimed as indefeasible, but also Magna Carta and that useful if undefined shield—the " rights of Englishmen ".[2]

When the struggle began again on the morrow of the Seven Years War with a Parliamentary majority in place of the Stuart King it was a struggle in which the successive protagonists on the British side were in no doubt as to the merits of their case both on the political and on the constitutional side. It seemed only fair that the colonies from whose doorstep the French and Indian menace had been removed should pay for part of the cost of the war which had brought this about. From the lawyers' point of view, the contention that Parliament had the right to tax any of the King's subjects for such a purpose was undeniable. On both scores it was the Americans who had to make the running.

The first element in the great debate to be emphasized, was the American belief in a fundamental law which should act as a restraint upon the activities even of Parliament itself. Such seems to be the purport of the speech by James Otis on the Writs of Assistance made in February 1761 (No. 1). The development of this idea of a fundamental law—an idea closely resembling the original Whig doctrine—was for some time indeed the major element in political

[1] Cf., V. F. Barnes, *The Dominion of New England* (Yale, U.P., 1923).

[2] C. F. Mullett, *Fundamental Law and the American Revolution, 1760-76* (Columbia U.P., 1933), p. 70.

thinking on the American side. It was thought of as
deriving from a threefold source, the colonial charters,
the British constitution assumed to consist of the common law and the great statutes, and finally natural
law.[1]

The writings of Otis provide an excellent illustration
of this aspect of American thought. In his pamphlet of
1762, *The Vindication of the Conduct of the House of
Representatives*, arising out of Governor Bernard's action in incurring naval expenditure unauthorized by
the legislature (which had not been in session in a time
of emergency), Otis proclaimed the doctrine that the
right of raising money in the colonies belonged solely
to their legislatures. Otherwise they would not enjoy
the full rights of British subjects, as they were entitled
to " by the common law, by their several charters, by
the law of nature and nations and by the law of God ".

When faced with the further development of British
policy in the shape of the proposed stamp tax, Otis
developed his ideas in *The Rights of the British Colonies
Asserted and Proved* (No. 2). Again the British constitution is assumed to derive from natural law. " In
theory and in the present administration of it ", he
declares, it " in general comes nearest the idea of perfection of any that has been reduced to practice ". It
is " from and under " the British Parliament " and its
acts, and from the common law that the political and
civil rights of the colonists are derived ". The abolition of the colonial charters, assuming Parliament were
to contemplate such an act, could not " shake one of
the essential, natural, civil or religious rights of the
colonists ".

[1] On the influence of natural law doctrines in Eighteenth Century America,
see the present writer's introduction to *The Federalist* (Oxford, 1948), and the
authorities referred to there.

25

The Empire within which these rights are enjoyed is seen by Otis as a single unit and he goes on to argue the advantages that would be derived from American representation in the Imperial Parliament. It was the same theme which the Englishman Thomas Pownall (1722–1805), a former governor of Massachusetts, elaborated in his work, *The Administration of the Colonies*, of which the first edition appeared in London in the same year. Such representation would entitle the Government to tax the colonists for Imperial purposes; at the same time they should have a common subordinate legislature to apportion the burdens and make local laws. But it was irreconcilable with the " first principles of law and justice " or with " many other fundamental maxims of the British constitution " and " the natural and civil rights, which by the laws of their country all British subjects are entitled to," that the colonists should be taxed by a Parliament in which they were unrepresented.

Nevertheless, in all matters other than taxation, Otis accepted " the supreme, sacred and uncontrollable legislative power not only in the realm but through the dominions " of the British Parliament.

The fiery language of Patrick Henry could not conceal the fact that the doctrine of the Virginia Resolves on the Stamp Act (No. 3) was no other. Only the last two Resolves, which the Assembly did not pass, went over from theory to practice and asserted the right of the colonists to disobey any tax-law imposed upon them from outside.

These ideas received a new refinement in the shape of a distinction between external taxation, that is to say customs duties which the Imperial Parliament had always imposed, and the new internal tax devised by

Grenville. The former were imposed primarily as a part of the regulation of trade for the common benefit of the Empire, the latter merely to raise revenue. Daniel Dulany, one of the foremost exponents of this distinction, also denied the applicability to American conditions of one of the stock arguments of British opponents of Parliamentary reform—that of virtual representation (No. 4). It might be true that, in a society so closely knit as that of Great Britain, it was difficult to find any major interest which was not in some way represented in Parliament, even if particular individuals or places were not. It was therefore difficult to pass legislation manifestly unjust. But the Americans formed a separate society and a tax upon them might not affect " a single actual elector in England ".

These opposition pamphlets received a powerful answer from Soames Jenyns in a widely read pamphlet (No. 5), in which he reversed the argument about virtual representation in order to show that, if the colonists were correct about the rights of Englishmen, the whole British representative system would stand condemned. The connection in orthodox English minds of the American complaint with Wilkes and the radicals, as well as with other opposition elements such as the country Tories, is well illustrated by Jenyns' remark that the phrase " the liberty of an Englishman " has within the past " few years been used as a synonymous term for blasphemy, bawdy, treason, libels, strong beer and cyder ". What it could not mean, he declared, was " an exemption from taxes imposed by the authority of the Parliament of Great Britain ". Even if the charters had granted it, they would have no force, since " no charter from the Crown can possibly supersede the right of the whole legislature". In America these arguments carried little weight with the opposition and, at the end of the same year, John Adams was arguing that the Stamp Act was something that Parliament had no right to enact, and that the courts were consequently not bound to enforce it.[1]

There was more than one way of defining the issues now being debated. It could either be done in terms of an alleged limitation upon the full sovereignty of Parliament, or in terms of a dispute about the status of the colonial legislatures. " In Britain ", pointed out the Governor of Massachusetts (No. 6), " the American Governments " were considered as " corporations empowered to make by-laws existing only during the pleasure of Parliament," which had never done anything to confirm their establishment and could at any time put an end to them. In America the colonies claimed to be " perfect States, no otherwise dependent upon Great Britain than by having the same King ". In 1765, this was perhaps going too far—certainly further than Otis had gone. But as a prognostication of the future development of the American case it was accurate enough. For the time being the question of taxation was the centre of attention, and a definition of inter-imperial relations was called for in vain. It was with such an argument about taxation that John Dickinson first appeared upon the national scene (No. 7).

Meanwhile the arguments over the Stamp Act were reflected in the English Parliament. But there, as Bernard pointed out, the dogma of Parliamentary supremacy was hardly challenged. It was indeed the keynote of Blackstone's constitutional doctrine and the first volume of the *Commentaries* appeared in the year of the Stamp Act itself (No. 8).

[1] John Adams, *Works*, II, pp. 157-9.

In the House of Commons, William Pitt, whose
" Whiggism was of that old order which placed the
fundamental law of the constitution beyond the reach
of Parliament ",[1] opposed the Stamp Act and the
principle behind it. In his view England had no right
to " lay a tax upon the colonies, to be sovereign and
supreme in every circumstance of government and
legislation whatsoever." The colonists were subjects
of the kingdom equally entitled with the others " to
all the natural rights of mankind and the peculiar
privileges of Englishmen ". The Americans were
" the sons not the bastards of England ". It was wrong
to confuse taxation with the general power of government. In taxing the country the Commons gave and
granted what was theirs. How could they grant the
property of the King's subjects in America ? (No. 9).
The main exponent of the contrary doctrine was
George Grenville who declared himself unable to
understand the alleged difference between external
and internal taxes. In his view, the power to tax was
part of the sovereign, the supreme legislative power
which Parliament was admitted to have over America
(No. 10). In his reply, Pitt made it clear that he did
not deny the latter contention. If he rejoiced that
America had resisted, it was because she had resisted
taxation which was unconstitutional. But the legislative power over the colonies was supreme (No. 11).

The direct question of the legislative authority of
Parliament arose in a debate in the House of Lords in
February, 1766 (No. 12). On the whole, the speakers
took the same line as Grenville had followed in the
Commons. Lord Lyttleton gave an admirable illustra-
tion of the way in which Locke's version of the social

[1] Guttridge, op. cit. p. 34.

contract had come to be regarded as justification for parliamentary sovereignty, and denied there could be a right in a government to make laws and at the same time a right in the people to disobey them. The emigration of the colonists to America could make no difference to their status as subjects. On the other hand, Lord Camden pointed out certain accepted limitations upon the powers of Parliament—they could not contravene the Divine Law, or take private property without compensation, or pass a bill of attainder upon a man without hearing him. The right of taxation rested, upon the principle of representation; the clergy had been exempt from Parliamentary taxation when they had taxed themselves in their own representative body, and other parallels could be drawn. The colonies were unrepresented and could not be taxed. The reply of Lord Northington to what he called " a paradox in every law " that he knew of followed familiar lines. " There must be a supreme dominion in every state . . . and all the subjects of each state are bound by the laws made by government ". The more elaborate argument of Lord Mansfield added little of substance. The Lord Chancellor and Lord Chief Justice were at one with Sir William Blackstone.

Camden repeated and elaborated his argument in another speech a fortnight later, with reference to the Declaratory Bill with which the ministry accompanied its repeal of the Stamp Act itself. Again he stressed that, under the constitution, taxation and representation were inseparable. The Declaratory Bill which laid down that Parliament had the right to tax the colonies was " illegal, absolutely illegal, contrary to the fundamental laws of nature, contrary to

the fundamental laws of this constitution " (No. 13).
But in their dislike of the central doctrine of the
Declaratory Act, that the taxing power was part of the
governing or legislative power, Pitt and Camden
stood almost alone. The great body of the Whigs
went along with Rockingham and Burke in support of
the Act. Indeed, Pitt was more disturbed by it than
the Americans who, having got the odious Stamp Act
repealed, were not over-anxious to probe the doctrines
of those who had done them this service.

What brought the Americans back into the debate,
was the Townshend policy. Townshend had thought
to make use of the American distinction between internal and external taxes, by raising money in the
form of taxes on colonial imports from Britain—that
is by external taxes. The Americans, as represented
for instance by John Dickinson, now shifted their
ground slightly. It was no longer a question of internal and external taxes, but of contrasting taxes for
the regulation of trade which only incidentally brought
in revenue, and taxes on trade whose real purpose was
simply to raise money (No. 14). Once again the idea
that there was a British constitution which Parliament
was violating was useful, and was indeed adequately
exploited by Samuel Adams (No. 15).

The adoption by the Americans of measures against
British commerce intended to coerce the ministry into
changing their policy was regarded by many in
England as an illegal act. Chatham, however, took
the view that however dangerous might be the possible
consequences of such actions they were well within
the colonists' rights (No. 16).

The attitude taken up in the colonies, culminating
in acts of violence such as the attack on the revenue

ship *Gaspee* made some Englishmen dispute the reality of the colonists' professed loyalty to the Imperial connection. In 1766, Josiah Tucker had argued that the Stamp Act and direct taxation were not the real causes of American factiousness. What they objected to was the whole system of commercial control which they were forced to accept while they remained part of the Empire. Now that the danger from France was removed, the Americans were bound to revolt. While himself believing that the colonists were virtually represented in Parliament, and therefore rightly subject to its taxing and legislative power, he advocated colonial independence as more in accordance with Britain's own interests. Tucker was a 'little Englander' before his time.[1]

But British Imperialists also argued that the colonists were insincere or mistaken when they drew their fine distinctions between what Parliament could and could not do. "I know of no line" declared Thomas Hutchinson in January, 1773, "that can be drawn between the supreme authority of Parliament and the total independence of the colonies. It is impossible there should be two legislatures in one and the same state." Once again a British governor was forecasting rather than describing the course of American thought (No. 17).

The passage of the Coercive Acts against Massachusetts in retaliation for the 'Boston tea-party', marked a further phase in the deepening rift between Britain and the colonies. It is important to note that in Britain, even the opponents of the ministry were mainly concerned with the inexpediency of their

[1] Josiah Tucker, *Selected Writings*, ed., R. L. Schuyler (Columbia, U.P., 1931).

recent policies, rather than with questions of right. This was above all true of Burke, the first of whose notable speeches on American affairs was made at this juncture. (No. 18). His point of view in no way differed from that of the Rockingham Whigs with whom he was associated, and the apparent profundity of his arguments must in some measure be attributed to the merits of his literary style. For what Burke was saying was that the old system of Imperial commercial control had worked well enough, and would have gone on working, but for the unfortunate insistence of first Grenville, and then Townshend, on trying to raise revenue from the colonies. His argument that usage had made the former endurable, while novelty made the latter intolerable, was good psychology, but overlooked the historical fact that the colonies were growing and developing societies which might well come to reject what they had accepted in earlier times. It was all very well to refuse to go into " distinctions of rights " and to declare one's hatred of these " metaphysical distinctions ". Once the Americans had raised these questions, each successive crisis in Imperial relations was certain to raise them again, and Burke himself, by ending with a vigorous defence of the Declaratory Act and of the principle enshrined in it showed that he had his own views on these subjects just as much as anyone else.

It was the practical statesman, Chatham, not the political philosopher, Burke, who saw more clearly into the heart of the matter. By repudiating the notion that the British Parliament could tax the colonies, and by declaring that exemption from such taxation by a body in which they were not represented was " an essential unalterable right in nature, ingrafted into the

British constitution as a fundamental law ", Chatham showed himself the better Whig and the more magnanimous statesman of the two (No. 19).

The logical conclusion of this train of thought was the complete repudiation of parliamentary authority, since the distinction between the taxing and the legislative authority was no easier to maintain than that between internal and external taxation. But this conclusion, and the corollary that the link of Empire was the Crown and not Parliament, had to wait to find expression in America itself. James Wilson and Thomas Jefferson share the credit for the enunciation of what, more than a century and a half later, became the guiding principle of the British Commonwealth of Nations (Nos. 20, 21 and 22). Jefferson's *Summary View* is, indeed, the best presentation of the American viewpoint on the eve of the final movement in opinion which led to outright secession from the Empire. It made much of the argument from history and from the " rights of Englishmen ", but it is also possible to see in it the extent to which this argument could be fortified by that of " natural rights ". The Americans were, in their own estimation, " a free people, claiming their rights as derived from the laws of nature and not as the gift of their chief magistrate ". The debate was now on a plane on which it was difficult if not impossible for any British statesman to answer the American case. The splendid theoretical fabric which Burke had erected, based upon usage, precedent and tradition, was falling before the frontiersman's axe.

Even in America it was still possible for loyalists to fight a rearguard action, and one finds Daniel Leonard arguing that the colonial legislatures must be subordinate, because there cannot be two co-ordinate authorities in one state, and denying as absurd the notion of a mere common allegiance to the Imperial Crown. The King could only appear under such a system as King of each separate colony and if these were constitutionally and not absolutely governed the consequence would be chaos. The whole comparison of the provincial legislatures with the British Parliament was pointless since the former had no houses of peers, and lacked many of the latter's essential powers. They were, and could only remain, essentially subordinate (No. 23).

In his reply, John Adams showed how great was the distance which now separated the two parties. The whole concept of a united Empire was superseded in the American mind by the idea that all the connections with Great Britain were either the old allegiance of the colonists to the Crown, or undertakings voluntarily entered into for the common good. Even the argument from the rights of Englishmen was abandoned. The New England laws were derived from the law of nature, and although the ancestors of the New Englanders had been entitled to the common law, they had not been bound to accept more of it than they chose (No. 24). The transition from this to an argument in favour of complete independence was no longer a difficult one to make, in spite of the conventional protestations of loyalty which the American pamphleteers still favoured.

In England there was direct discussion of independence both by Josiah Tucker and by radicals such as John Cartwright. But responsible statesmen were still endeavouring to save the Imperial structure. Chatham continued to oppose the coercive measures of the ministry, and both Whigs and radicals found an added cause of dismay in the Quebec Act of May 1774, which was held to provide a dangerous model of a despotism. Chatham's attitude throughout had at least the merit of consistency. In January, 1775, he was still arguing in favour of the distinction between commercial regulation and taxation, and referring to the justice of American resistance and the vanity of " declarations of the omnipotence of Parliament " (No. 25). His actual proposals, cast in the form of a bill, proclaimed the legislative supremacy of Parliament over the whole Empire, but limited this by denying to Parliament the right to use military force " to violate and destroy the just rights of the people ", as well as the right to tax Americans other than through their own assemblies. The American Congress should be invited to meet again to acknowledge the supremacy of Parliament within these limits, and to take into consideration the question of making a financial contribution towards meeting the burdens of the Imperial Government (No. 26).

But by now any scheme for solving the problem by formalizing the Imperial tie and by creating new institutions for the purpose of strengthening it, had to face the increasing tide of what can only be described as American nationalism. Americans were becoming convinced that the whole Imperial connection, however limited, was a handicap to their autonomous development, and Franklin's views at this time, as well as his reluctance to face an armed conflict if this could be avoided, may be taken as typical enough (No. 27).

Burke's contribution at this stage of the discussion showed little advance in his thinking. He was still determined to uphold the doctrine of full Parliamentary sovereignty, and still believed that peace could be obtained by returning to the legal position as it stood in 1767, and by abandoning all attempts at further definition of the constitutional relationship between the different parts of the Empire. Eloquent as was his description of the historical causes which had made the colonists jealous of their liberties, he drew back from the natural conclusion that they would not allow others to define what these liberties were (No. 28). Josiah Tucker, whose political development had brought him into strong opposition to the whole idea of natural rights and of the contractual theory of the State, was a better judge of what was really going on. In an open letter to Burke, dealing with the latter's speech of 22 March 1775, he showed the first clear understanding of the fact that the doctrines of Locke, which had become in England a conventional support for an essentially conservative system, were being acted on in America, in a spirit much closer to the original:

" They (the colonists) are now Mr Locke's Disciples; who has laid down such Maxims in his Treatise on Government, that if they were to be executed according to the letter and in the Manner the Americans pretend to understand them, they would necessarily unhinge and destroy every Government upon earth."

But it was an Englishman only recently arrived in America who gave the final, and from the political point of view, convincing, answer to Burke. Nothing could be less like Burke, in its matter or its manner, than the political writing of Thomas Paine. In *Common Sense* the idea of natural rights and a radical suspicion of all government other than the simplest and most directly representative, are brought together to form a justification of American independence in

D   37

terms which commended themselves at once to minds prepared for such doctrine by the whole tenor of the previous debate and the no less cogent logic of events (No. 29). But, in England, opinion, even among men of a comparatively advanced frame of mind, still lagged behind. Richard Price, the protégé of Shelburne, while condemning the Declaratory Act and the whole doctrine of the omnipotence of Parliament, which he regarded as a simple trustee of the true sovereignty of the people it represented, was still in favour of retaining for Great Britain the right of regulating the Imperial trade of the colonies (No. 30).

It was too late for any form of compromise. The Declaration of Independence, in language less robustly utilitarian than Paine's, but with substantially the same attitude to natural rights and the liberties springing from them, set out the completed doctrinal basis for American nationhood. The pursuit of happiness had replaced property among man's unalienable rights, and with this momentous declaration, the history of American political thought finally separates from the parent stem (No. 31).[1]

In England, even after the outbreak of hostilities the Whigs continued to resist the implications of what had been done and said. The Whig claim that the war was one waged by the Ministry and its supporters and not by the country as a whole was a foredoomed attempt to escape from their dilemma. In April, 1777, Burke was still adumbrating the Rockingham doctrines of 1766 (No. 32), and Chatham, in November, still believed that his old views could provide a basis for reconciliation (No. 33). When the French

[1] The intellectual antecedents of the Declaration are examined in Carl Becker, *The Declaration of Independence* (New York, 1922).

alliance with the Americans showed that such hopes would have to be abandoned, the logic of Chatham's position led him strongly to oppose any talk of accepting the American claim to independence, to which other Whigs were becoming reconciled, and which they preferred to the idea of a federal link through the Crown alone, with its possible implications for English politics. (No. 34.) It was left for Josiah Tucker to utter the final comment on the struggle and to represent the cynical pessimism about the possibility of any ties between peoples but those of interest and subordination which so long stood in the way of a new constructive approach to the Imperial problem (No. 35).

But this was not the end of the effect of the American Revolution upon British political thought in either the Imperial or the domestic sphere. The later sequence of British theories of Empire will be traced in a separate volume in this series. Here we need only note that the Quebec Act of 1791, in spite of its apparent faithfulness to the old formulae, was in fact the beginning of a new age. The claim that its object was " to give Canada a free constitution in the British sense of the word " marked a decisive change from the atmosphere of the debates on the position of the thirteen colonies.[1]

Internally the effect was perhaps harder to follow. In the volume on English radical thought in the present series,[2] the development of English democratic ideas at this time will be further illustrated. They centred mainly around the question of Parliamentary reform. The reformers had of course been influenced

[1] See R. Coupland, *The American Revolution and the British Empire* (London, 1930).
[2] See *The Radical Tradition 1780-1914*. Edited by S. Maccoby.

profoundly by the discussion on the nature and purpose of representative institutions which had been
carried on in connection with the American claims.
" It was, in fact, the dispute with America which had
first led some of them to examine the doctrine of
representation upon which that dispute ultimately
turned, and which had converted them, almost insensibly, into advocates of a reform of Parliament.
Some, no doubt, it led even further."[1] But the some
were few. Indeed with the purging of some of the
impediments to the working of the existing system by
the Whigs' measure of " economical reform " in 1782,
much of the political backing for real reform vanished.
Pitt's attempt at a comparatively minor improvement
in the representative quality of the House of Commons
failed in 1785, and was not renewed. There was great
disappointment among the radicals and it looked as
though only some Dissenting interests, with the Uni-
tarians prominent among them, would have sufficient
incentive to continue the struggle. After a year or
two indeed, there were some signs of a revival of
radical activity. But the coming of the French Revolution in 1789 created currents in British thought so
profound as to obliterate most traces of the earlier
American influence. With undoubted justice, the
treatment of this theme has also been left for another
volume in the present series.[2] Later contacts between
British and American political thought were to be
contacts between two wholly independent systems.
The effect of the American Revolution as such can
properly be confined to the period covered in the
present volume.

[1] G. S. Veitch, *The Genesis of Parliamentary Reform* (London, 1913).
[2] See the volume in this series by Alfred Cobban, *The Debate on the French Revolution.*

CHRONOLOGY OF PRINCIPAL EVENTS

	1760
25 October	Accession of George III

	1761
5 October	Resignation of Pitt

	1762
26 May	Bute, Prime Minister

	1763
20 February	The Peace of Paris
16 April	Grenville, Prime Minister
May	Pontiac's Rising
7 October	The Proclamation of 1763

	1764
March	Grenville's Sugar Act
	Colonial Currency Act

	1765
March	Stamp Act
	Quartering Act
May	Virginia Resolves
13 July	Rockingham, Prime Minister
August	Boston Stamp Act Riots
October	Stamp Act Congress, New York

	1766
March	Repeal of Stamp Act
	Declaratory Act
30 July	Chatham, Prime Minister

	1767
May	Townshend Acts

41

1768

February	Massachusetts Circular Letter
March	Non-importation agreements begin
June	*Liberty* riot at Boston
September	Massachusetts Convention
4 October	Grafton, Prime Minister
	Arrival of British troops in Boston

1769

May	Virginia Non-importation agreement

1770

28 January	North, Prime Minister
March	Partial Repeal of Townshend Duties
	Boston " Massacre "
August	Breakdown of non-importation agreements

1772

June	Burning of the *Gaspee*
December	Boston Committee of Correspondence established

1773

March	Virginia Committee of Correspondence established
May	North's Tea Act
December	" Boston Tea Party "

1774

January	Franklin's appearance before Privy Council
February	Additional Instructions to Governors on Land Policy
March-June	The Coercive Acts
June	The Quebec Act
September	The First Continental Congress
October	The Adoption of the Continental Association

1775

February	Lord North's proposals for settlement

April	Battles of Lexington and Concord
May	Second Continental Congress
June	Washington, Commander-in-Chief
October	Invasion of Canada

1776

May	Virginia Convention declares in favour of independence
2 July	Congress votes for Independence

1777

October	Burgoyne surrenders at Saratoga

1778

February	French Alliance
	North's proposals for conciliation
May	Congress ratifies treaties with France
	Death of Chatham

1782

30 November	Preliminary Articles of Peace

1783

3 September	Peace of Paris

43

1: JAMES OTIS. Speech on the Writs of Assistance

February 1761

The widespread activities of smugglers led the British government to seek new methods of enforcing the commercial regulations. From 1755, use was made in Massachusetts of " writs of assistance " issued by judges and empowering the customs officers to receive the assistance of constables and other local officials and to enter warehouses and private homes in search of smuggled goods. When the death of George II obliged the administration to seek new writs from the Massachusetts court, James Otis (1725–83) was engaged by the Boston merchants to oppose their issue. Although he was ultimately unsuccessful, the constitutional issues raised in his speech helped to crystallize opposition feeling.

No text of the speech exists, but John Adams took notes which are here printed from his *Works* (C. F. Adams, ed.), (10 v., Boston, 1856), II, p. 522. Their significance is brought out in an appended note by Horace Gray, Associate Justice of the U.S. Supreme Court, 1881–1902.

As to Acts of Parliament. An Act against the Constitution is void; an Act against natural equity is void; and if an Act of Parliament should be made in the very words of this petition, it would be void. The executive courts must pass such Acts into disuse. 8 Rep. 118 from Viner. Reason of the common law to control an Act of Parliament.

45

Note

The Adams notes were republished in the *Massachusetts Bay Reports*, *1761–72*, ed., Josiah Quincy jun. (Boston, 1865). In Appendix I to this volume there is a discussion by Horace Gray on Otis' argument, from which the following is quoted: " But Otis, while he recognized the jurisdiction of Parliament over the Colonies, denied that it was the final arbiter of the justice and constitutionality of its own acts; and relying upon words of the greatest English lawyers, and putting out of sight the circumstances under which they were uttered, contended that the validity of statutes must be judged by the Courts of Justice; and thus foreshadowed the principle of American Constitutional Law, that it is the duty of the judiciary to declare unconstitutional statutes void.

" His main reliance was the well-known statement of Lord Coke in Dr. Bonham's case—' It appeareth in our books, that in many cases the common law will control Acts of Parliament and adjudge them to be utterly void; for where an Act of Parliament is against common right and reason, or repugnant or impossible to be performed, the common law will control it and adjudge it to be void.' Otis seems also to have had in mind the equally familiar dictum of Lord Hobart, ' Even an Act of Parliament made against natural equity, as to make a man judge of his own case, is void in itself: for *jura naturæ sunt immutabilia*, and they are *leges legum.* ' Lord Holt is reported to have said, ' What my Lord Coke says in Dr. Bonham's case in his 8 Rep. is far from any extravagancy, for it is a very reasonable and true saying, that if an Act of Parliament should ordain that the same person should be party and judge, or what is the same thing, judge in his own cause, it would be à void Act of Parliament.' "

The law was laid down in the same way, on the authority of the above cases, in Bacon's Abridgment, first published in 1735; in Viner's Abridgment, published in 1741–51, from which Otis quoted it; and in Comyn's Digest, published 1762–67, but written more than twenty years before. And there are older authorities to the same effect. So that at the time of Otis's agreement (i.e., argument) his position appeared to be supported by some of the highest authorities in the English law.

2: JAMES OTIS. *The Rights of the British Colonies Asserted and Proved*

Boston July 1764

The pamphlet, *The Rights of the British Colonies Asserted and Proved*, was published by Otis after it had become clear that Parliament's efforts to tighten up the Imperial System after the Peace of Paris of 1763, would include, not merely new and better enforced commercial regulations, but also an attempt to raise revenue from the colonies for the first time in the form of a stamp tax, the introduction of which in the next session had already been announced.

The extracts given here are taken from the text in Vol. I of his *Political Writings*, edited by C. F. Mullett (2 vols.), in the *University of Missouri Studies*, 1929. A reply was commissioned by Grenville from Thomas Whately.

OF THE ORIGIN OF GOVERNMENT

THE origin of *government* has in all ages no less perplexed the heads of lawyers and politicians, than the origin of *evil* has embarrassed divines and philosophers; and 'tis probable the world may receive a satisfactory solution on *both* those points of enquiry at the *same* time.

The various opinions on the origin of *government* have been reduced to four.

1st. That dominion is founded in *grace*.

2. On *force* or mere *power*.

3. On *compact*.

4. On *property*.

The first of these opinions is so absurd, and the world has paid so very dearly for embracing it, especially under the administration of the *roman pontiffs*, that mankind seem at this day to be in a great measure cured of their madness in this particular; and the notion is pretty generally exploded, and hiss'd off the stage.

To those who lay the foundation of government in *force* and mere *brutal power*, it is objected: that their system destroys all distinctions between right and wrong; that it overturns all morality, and leaves it to every man to do what is right in his own eyes; that it leads directly to *scepticism*, and ends in *atheism*. When a man's will and pleasure is his only rule and guide, what safety can there be either for him or against him, but in the point of a sword?

On the other hand the gentlemen in favour of the *original compact* have been often told that *their* system is chimerical and unsupported by reason or experience. Questions like the following have been frequently asked them, and may be again. " When and where was the original compact for introducing government into any society, or for creating a society, made? Who were present and parties to such a compact? Who acted for infants and women, or who appointed guardians for them? Had these guardians power to bind both infants and women during life, and their posterity after them? Is it in nature or reason that a guardian should by his own act perpetuate his power over his ward, and bind him and his posterity in chains? Is not every man born as free by nature as his father? Has he not the same natural right to think and act an contract for himself? Is it possible for a man to have a natural right to make a slave of himself or of his posterity? Can a father supersede the laws of nature?

48

What man is or ever was born free, if every man is not? What will there be to distinguish the next generation of men from their forefathers, that they should not have the same right to make original compacts as their ancestors had? If every man has such right, may there not be as many original compacts as there are men and women born or to be born? Are not women born as free as men? Would it not be infamous to assert that the ladies are all slaves by nature? If every man and woman born or to be born has, and will have, a right to be consulted, and must accede to the original compact before they can with any kind of justice to be said to be bound by it—will not the compact be ever forming and never finished ever making but never done? Can it with propriety be called a compact original or derivative, that is ever in treaty but never concluded?"

When it has been said that each man is bound as soon as he accedes, and that the consent may be either express or tacit, it has been asked: "What is a *tacit* consent or compact? Does it not appear plain that those who refuse their assent can not be bound? If one is at liberty to accede or not, is he not also at liberty to *recede* on the discovery of some intolerable fraud and abuse that has been palm'd upon him by the rest of the high contracting parties? Will not natural equity in several special cases rescind the original compacts of great men as effectually, as those of little men are rendered null and void in the ordinary course of a court of chancery?"

There are other questions which have been started, and a resolution of them demanded, which may perhaps be deemed indecent to those who hold the prerogatives of an earthly monarchy, and even the power

of a plantation government, so sacred as to think it
little less than blasphemy to enquire into their origin
and foundation: while the government of the supreme
ruler of the universe is every day discussed with less
ceremony and decency than the administration of a
petty German prince. I hope the reader will consider
that I am at present only mentioning such questions
as have been put by highflyers and others in Church
and State, who would exclude all compact between a
Sovereign and his people, without offering my own
sentiments upon them; this however I presume I may
be allowed hereafter to do without offence. Those who
want a full answer to them may consult Mr. Locke's
discourses on government, M. de Vattel's law of
nature and nations, and their own consciences.
" What state were Great Britain, Ireland and the
Plantations left in by the abdication of James II ?
Was it a state of natural or of civil government ? If
a state of civil government where were the supreme
legislative and executive powers from the abdication
to the election of William and Mary ? Could the
Lords and Commons be called a complete parliament
or supreme power without a king to head them ? Did
any law of the land or any original compact previous
to the abdication provide that, on such an event, the
supreme power should devolve on the two houses ?
Were not both houses so manifestly puzzled with the
novelty and strangeness of the event, and so far from
finding any Act of Parliament, book-case, or precedent
to help them, that they disputed in solemn conference
by what name to call the action, and at last gave it
one, as new in our language and in that of Parliament
as the thing itself was in fact ? "

If on this memorable and very happy event the

three kingdoms and the dominions fell back into a state of *nature*, it will be asked, " Whether every man and woman were not then equal ? If so, had not every one of them a natural and equitable right to be consulted in the choice of a new king, or in the formation of a new and original compact or government, if any new form had been made ? Might not the nation at that time have rightfully changed the Monarchy into a republic or any form, that might seem best ? Could any change from a state of nature take place without universal consent, or at least without the consent of the *majority* of the individuals ? Upon the principles of the original compact as commonly explained and understood, could a few hundred men who before the dissolution of the Government had been called, and in fact were, lords, knights and gentlemen, have lawfully made that glorious deliverer and defender, William III, rightful king ? " Such a one he certainly was, and such have been all his illustrious successors to the present happy times: when we have the joy to see the sceptre sway'd in justice, wisdom and mercy, by our lawful sovereign George III; a prince who glories in being a Briton born, and whom may God long preserve and prosper.

" If upon the abdication all were reduced to a state of nature, had not the apple women and orange girls as good a right to give their respectable suffrages for a new king as the philosopher, courtier, *petit maitre* and politician ? Were these and ten million of others such ever more consulted on that occasion, than the multitude now are in the adjustment of that real modern farce, an election of a King of the Romans; which serves as a contrast to the grandeur of the ancient republics and shows the littleness of the modern

51

German and some other Gothic constitutions in their present degenerate state

" In the election of William III, were the votes of Ireland and the plantations ever called for or once tho't of till the affair was settled ? Did the lords and commons who happened to be then in and about William represent, and act, for the individuals, not only of the three kingdoms, but for all the *freeborn and as yet unconquered possessors and proprietors of their own money-purchased, blood-purchased plantations, which, till lately, have been defended with little or no assistance from Great Britain* ? Were not those who did vote in or for the new model at liberty upon the principles of the compact to remain in what some call the delectable state of nature, to which by the hypothesis they were reduced, or to join themselves to any other state, whose solemn league and covenant they could subscribe ? Is it not a first principle of the original compact that all who are bound should bind *themselves* ? Will not common sense without much learning or study dictate obvious answers to all the above questions ?—and, say the opposers of the original compact and of the natural equality and liberty of mankind, will not those answers infallibly show that the doctrine is a piece of *metaphysical* jargon and *systematical* nonsense ? " Perhaps not.

With regard to the fourth opinion, that *dominion is founded in property*, what is it but playing with words ? Dominion in one sense of the term is synonymous with power, so one cannot be called the foundation of the other, but as one *name* may appear to be the foundation or cause of another.

Property cannot be the foundation of dominion as synonymous with government for on the supposition that property has a precarious existence antecedent to government, and tho' it is also admitted that the security of property is one end of government, but that of little estimation even in the view of a *miser* when life and liberty of locomotion and further accumulation are placed in competition, it must be a very absurd way of speaking to assert that *one* end of government is the foundation of government. If the ends of government are to be considered as its foundation, it cannot with truth or propriety be said that government is founded on any *one* of those ends: and therefore government is not founded on power or its security *alone*, but at least on something else in conjunction.

It is, however, true in fact and *experience*, as the great, the incomparable Harrington has most abundantly demonstrated in his *Oceana*, and other divine writings, that Empire follows the balance of *Property*: 'Tis also certain that *property* in fact generally *confers* power, tho' the possessor of it may not have much more wit than a mole or a musquash. And this is too often the cause, that riches are sought after, without the least concern about the right application of them. But is the fault in the riches, or the general law of nature, or the unworthy possessor? It will never follow from all this, that government is *rightfully* founded on *property*, alone. What shall we say then? Is not government founded on grace? No. Nor on *force*? No. Nor on *compact*? Nor *property*? Not altogether on either. Has it *any* solid foundation? Any chief corner stone, but what accident, chance or confusion may lay one moment and destroy the next? I think it has an everlasting foundation in the *unchangeable will* of God, the author of nature, whose laws never vary. The same omniscient, omnipotent, infinitely good and gracious

Creator of the universe, Who has been pleased to make it necessary that what we call matter should *gravitate*, for the celestial bodies to roll round their axes, dance their orbits and perform their various revolutions in that beautiful order and concert, which we all admire, has made it *equally* necessary that from Adam and Eve to these degenerate days, the different sexes should sweetly *attract* each other, form societies of *single* families, of which *larger* bodies and communities are as naturally, mechanically, and necessarily combined, as the dew of Heaven and the soft distilling rain is collected by the all enliv'ning heat of the sun. *Government* is therefore most evidently founded *on the necessities of our nature.* It is by no means an *arbitrary thing*, depending merely on *compact or human will* for its existence.

We come into the world forlorn and helpless; and if left alone and to ourselves at any one period of our lives, we should soon die in want, despair or distraction. So kind is that hand, tho' little known or regarded, which feeds the rich and the poor, the blind and the naked; and provides for the safety of infants by the principle of parental love, and for that of men by government! We have a king, who neither slumbers nor sleeps, but eternally watches for our good; whose rain falls on the just and the unjust: yet while they live, move and have their being in him, and cannot account for either, or for any thing else, so stupid and wicked are some men, as to deny his existence, blaspheme his most evident government, and disgrace their nature.

Let no man think I am about to commence advocate for *despotism*, because I affirm that government is founded on the necessity of our natures; and that an

original, supreme sovereign, absolute and uncontrol-
able, *earthly* power *must* exist in and preside over every
society, from whose final decisions there can be no
appeal but directly to Heaven. It is therefore *originally*
and *ultimately* in the people. I say supreme absolute
power is *originally* and *ultimately* in the people and they
never did in fact *freely*, nor can they *rightfully*, make an
absolute, unlimited renunciation of this divine right.
It is ever in the nature of the thing given in *trust*, and
on a condition, the performance of which no mortal
can dispense with; namely, that the person or persons
on whom the sovereignty confer'd by the people, shall
incessantly consult *their* good. Tyranny of all kinds is to
be abhor'd, whether it be in the hands of one, or of
the few, or of the many. And tho' " in the last age a
generation of men sprung up that would flatter princes
with an opinion that *they* have a *divine right* to absolute
power," yet " slavery is so vile and miserable an estate of
man, and so directly opposite to the generous temper and
courage of our nation, that 'tis hard to be conceived that
an *Englishman* much less a *gentleman*, should plead for
it:" Especially at a time when the finest writers of the
most polite nations on the continent of Europe, are en-
raptured of the beauties of the civil constitution of *Great
Britain*, and envy her, no less for the *freedom* of her
sons, than for her immense *wealth* and *military* glory.

But let the *origin* of government be placed where it
may, the *end* of it is manifestly the good of the *whole*.
Salus populi suprema le esto, is of the law of nature, and
part of that grand charter given the human race (tho'
too many of them are afraid to assert it), by the only
monarch of the universe, who has a clear and indisputable right to *absolute* power; because he is the *only*
One who is *omniscient* as well as *omnipotent*.

It is evidently contrary to the first principles of reason, that supreme *unlimited* power should be in the hands of *one* man. It is the greatest " *idolatry*, begotten by *flattery*, on the body of *pride*," that could induce one to think that a *single mortal* should be able to hold so great a power, if ever so well inclined. Hence the origin of *deifying* princes: It was from the trick of gulling the vulgar into a belief that their tyrants were *omniscient* and that it was therefore right that they should be considered as *omnipotent*. Hence the *Dii majorum et minorum gentium*, the great, the monarchical, the little provincial subordinate and subaltern gods, demi-gods, and semidemi-gods, ancient and modern. Thus deities of all kinds were multiplied and increased in *abundance*: for every devil incarnate, who could enslave a people, acquired a title to *divinity*: and thus the " rabble of the skies " was made up of locusts and caterpillars; liars, tygers and harpies; and other devourers translated from plaguing the earth!

The *end* of government being the *good* of mankind, points out its great duties: It is above all things to provide for the security, the quiet, and happy enjoyment of life, liberty and property. There is no one act which a government can have a *right* to make, that does not tend to the advancement of the security, tranquillity and prosperity of the people. If life, liberty and property could be enjoyed in as great perfection in *solitude*, as in *society*, there would be no need of government. But the experience of ages has proved that such is the nature of man, a weak, imperfect being; that the valuable ends of life cannot be obtained without the union and assistance of many. Hence 'tis clear that men cannot live apart of independent of each other. In solitude men would perish; and yet they cannot live together without contests. These contests require some arbitrator to determine them. The necessity of a common, indifferent, and impartial judge, makes all men seek one; tho' few find him in the *sovereign power*, of their respective states or anywhere else in subordination to it.

Government is founded *immediately* on the necessities of human nature, and *ultimately* on the will of God, the author of nature, who has not left it to man in general to choose, whether they will be members of society or not, but at the hazard of their senses if not of their lives. Yet it is left to every man as he comes of age to choose *what society* he will continue to belong to. Nay if one has a mind to turn to *Hermit*, and after he has been born, nursed and brought up in the arms of society, and acquired the habits and passions of social life, is willing to run the risque of starving alone, which is generally most unavoidable in a state of hermitage, who shall hinder him? I know of no human law, founded on the law of nature to restrain him from separating himself from the species, if he can find it in his heart to leave them; unless it should be said, it is against the great law of *self-preservation*: But of this every man will think himself *his own judge*.

The few *Hermits* and *Misanthropes* that have ever existed, show that those states are *unnatural*. If we were to take out from them, those who have made great *worldly* gain of their *godly* hermitage, and those who have been under the madness of *enthusiasm*, or *disappointed* hopes in their *ambitious* projects, for the detriment of mankind: perhaps there might not be left ten from Adam to this day.

The form of government is by *nature* and by *right* so far left to the individuals of each society, that they may alter it from a simple democracy or government of all over all, to any other form they please. Such alteration may and ought to be made by express compact. But how seldom this right has been asserted, history will abundantly show. For once that it has been fairly settled by compact, *fraud, force or accident* have determined it an hundred times. As the people have gained upon tyrants, these have been obliged to relax, *only* till a fairer opposition has put it in their power to encroach again.

But if every prince since *Nimrod* has been a tyrant, it would not prove a *right* to tyranize. There can be no prescription old enough to supersede the law of nature, and the grant of God almighty, who has given to all man a natural right to be *free* and they have it ordinarily in their power to make themselves so, if they please.

Government having been proved to be necessary by the law of nature, it makes no difference in the thing to call it from a certain period, *civil.* This term can only relate to form, to additions to, or deviations from, the substance of government: This being founded in nature, the superstructures and the whole administration should be conformed to the law of universal reason. A supreme legislative and supreme executive power, must be placed *somewhere* in every commonwealth: Where there is no other positive provision or compact to the contract, those powers remain in the *whole body of the people.* It is also evident there can be but *one* best way of depositing those powers: but what that way is, mankind have been disputing in peace and in war more than five thousand years. If we could suppose the individuals of a community met to deliberate, whether it were best to keep these powers in *their own* hands, or dispose of them in *trust*, the following questions would occur—Whether these two great powers of Legislation and Execution should remain united? If so, whether in the hands of the many, or jointly or severally in the hands of a few, or jointly in some one individual? If both these powers are retained in the hands of the many, where nature seems to have placed them originally, the government is a simple *democracy*, or a government of all over all. This can be administered, only by establishing it as a first principle, that the votes of the majority shall be taken as the voice of the whole. If those powers are lodged in the hands of a few, the government is an *Aristocracy* or *Oligarchy*. Here too, the first principle of a practicable administration is that the majority rules the whole. If those great powers are both lodged in the hands of one man, the government is a *simple Monarchy*, commonly, though falsely called *absolute*, if by that term is meant a right to do as one pleases. *Sic volo, sic jubeo, stet pro ratione voluntas*, belongs not of right to any mortal man.

The same law of nature and of reason is equally obligatory on a *democracy*, an *aristocracy* and a *monarchy*. Whenever the administrators, in any of those forms, deviate from truth, justice and equity, they verge towards tyranny, and are to be opposed; and if they prove incorrigible, they will be *deposed* by the people if the people are not rendered too abject. Deposing the administrators of a *simple democracy* may sound oddly, but it is done every day, and in almost every vote. A, B & C, for example, make a *democracy*. Today A and B are for so vile a measure as a standing army. Tomorrow B and C vote it out. This is as really deposing the former administration as setting up and making a new king is deposing the old one. *Democracy* in the one case, and *monarchy* in the other, still remain; all that is done is to change the administration.

The first principle and great end of government being to provide for the best good of all the people, this can be done only by a supreme legislature and executive ultimately in the people, or whole community where God has placed it, but the inconveniences, not to say impossibility attending the consultations and operations of a large body of people have made it necessary to transfer the power of the whole to a few: This necessity gave rise to deputation, proxy or a right of representation.

A power of legislature without a power of execution in the same or other hands, would be futile and in vain: on the other hand, a power of execution, supreme or subordinate, without an *independent* legislature would be perfect despotism.

The difficulties attending an universal congress, especially when society became large, have bro't men to consent to a delegation of the power of all: The weak and the wicked have too often been found in the same interest, and in most nations have not only bro't these powers *jointly*, into the hands of one, or some few of their number; but made them *hereditary* in the families of despotic nobles and princes.

The wiser and more virtuous states, have always provided that the representation of the people should be *numerous*. Nothing but life and liberty are *naturally* hereditable: this has never been considered by those, who have *tamely* given up both in the hands of a tyrannical Oligarchy or despotic *Monarchy*.

The analogy between the natural or material as it is called and the moral world is very obvious; God himself appears to us at some times to cause the inter-

vention or combination of a *number* of simple principles
tho' never when *one* will answer the end; gravitation
and attraction have place in the revolution of the
planets, because the one would fix them to a centre,
and the other would carry them off indefinitely; so in
the moral world, the first simple principle is *equality*
of the power of the whole. This will answer in small
numbers; so will a tolerably virtuous Oligarchy or a
Monarchy. But when the society grows in bulk, none
of them will answer well *singly*, and none worse than
absolute monarchy. It becomes necessary, therefore,
as numbers increase, to have these several powers
properly combined so as from the whole to produce
that harmony of government so often talked of and
wished for, but too seldom found in ancient or modern
states. The grand political problem in all ages has
been to invent the best combination or distribution of
the supreme powers of legislation and execution.
Those states have ever made the greatest figure, and
have been most durable, in which these powers have
not only been separated from each other, but placed
each in more hands than one, or a few. The *Romans*
are the most shining example: but they never had a
balance between the senate and the people, and the
want of this, is generally agreed by the few who know
any thing of the matter, to have been the cause of
their fall. The *British* Constitution in theory and in the
present administration of it, in general comes nearest
the idea of perfection, of any that has been reduced to
practice; and if the principles of it are adhered to, it
will according to the infallible prediction of *Harrington*
always keep the *Britons* uppermost in *Europe*, till their
only rival nation shall either embrace that perfect
model of a commonwealth given us by that author, or

come as near it as *Great Britain* is. Then indeed and not till then, will that rival and our nation either be eternal confederates, or contend in greater earnest than they have ever yet done, till one of them shall sink under the power of the other, and rise no more.

In order to form an idea of the natural rights of the Colonists, I presume it will be granted that they are men, the common children of the same Creator with their brethren of Great Britain. Nature has placed all such in a state of equality and perfect freedom, to act within the bounds of the laws of nature and reason without consulting the will or regarding the humor, the passions or whims of any other men, unless they are formed into a society or body politic. This it must be confessed is rather an abstract way of considering men than agreeable to the real and general course of nature. The truth is, as has been shown, men come into the world and into society at the same instant. But this hinders not but that the natural and original rights of each individual may be illustrated and explained in this way better than in any other. We see here by the way a probability that this abstract consideration of men, which has its use in reasoning on the principles of government, has insensibly led some of the greatest men to imagine, some real general state of nature agreeable to this abstract conception, antecedent and independent of society. This is certainly not the case in general, for most men become members of society from their birth, tho' separate individual states are really in the same condition of perfect freedom and equality with regard to each other, and so are any number of individuals who separate themselves from a society of which they have formerly been members, for ill treatment or other good cause, with express design to found another. If in such case, there is a real interval, between the separation of the new conjunction, during such interval the individuals are as much detached, and under the law of nature only, as would be two men who should chance to meet on a desolate island.

The Colonists are by the law of nature free born, as indeed all men are, white or black.

I also lay it down as one of the first principles from whence I intend to deduce the civil rights of the British colonies that all of them are subject to, and dependent on Great Britain; and that therefore as over subordinate governments, the Parliament of Great Britain has an undoubted power and lawful authority to make Acts for the general good, that by naming them, shall and ought to be equally binding, as upon the subjects of Great Britain within the realm. This principle, I presume, will be readily granted on the other side of the Atlantic. It has been practised upon for twenty years to my knowledge, in the province of the *Massachusetts-Bay*; and I have ever received it, that it has been so from the beginning, in this and the sister provinces, thro' the continent.

I am aware, some will think it is time for me to retreat, after having expressed the power of the British parliament in quite so strong terms. But 'tis from and under this parliament and its acts, and from the common law, that the political and civil rights of the Colonists are derived: And upon these grand pillars of liberty shall my definition be rested. At

63

present therefore the reader may suppose, that there is not one provincial charter on the continent, he may, if he pleases imagine all taken away, without fault, without forfeiture, without tryal or notice. All this really happened to some of them in the last century. I would have the reader carry his imagination still further, and suppose a time may come, when instead of a process at common law, the parliament shall give a decisive blow to every charter in America and declare them all void. Nay it shall also be granted, that 'tis barely possible the time may come, when the real interest of the whole may require an act of parliament to annihilate all those charters. What could follow from all this, that would shake one of the essential, natural, civil or religious rights of the Colonists ? Nothing. They would be men, citizens and brother subjects after all. No act of parliament can deprive them of the liberties of such, unless any will contend that an act of parliament can make slaves not only of one, but of two millions of the commonwealth. And if so, why not of the whole ? I freely own, that I can find nothing in the laws of my country, that would justify the parliament in making one slave, nor did they ever professedly undertake to make one.

Two or three innocent colony charters have been threatened with destruction an hundred and forty years past. I wish the present enemies of those harmless charters would reflect a moment, and be convinced that an act of parliament that should demolish those bugbears to the foes of liberty would not reduce the Colonists to a state of absolute slavery. The worst enemies of the charter governments are by no means to be found in England. 'Tis a piece of justice due to Great-Britain to own, they are and have ever been natives of or residents in the colonies. A set of men in America, without honour or love to their country, have been long grasping at powers, which they think unattainable while these charters stand in the way. But they will meet with unsurmountable obstacles to their project for enslaving the British colonies, should these, arising from provincial charters be removed. It would indeed seem very hard and severe, for those of the colonists, who have charters, with peculiar privileges, to loose them. They were given to their ancestors, in consideration of their sufferings and merit, in discovering and settling America. Our fore-fathers were soon worn away in the toils of hard labour on their little plantations, and in war with the Savages. They thought they were earning a sure inheritance for their posterity. Could they imagine it would ever be tho't just to deprive them or theirs of their charter privileges ? Should this ever be the case, there are, thank God, natural, inherent and inseparable rights as men, and as citizens that would remain after the so much wished for catastrophe, and which, whatever became of charters, can never be abolished *de jure*, if *de facto*, till the general conflagration. Our rights as men and free born British subjects give all the Colonists enough to make them very happy in comparison with the subjects of any other prince in the world.

Every British subject born on the continent of America or in any other of the British dominions, is by the law of God and nature, by the common law, and by act of parliament (exclusive of all charters from the Crown) entitled to all the natural, essential, inherent and inseparable rights of our fellow subjects in Great Britain. Among these rights are the following, which it is humbly conceived no man or body of men, not excepting the parliament, justly, equitably and consistently with their own rights of the constitution, can take away.

1st. *That the supreme and subordinate power of the legislature should be free and sacred in the hands where the community have once rightfully placed them.*

2dly. *The supreme natural legislative cannot be altered justly until the commonwealth is dissolved, nor a subordinate legislative taken away without forfeiture or other good cause.*

Nor then can the subjects in the subordinate government be reduced to a state of slavery and subjected to the despotic rule of others. A state has no right to make slaves of the conquered. Even when the subordinate right of legislature is forfeited and so declared, this cannot affect the natural persons either of those who were invested with it, or the inhabitants so far as to deprive them of the rights of subjects and of men. The colonists will have an equitable right notwithstanding any such forfeiture of charter, to be represented in Parliament or to have some new subordinate legislature among themselves. It would be best if they had both. Deprived however of their common rights as subjects, they cannot lawfully be, while they remain such. A representation in Parliament from the several Colonists, since they are become so large and numerous, as to be called on not to maintain provincial government, civil and military among themselves, for this they have cheerfully done, but to contribute towards the support of a national standing army, by reason of the heavy national debt, when they themselves owe a large one, contracted in the common cause, cannot be tho't an unreasonable thing, nor if asked, could it be called an immodest request. *Qui sentit commodum sentire debet et onus.* He who feels

66

the benefit should also feel the burden has been tho't
a maxim of equity.

But that a man should bear a burthen· for other
people, as well as for himself, without a return, never
long found a place in any law-book, or decrees, but
those of the most despotic princes. Besides the equality
of an American representation in parliament, a thousand advantages would result from it. It would be the
most effectual means of giving those of both countries
a thorough knowledge of each others interests; as well
as that of the whole, which are inseparable.

Were this representation allowed, instead of the
scandalous memorials and depositions that have been
sometimes, in days of old, privately cooked up in an
inquisitorial manner, by persons of bad minds and
wicked views, and sent from America to the several
boards, persons of the first reputation among their
countrymen, might be on the spot, from the several
colonies, truly to represent them. Future ministers
need not, like some of their predecessors have recourse
for information in American affairs, to every vagabond
stroller, that has run or rid post thro' America, from his
creditors, or to people of no kind of reputation from the
colonies; some of whom, at the time of administering
their sage advice, have been as ignorant of the state
of the country as of the regions in Jupiter and Saturn.

No representation of the Colonies in parliament alone,
would however be equivalent to a subordinate legislative among themselves: nor so well answer the ends of
increasing their prosperity and the commerce of Great-
Britain. It would be impossible for the people to judge
so well, of their abilities to bear taxes, impositions on
trade, and other duties and burthens, or of the local
laws that might be really needful, as a legislative here.

3rdly. *No legislative supreme or subordinate has a right to make itself arbitrary.* It would be manifestly contrary, for a free legislative, like that of Great-Britain, to make itself arbitrary.

4thly. *The supreme legislative cannot justly assume a power of ruling by extempore arbitrary decrees, but is bound to dispense justice by known settled rules, and by duly authorized individual judges.*

5thly. *The supreme power cannot take from any man any part of his property without his consent in person or by representation.*

6thly. *The legislature cannot transfer the power of making laws to any other hands.*

These are their bounds, which by God and nature are fixed, hitherto have they a right to come and no further.

1. To govern by stated laws.

2. These laws should have no other end ultimately but the good of the people.

3. Taxes are not to be laid on the people, but by their consent in person, or by deputation.

4. Their whole power is not transferable.

These are the first principles of law and justice and the great barriers of a free state, and of the British constitution in part. I ask, I want no more—Now let it be shown how 'tis reconcileable with these principles or to many other fundamental maxims of the British constitution, as well as the natural and civil rights, which by the laws of their country all British subjects are intitled to, as their best inheritance and birth-right, that all the northern colonies, who are without legal representation in the house of Commons should be taxed by the British parliament.

The sum of my argument is, that civil government is of God: that the administrators of it were originally the whole people: that they might have devolved it on whom they pleased: that this devolution is fiduciary, for the good of the whole; that by the British constitution, this devolution is on the King, lords and commons, the supreme, sacred and uncontroulable legislative power, not only in the realm, but thro' the dominions: that by the abdication, the original compact was broken to pieces: that by the revolution, it was renewed, and more firmly established, and the rights and liberties of the subjects in all parts of the dominions more fully explained and confirmed: that in consequence of this establishment, and the Acts of Succession and Union, His Majesty George III is rightful king and sovereign, and with his Parliament, the supreme legislative of Great Britain, France, and Ireland, and the dominions thereto belonging: that this constitution is the most free one, and by far the best, now existing on earth: that by this constitution, every man in the dominions is a free man: that no parts of his Majesty's dominions can be taxed without their consent: that every part has a right to be represented in the supreme or some subordinate legislature: that the refusal of this would seem to be a contradiction in practice to the theory of the constitution: that the colonies are subordinate dominions, and are now in such a state, as to make it best for the good of the whole, that they should not only be continued in the enjoyment of subordinate legislation, but be also represented in some proportion to their number and estates, in the grand legislature of the nation: that this would firmly unite all parts of the British empire, in the greatest peace and prosperity; and render it invulnerable and perpetual.

3: PATRICK HENRY. *Virginia resolves on the Stamp Act*

30 May 1765

The news of the passage of the Stamp Act by the British Parliament on 22 March, 1765, caused widespread protest in the colonies. In Virginia, the lead was taken by Patrick Henry (1736–99) who had already attained prominence as the leader of the opposition to the planter oligarchy which controlled the colony's affairs. He introduced into the Assembly a series of resolves. The last of these was certainly not passed by the Assembly and the fifth probably not also; but since all of them were published together in newspapers outside Virginia, Henry's propagandist purposes were not thereby much impeded.

The text is here taken from that reprinted in Morison, *Sources and Documents*, pp. 17–18; Morison also prints (pp. 32–4) the more moderate resolutions passed by the inter-colonial " Stamp Act Congress" in October. See E. S. and H. M. Morgan, *The Stamp Act Crisis* (Chapel Hill, N.C., 1953).

RESOLVED, That the first adventurers and settlers of this His. Majesty's Colony and Dominion of Virginia brought with them, and transmitted to their posterity, and all other of His Majesty's subjects since inhabiting this His Majesty's said Colony, all the liberties, privileges, franchises, and immunities, that have at any time been held, enjoyed, and possessed, by the people of Great Britain.

Resolved, That by two royal charters, granted by King James the First, the colonists aforesaid are declared entitled to all liberties, privileges, and immunities of denizens and natural subjects, to all intents and purposes, as if they had been abiding and born within the realm of England.

Resolved, That the taxation of the people by themselves, or by persons chosen by themselves to represent them, who can only know what taxes the people are able to bear, or the easiest method of raising them, and must themselves be affected by every tax laid on the people, is the only security against a burthensome taxation, and the distinguishing characteristick of British freedom, without which the ancient constitution cannot exist.

Resolved, That His Majesty's liege people of this his most ancient and loyal Colony have without interruption enjoyed the inestimable right of being governed by such laws, respecting their internal polity and taxation, as are derived from their own consent, with the approbation of their sovereign, or his substitute; and that the same hath never been forfeited or yielded up, but hath been constantly recognized by the kings and people of Great Britain.

Resolved therefore, That the General Assembly of this Colony have the only and sole exclusive right and power to lay taxes and impositions upon the inhabitants of this Colony, and that every attempt to vest such power in any person or persons whatsoever other than the General Assembly aforesaid has a manifest tendency to destroy British as well as American freedom.

Resolved, That His Majesty's liege people, the inhabitants of this Colony are not bound to yield obedience to any law or ordinance whatever, designed to impose any taxation whatsoever upon them other than the laws or ordinances of the General Assembly aforesaid.

Resolved, That any person who shall, by speaking or writing, assert or maintain that any person or persons other than the General Assembly of this Colony, have any right or power to impose or lay any taxation on the people here, shall be deemed an enemy to His Majesty's Colony.

4: DANIEL DULANY. *Considerations on the Propriety of imposing Taxes in the British Colonies for the purpose of raising a Revenue, by Act of Parliament.*

Annapolis, October 1765

Daniel Dulany (1722–97), the author of this pamphlet which was published anonymously, was the leading lawyer of the colony, and had for many years been its Secretary. He had been educated in England and never wavered in his belief that, although the British parliament had no right to tax the colonies internally, it had the right of external taxation for the benefit of the empire as a whole. It was this sentiment which eventually brought him into the loyalist camp.

The extracts here are taken from the reprint of the second edition, issued in London in 1766. It has been pointed out that Pitt's speech of 14 January, 1766 (No. 9), admittedly owed much to the arguments set forth in this pamphlet by his fellow-Etonian.

I SHALL undertake to disprove the supposed similarity of situations, whence the same kind of Representation is deduced of the inhabitants of the colonies of the *British* non electors; and, if I succeed, the Notion of a *virtual representation* of the colonies must fail, which, in Truth is a mere cob-web, spread to catch the unwary and intangle the weak. I would be understood. I am upon a question of propriety, not of power; and though some may be inclined to think it is to little purpose to discuss the one when the other is irresistible,

73

yet they are different considerations; and, at the same time that I invalidate the claim upon which it is founded, I may very consistently recommend a submission to the law, whilst it endures. . . .

Lessees for years, copyholders, proprietors of the public funds, inhabitants of Birmingham, Leeds, Halifax and Manchester, merchants of the City of London, or members of the corporation of the East India Company, are, *as such*, under no personal incapacity to be electors; for they may acquire the right of election, and there are not only a considerable number of electors in each of the classes of lessees for years etc., but in many of them, if not all, even members of Parliament. The interests therefore of the non-electors, the electors, and the representatives, are individually the same; to say nothing of the connection among neighbours, friends and relations. The security of the non-electors against oppression, is that their oppression will fall also upon the electors and the representatives. The one can't be injured and the other indemnified.

Further if the non-electors should not be taxed by the British Parliament, they would not be taxed at all; and it would be iniquitous, as well as a solecism in the political system, that they should partake of all the benefits resulting from the imposition and application of taxes, and derive an immunity from the circumstances of not being qualified to vote. Under this Constitution, then a double or virtual representation may be reasonably supposed. . . .

There is not that intimate and inseparable relation
74

between the electors of Great Britain and the inhabitants of the colonies which must inevitably involve both in the same taxation; on the contrary, not a single actual elector in England might be immediately affected by a taxation in America, imposed by a statute which would have a general operation and effect upon the properties of the inhabitants of the colonies . . . wherefore a relation between the British Americans and the English electors is a knot too infirm to be relied on. . . .

It appears to me that there is a clear and necessary Distinction between an Act imposing a tax for *the single purpose of revenue*, and those Acts which have been made for the *regulation of trade*, and have produced some revenue in consequence of their effect and operation as regulations of trade.

The colonies claim the privileges of British subjects. It has proved to be inconsistent with those privileges to tax them without their own consent, and it hath been demonstrated that a tax imposed by Parliament is a tax without their consent.

The subordination of the colonies and the authority of Parliament to preserve it, have been fully acknowledged. Not only the welfare, but perhaps the existence of the mother country as an independent kingdom, may rest upon her trade and navigation, and these so far upon her intercourse with the colonies, that if this should be neglected, there would soon be an end to that commerce whence her greatest power is derived and upon which her maritime power is principally founded. From these considerations, the right of the British Parliament to regulate the trade of the colonies, may be justly deduced; a denial of it would contradict the admission of the subordination, and of the authority to preserve it, resulting from the nature of the relation between the mother country and her colonies. It is a common and frequently the most proper method to regulate trade by duties on imports and exports. The authority of the mother country to regulate the trade of the colonies being unquestionable, what regulations are the most proper, are of course submitted to the determination of the Parliament; and if an incidental revenue should be produced by such regulations, these are not therefore unwarrantable.

A right to impose an internal tax on the colonies without their consent *for the single purpose of revenue* is denied; a right to regulate their trade without their consent is admitted. The imposition of a duty may in some circumstances, be the proper regulation. If the claims of the mother country and the colonies should seem on such an occasion to interfere and the point of right to be doubtful (which I take to be otherwise) it is easy to guess that the determination will be on the side of power, and the inferior will be constrained to submit.

5: SOAME JENYNS. *The Objections to the Taxation of Our American Colonies by the Legislature of Great Britain, briefly consider'd*

London 1765

Soame Jenyns (1704–87), who was a member of Parliament from 1754 to 1780 and who had in 1765 been for some years one of the commissioners of the Board of Trade, was well known as a writer and politician. The pamphlet achieved instant success in England and provoked a number of replies in the colonies of which the most effective was James Otis' *Considerations on Behalf of the Colonies in a Letter to a Noble Lord*, which first appeared at Boston in October of the same year.

THE right of the Legislature of Great Britain to impose taxes on her American colonies, and the expediency of exerting that right in the present conjuncture, are propositions so indisputably clear that I should never have thought it necessary to have undertaken their defence, had not many arguments been lately flung out both in papers and conversation, which with insolence equal to their absurdity deny them both. As these are usually mixt up with several patriotic and favorite words such as liberty, property, Englishmen, etc., which are apt to make strong impressions on that more numerous part of mankind who have ears but no understanding, it will not, I think, be improper to give them some answers. To this, therefore,

77

I shall singly confine myself, and do it in as few words as possible, being sensible that the fewest will give least trouble to myself, and probably most information to my reader.

The great capital argument which I find on this subject, and which, like an elephant at the head of a Nabob's army, being once overthrown must put the whole into confusion, is this; that no Englishman is, or can be taxed, but by his own consent: by which must be meant one of these three propositions; either that no Englishman can be taxed without his own consent as an individual; or that no Englishman can be taxed without the consent of the persons he chuses to represent him; or that no Englishman can be taxed without the consent of the majority of all those who are elected by himself and others of his fellow subjects to represent them. Now let us impartially consider whether any one of these propositions are in fact true: if not, then this wonderful structure which has been erected upon them falls at once to the ground, and like another Babel, perishes by a confusion of words, which the builders themselves are unable to understand.

First then, that no Englishman is or can be taxed but by his own consent as an individual: this is so far from being true, that it is the very reverse of truth; for no man that I know of is taxed by his own consent, and an Englishman, I believe, is as little likely to be so taxed as any man in the world.

Secondly, that no Englishman is or can be taxed but by the consent of those persons whom he has chose to represent him. For the truth of this I shall appeal only to the candid representatives of those unfortunate counties which produce cyder, and shall willingly acquiesce under their determination.

78

Lastly, that no Englishman is or can be taxed without the consent of the majority of those who are elected
by himself and others of his fellow subjects to represent
them. This is certainly as false as the other two; for every
Englishman is taxed, and not one in twenty represented:
copyholders, leaseholders, and all men possessed of personal property only, chuse no representatives; Manchester, Birmingham, and many more of our richest and
most flourishing trading towns send no members to
Parliament, consequently cannot consent by their representatives, because they chuse none to represent them;
yet are they not Englishmen ? or are they not taxed ?

I am well aware that I shall hear Locke, Sidney,
Selden, and many other great names quoted to prove
that every Englishman, whether he has a right to vote
for a representative or not, is still represented in the
British Parliament, in which opinion they all agree.
On what principle of common-sense this opinion is
founded I comprehend not, but on the authority of
such respectable names I shall acknowledge its truth;
but then I will ask one question, and on that I will rest
the whole merits of the cause. Why does not this
imaginary representation extend to America as well as
over the whole Island of Great Britain ? If it can
travel three hundred miles, why not three thousand ?
If it can jump over rivers and mountains, why cannot
it sail over the ocean ? If the towns of Manchester and
Birmingham, sending no representatives to Parliament, are notwithstanding there represented, why are
not the cities of Albany and Boston equally represented
in that Assembly? Are they not alike British subjects? are
they not Englishmen? or are they only Englishmen when
they sollicit for protection, but not Englishmen when
taxes are required to enable this country to protect them?

But it is urged that the colonies are by their charters placed under distinct Governments each of which has a legislative power within itself, by which alone it ought to be taxed; that if this privilege is once given up, that liberty which every Englishman has a right to, is torn from them, they are all slaves, and all is lost.

The liberty of an Englishman is a phrase of so various a signification, having within these few years been used as a synonymous term for blasphemy, bawdy, treason, libels, strong beer, and cyder, that I shall not here presume to define its meaning; but I shall venture to assert what it cannot mean; that is, an exemption from taxes imposed by the authority of the Parliament of Great Britain; nor is there any charter that ever pretended to grant such a privilege to any colony in America; and had they granted it, it could have had no force; their charters being derived from the Crown, and no charter from the Crown can possibly supersede the right of the whole legislature. Their charters are undoubtedly no more than those of all corporations, which impower them to make bye-laws, and raise duties for the purposes of their own police, for ever subject to the superior authority of Parliament; and in some of their charters the manner of exercising these powers is specifyed in these express words, " according to the course of other corporations in Great Britain ". And therefore they can have no more pretence to plead an exemption from this parliamentary authority, than any other corporation in England.

It has been moreover alleged, that though Parliament may have power to impose taxes on the colonies, they have no right to use it, because it would be an unjust tax; and no supreme or legislative power can have a right to enact any law in its nature unjust. To this, I shall only make this short reply, that if Parliament can impose no taxes but what are equitable, and if the persons taxed are to be the judges of that equity, they will in effect have no power to lay any tax at all. No tax can be imposed exactly equal on all, and if it is not equal it cannot be just, and if it is not just, no power whatever can impose it; by which short syllogism all taxation is at an end; but why it should not be used by Englishmen on this side the Atlantic as well as by those on the other, I do not comprehend.

Thus much for the right. Let us now a little inquire into the expediency of this measure, to which two objections have been made; that the time is improper, and the manner wrong.

As to the first, can any time be more proper to require some assistance from our colonies, to preserve to themselves their present safety, than when this country is almost undone by procuring it? Can any time be more proper to impose some tax upon their trade, than when they are enabled to rival us in our manufactures, by the encouragement and protection which we have given them? Can any time be more proper to oblige them to settle handsome incomes on their Governors, than when we find them unable to procure a subsistence on any other terms than those of breaking all their instructions, and betraying the rights of their sovereign? Can there be a more proper time to compel them to fix certain salaries on their judges, than when we see them so dependent on the humours of their Assemblies, that they can obtain a livelihood no longer than *quam diu se male gesserint*? Can there be a more proper time to force them to maintain an army at their expence, than when that army is necessary for their own protection, and we are utterly unable to support it? Lastly; can there be a more proper time for this mother country to leave off feeding out of her own vitals these children whom she has nursed up, than when they are arrived at such strength and maturity as to be well able to provide for themselves and ought rather with filial duty to give some assistance to her distresses?

As to the manner; that is, the imposing taxes on the colonies by the authority of Parliament, it is said to be harsh and arbitrary; and that it would have been more consistent with justice, at least with maternal tenderness, for administration here to have settled quotas on each of the colonies, and have then transmitted them with injunctions that the sums allotted should be immediately raised by their respective legislatures, on the penalty of their being imposed by Parliament in case of their non-compliance. But was this to be done, what would be the consequence? Have their Assemblies shewn so much obedience to the orders of the Crown, that we could reasonably expect that they would immediately tax themselves on the arbitrary command of a minister? Would it be possible here to settle those quotas with justice, or would any one of the colonies submit to them, were they ever so just? Should we not be compared to those Roman tyrants, who used to send orders to their subjects to murder themselves within so many hours, most obligingly leaving the method to their own choice, but on their disobedience threatening a more severe fate from the hands of an executioner? And should we not receive votes, speeches, resolutions, petitions, and remonstrances in abundance, instead of taxes? In short, we either have a right to tax the colonies, or we have not. If Parliament is possessed of this right, why should it be exercised with more delicacy in America than it has ever been even in Great Britain itself? If on the other hand, they have no such right, sure it is below the dignity as well as the justice of the Legislature to intimidate the colonies with vain threats, which they have really no right to put in execution.

One method indeed has been hinted at, and but one, that might render the exercise of this power in a British Parliament just and legal, which is the introduction of representatives from the several colonies into that body; but as this has never seriously been proposed, I shall not here consider the impracticability of this method, nor the effects of it if it could be practised; but only say that I have lately seen so many specimens of the great powers of speech of which these American gentlemen are possessed, that I should be much afraid that the sudden importation of so much eloquence at once, would greatly endanger the safety and government of this country; or in terms more fashionable, though less understood, this our most excellent Constitution. If we can avail ourselves of these taxes on no other condition, I shall never look upon it as a measure of frugality; being perfectly satisfyed that in the end it will be much cheaper for us to pay their army than their orators.

I cannot omit taking notice of one prudential reason which I have heard frequently urged against this taxation of the colonies, which is this: That if they are by this means impoverished, they will be unable to purchase our manufactures, and consequently we shall lose that trade from which the principal benefit which we receive from them must arise. But surely, it requires but little sagacity to see the weakness of this argument; for should the colonies raise taxes for the purposes of their own government and protection, would the money so raised be immediately annihilated? What some pay, would not others receive? Would not those who so receive it, stand in need of as many of our manufactures, as those who pay? Was the army there maintained at the expence of the Americans, would the soldiers want fewer coats, hats, shirts, or shoes than at present? Had the judges salaries ascertained to them, would they not have occasion for as costly perriwigs, or robes of as expensive scarlet, as marks of their legal abilities, as they now wear in their present state of dependency? Or had their Governors better incomes settled on them for observing their instructions, than they can now with difficulty obtain for disobeying them, would they expend less money in their several Governments, or bring home at their return less riches to lay out in the manufactories of their native country?

It has been likewise asserted that every shilling which our colonies can raise either by cultivation or commerce, finally centers in this country and therefore it is argued we can acquire nothing by their taxation, since we can have no more than their all; and whether this comes in by taxes or by trade, the consequence is the same. But allowing this assertion to be true, which it is not, yet the reasoning upon it is glaringly false; for surely it is not the same whether the wealth derived from these colonies flows immediately into the coffers of the public, or into the pockets of individuals from whence it must be squeezed by various domestic taxes before it can be rendered of any service to the nation. Surely it is by no means the same, whether this money brought in by taxes enables us to diminish part of that enormous debt contracted by the last expensive war, or whether coming in by trade it enables the merchant, by augmenting his influence together with his wealth, to plunge us into new wars and new debts for his private advantage.

From what has been here said, I think that not only the right of the legislature of Great Britain to impose taxes on her colonies, not only the expediency, but the absolute necessity of exercising that right in the present conjuncture, has been so clearly though concisely proved, that it is to be hoped that in this great and important question all parties and factions, or in the more polite and fashionable term, all connections will most cordially unite; that every member of the British Parliament, whether in or out of humour with Administration, whether he has been turned out because he has opposed, or whether he opposes because he has been turned out, will endeavour to the utmost of his power to support this measure. A measure which must not only be approved by every man who has any property or common sense, but which ought to be required by every English subject of an English Administration.

6: SIR FRANCIS BERNARD. Letter to Lord Barrington

23 November 1765

Sir Francis Bernard (?1711–79) was Governor of Massachusetts Bay from 1760 to 1769. As such he faithfully upheld the views of the home government and engaged in a long series of disputes with the Assembly. The problems he had to face are illustrated by his correspondence with William Wildman, second Viscount Barrington (1717–93), who was successively Chancellor of the Exchequer, Treasurer of the Navy and Secretary at War—holding the latter post from 1765 to 1778.

The letter from which these extracts are taken is printed in *Barrington-Bernard Correspondence*, ed. E. Channing and A. C. Coolidge (Harvard, U.P., 1912), pp. 93–102.

IT is my opinion that all the political evils in America arise from the want of ascertaining the relation between Great Britain and the American Colonies. Hence it is that ideas of that relation are formed in Britain and America, so very repugnant and contradictory to each other. In Britain the American Governments are considered as corporations empowered to make by-laws, existing only during the pleasure of parliament, who have never yet done anything to confirm their establishment and hath at any time a power to dissolve them. In America they claim (I mean in publick papers) to be perfect States, no otherwise dependent upon Great Britain than by

86

having the same king, which having compleat legislatures within themselves are no ways subject to that of
Great Britain; which in such instances as it has heretofore exercised a legislative power over them has
usurped it. In a difference so very wide who shall
determine?

So much is America altered by the late financial
acts, that a new system of policy and of a more refined
kind than was wanted heretofore, has now become
needful. The patchwork government of America will
last no longer: the necessity of a parliamentary establishment of a government of America upon fixed constitutional principles is brought on with a precipitation
which could not have been foreseen but a year ago,
and is become more urgent by the very incidents which
make it more difficult. The circumstance of the
Americans justifying their obedience by their not being
represented points out a method to enforce their obedience upon their own principles. Take them at their
word: let them seek representatives at the present time
and for the present purposes: 30 for the Continent and
15 for the islands would be sufficient. In this Parliament, the Colonies being actually represented, let the
affair of the American governments be canvassed to
the bottom; and let a general uniform system of government be formed and established by Act of Parliament, by which the Americans according to their own
principles will be bound; and let the relation of America
to Great Britain be determined and ascertained by a
solemn recognition: so that the rights of the American
government and their subordination to that of Great

Britain may no longer be a subject of doubt and dispute. When the great work is done, the American representatives may be dismissed and left to attend their own legislatures which will then know the bounds of their own authority.

7: JOHN DICKINSON.   Address on the Stamp Act

Stamp Act Congress, New York, November 1765

John Dickinson (1732–1808) played a leading part in the political life of Pennsylvania in the revolutionary period. He represented the colony at the Stamp Act Congress held in New York in October, 1765, and has been credited with the authorship of the resolutions passed by that gathering on 19 October. (They are given in Morison, *Sources and Documents*, pp. 32–4.)

His own views were given in the document from which this extract is taken and which is printed in his *Writings* (ed., P. L. Ford). Memoirs of the Pennsylvania Historical Society Vol. XIV, 1891, pp. 199–205.

THAT this is the fatal Tendency of that Statute, appears from Propositions so evident, that he who runs may read and understand. To mention them is to convince. Men cannot be happy, without Freedom; nor free, without Security of Power; nor so secure, unless the sole Power to dispose of it be lodged in themselves: therefore no People can be *free*, but where Taxes are imposed on them *with their own Consent* given personally, or by their Representatives. If then the Colonists are equally intitled to Happiness with the inhabitants of *Great-Britain* and Freedom is essential to Happiness, they are equally intitled to Freedom. If they are equally intitled to Freedom, and an exclusive Right of Taxation is essential to Freedom, they are equally intitled to such Taxation.

8: SIR WILLIAM BLACKSTONE. Commentaries on the Laws of England

1765-69

Sir William Blackstone (1723-80) was professor of English law at Oxford from 1758-66. His lectures were published under the above title in four volumes which appeared between 1765 and 1769. They achieved wide circulation and influence in Great Britain and were subsequently widely studied in America.

The extracts are taken from Volume 1.

THE power and jurisdiction of Parliament says Sir Edward Coke, is so transcendent and absolute, that it cannot be confined, either for causes or persons within any bounds. . . . It hath sovereign and un-controllable authority in the making, confirming, enlarging, restraining, abrogating, repealing, reviving, and expounding of laws, concerning matters of all possible denominations, ecclesiastical or temporal, civil, military, maritime, or criminal: this being the place where that absolute despotic power, which must in all governments reside somewhere, is entrusted by the constitution of these kingdoms. All mischiefs and grievances, operations and remedies, that transcend the ordinary course of the laws, are within the reach of this extraordinary tribunal. It can regulate or new-model the succession to the Crown; as was done in the reign of Henry VIII and William III. It can alter the established religion of the land; as was done in a variety of instances, in the reigns of Henry VIII and his three children. It can change and create afresh even the constitution of the kingdom and of parliaments themselves; as was done by the act of union, and the several statutes for triennial and septennial elections. It can, in short, do everything that is not naturally impossible; and therefore some have not scrupled to call its power, by a figure rather too bold, the omnipotence of Parliament. True it is, that what the Parliament doth, no authority upon earth can undo . . . and, as Sir Matthew Hale observes, this being the highest and greatest court over which none other can have jurisdiction in the kingdom, if by any means a misgovernment should fall upon it, the subjects of this kingdom are left without all manner of remedy.

9: WILLIAM PITT: Speech in the Debate on the Address, House of Commons

14 January 1766

William Pitt (1708–78) had been out of office since his resignation in October, 1761, and was regarded as the principal leader of the Whigs, although incapacitated by ill-health from any participation in public business during the year 1765 in the course of which the Rockingham ministry had been formed. He had declined to participate in that ministry. He supported the ministry's decision to repeal the Stamp Act, which was taken on 17 January, three days after this debate.

No Eighteenth-Century parliamentary speeches were accurately reported. They were sometimes published from the speaker's manuscript like some of Burke's. For the source problems of Chatham's speeches, see Basil Williams, *Life of William Pitt, Earl of Chatham,* App. A. The text from which these extracts are drawn is that given in *Correspondence of William Pitt, Earl of Chatham* (4 v., 1838–40), II, pp. 369–72.

HE commended the king's speech, approved of the address in answer, as it decided nothing, every gentleman being left at perfect liberty to take such a part concerning America, as he might afterwards see fit. One word only he could not approve of: " early " is a word that does not belong to the notice the ministry have given to parliament of the troubles in America.

92

In a matter of such importance, the communication ought to have been immediate: I speak not with respect to parties, I stand up in this place singly and unconnected. As to the late ministry, (turning himself to Mr. Grenville,) every capital measure they have taken, has been entirely wrong. . . .

It is a long time, Mr. Speaker, since I have attended in parliament. When the resolution was taken in the house to tax America, I was ill in bed. If I could have endured to have been carried in my bed, so great was the agitation of my mind for the consequence, I would have solicited some kind hand to have laid me down on this floor, to have borne my testimony against it. It is now an act that has passed: I would speak with decency of every act of this house, but I must beg the indulgence of the house to speak of it with freedom.

I hope a day may soon be appointed to consider the state of the nation with respect to America. I hope gentlemen will come to this debate with all the temper and impartiality that his Majesty recommends, and the importance of the subject requires—a subject of greater importance than ever engaged the attention of this house, that subject only excepted, when, near a century ago, it was the question, whether you yourselves were to be bound or free.

In the mean time, as I cannot depend upon health for any future day, such is the nature of my infirmities, I will beg to say a few words at present, leaving the justice, the equity, the policy, the expediency of the act, to another time. I will only speak to one point, a point which seems not to have been generally under-stood—I mean to the right. Some gentlemen (alluding to Mr. Nugent) seem to have considered it as a point of honour. If gentlemen consider it in that light, they leave all measures of right and wrong, to follow a delusion that may lead to destruction. It is my opinion that this kingdom has no right to lay a tax upon the colonies, to be sovereign and supreme in every circum-stance of government and legislation whatsoever. They are the subjects of this kingdom, equally entitled with yourselves to all the natural rights of mankind and the peculiar privileges of Englishmen.

Equally bound by its laws, and equally participating of the constitution of this free country, the Americans are the sons, not the bastards of England. Taxation is no part of the governing or legislative power. The taxes are a voluntary gift and grant of the Commons alone. In legislation the three estates of the realm are alike con-cerned; but the concurrency of the Peers and the Crown to a tax, is only necessary to close with the form of a law.

The gift and grant is of the Commons alone. In ancient days, the Crown, the Barons, and the Clergy, possessed the lands. In those days, the Barons and the clergy gave and granted to the crown. They gave and granted what was their own. At present, since the discovery of America, and other circumstances per-mitting, the Commons are become the proprietors of the land. The Crown has divested itself of its great estates. The Church (God bless it) has but a pittance. The property of the Lords, compared with that of the Commons, is as a drop of water in the ocean; and this House represents these Commons, the proprietors of the lands; and those proprietors virtually represent the rest of the inhabitants.

94

When, therefore, in this house we give and grant, we give and grant what is our own. But in an American tax, what do we do? We, your majesty's commons of Great Britain, give and grant to your Majesty, what? our own, property?—No, we give and grant to your majesty the property of your Majesty's commons of America. It is an absurdity in terms.

The distinction between legislation and taxation is essentially necessary to liberty. The Crown, the Peers, are equally legislative powers with the Commons. If taxation be a part of simple legislation, the Crown, the Peers, have rights in taxation as well as yourselves; rights they will claim, which they will exercise, whenever the principle can be supported by power.

There is an idea in some, that the colonies are virtually represented in this House. I would fain know by whom an American is represented here? Is he represented by any knight of the shire, in any county in this kingdom? Would to God that respectable representation was augmented to a greater number. Or will you tell him that he is represented by any representative of a borough,—a borough which, perhaps, no man ever saw? That is what is called the " rotten part of the constitution ". It cannot continue a century. If it does not drop it must be amputated. The idea of a virtual representation of America in this House, is the most contemptible idea that ever entered into the head of man.—It does not deserve a serious consideration.

The Commons of America, represented in their several assemblies, have ever been in possession of the exercise of this, their constitutional right, of giving and granting their own money. They would have been slaves if they had not enjoyed it. At the same time, this kingdom, as the supreme governing and legislative power, has always bound the colonies by her laws, by her regulations, and restrictions in trade, in navigation, in manufactures, in every thing, except that of taking their money out of their pockets without their consent. Here I would draw the line,

" *Sunt certi denique fines. Quam ultra citraque nequit consistere rectum.*"

[" There are fixed limits beyond which, and short of which, right cannot find a resting-place." Horace *Satires*, I, i, 106.]

10: GEORGE GRENVILLE. Speech in the Debate on the Address: House of Commons

14 January 1766

George Grenville (1712–70) had been Prime Minister from April 1763 to July 1765, and was thus primarily responsible for the series of Acts and actions which brought about the crisis in the relations with the American colonies. He was now the chief of those who opposed the Rockingham government's more conciliatory policy.

The text is that given in Cobbett's *Parliamentary History*, XVI, p. 102.

HE began with censuring the ministry very severely, for delaying to give earlier notice to parliament of the disturbances in America. He said they began in July, and now we are in the middle of January; lately they were only occurrences; they are now grown to disturbances, to tumults, and riots. I doubt they border on open rebellion; and if the doctrine I have heard this day be confirmed, I fear they will lose that name, to take that of a revolution. The government over them being dissolved, a revolution will take place in America. I cannot understand the difference between external and internal taxes. They are the same in effect, and differ only in name. That this kingdom has the sovereign, the supreme legislative power over America, is granted. It cannot be denied;

and taxation is a part of that sovereign power. It is one branch of the legislation. It is, it has been exercised, over those who are not, who were never represented. It is exercised over the India Company, the merchants of London, and the proprietors of the stocks, and over great manufacturing towns. It was exercised over the county palatine of Chester, and the bishoprick of Durham, before they sent any representatives to parliament . . . Which being done, he said: When I proposed to tax America, I asked the house, if any gentleman would object to the right; I repeatedly asked it, and no man would attempt to deny it. Protection and obedience are reciprocal. Great Britain protects America, America is bound to yield obedience. If not, tell me when the Americans were emancipated? When they want the protection of this kingdom, they are always very ready to ask it. That protection has always been afforded them in the most full and ample manner. The nation has run itself into an immense debt to give them this protection; and now they are called upon to contribute a small share towards the public expence, an expence arising from themselves, they renounce your authority, insult your officers, and break out, I might almost say, in open rebellion.

The seditious spirit of the colonies owes its birth to factions in this house. Gentlemen are careless of the consequences of what they say, provided it answers the purposes of opposition.

We were told we trod on tender ground; we were bid to expect disobedience. What was this, but telling the Americans to stand out against the law, to encourage their obstinacy with expectation of support from hence? let us only hold out a little, they would

say, our friends will soon be in power. Ungrateful
people of America! bounties have been extended to
them. When I had the honour of serving the crown,
while you yourselves were loaded with an enormous
debt, you have given bounties on their lumber, on
their iron, their hemp, and many other articles. You
have relaxed, in their favour, the act of navigation,
that palladium of British commerce; and yet I have
been abused in all the public papers as an enemy to
the trade of America. I have been particularly charged
with giving orders and instructions to prevent the
Spanish trade, and thereby stopping the channel by
which alone North America used to be supplied with
cash for remittances for this country. I defy any man
to produce any such orders or instructions. I dis-
couraged no trade but what was illicit, what was prohibited by act of parliament. . . . I offered to do every
thing in my power to advance the trade of America. I
was above giving an answer to anonymous calumnies;
but in this place, it becomes me to wipe off the
aspersion.

11 : WILLIAM PITT (subsequently Earl of Chatham). Speech in reply to Grenville, House of Commons

14 January 1766

The text from which these extracts are given is that in *Chatham Correspondence*, II, pp. 369–72.

GENTLEMEN, Sir, (to the speaker) I have been charged with giving birth to sedition in America. They have spoken their sentiments with freedom against this unhappy act, and that freedom has become their crime. Sorry I am to hear the liberty of speech in this house, imputed as a crime. But the imputation shall not discourage me. It is a liberty I mean to exercise.

No gentleman ought to be afraid to exercise it—it is a liberty by which the gentleman who calumniates it might have profited, by which he ought to have profited. He ought to have desisted from his project. The gentleman tells us America is obstinate; America is almost in open rebellion. I rejoice that America has resisted. Three millions of people, so dead to all feelings of liberty as voluntarily to submit to be slaves, would have been fit instruments to make slaves of the rest. I come not here armed at all points, with law cases and acts of parliament, with the statute book doubled down in dogs'-ears, to defend the cause of liberty: if I had, I myself would have cited the two cases of Chester and Durham: I would have cited them, to have shewn that even under the most arbitrary reigns, parliaments were ashamed of taxing people without their consent, and allowed them representatives. Why did the gentleman confine himself to Chester and Durham? He might have taken a higher example in Wales; Wales, that never was taxed by parliament till it was incorporated. I would not debate a particular point of law with the gentleman: I know his abilities: I have been obliged by his diligent researches. But for the defence of liberty upon a general principle, upon a constitutional principle, it is a ground upon which I stand firm; on which I dare meet any man. The gentleman tells us of many who are taxed, and are not represented. The India Company, merchants, stock-holders, manufacturers. Surely many of these are represented in other capacities, as owners of land, or as freemen of boroughs. It is a misfortune that more are not actually represented. But they are all inhabitants, and, as such, are virtually represented. They have connections with those that elect, and they have influence over them. The gentleman mentioned the stock-holders. I hope he does not reckon the debts of the nation a part of the national estate. Since the accession of king William, many ministers, some of great, others of more moderate abilities, have taken the lead of government. (He then went through the list of them, bringing it down till he came to himself, giving a short sketch of the characters of each of them. None of these, he said, thought or ever dreamed of robbing the colonies of their constitutional rights. That was reserved to mark the era of the late administration: not that there were wanting some, when I had the honour to serve his majesty, to propose to me to burn my fingers with an American stamp act. With the enemy at their back, with our bayonets at their breasts, in the day of their distress, perhaps the Americans would have submitted to the imposition; but it would have been taking an ungenerous, an unjust advantage. The gentleman boasts of his bounties to America! Are not these bounties intended finally for the benefit of this kingdom? If they are not, he has misapplied the national treasures. I am no courtier of America, I stand up for this kingdom. I maintain that the parliament has a right to bind, to restrain America.

Our legislative power over the colonies is supreme. When it ceases to be sovereign and supreme, I would advise every gentleman to sell his lands, if he can, and embark for that country. Where two countries are connected together like England and her colonies, without being incorporated, the one must necessarily govern; the greater must rule the less; but so rule it, as not to contradict the fundamental principles that are common to both. If the gentleman does not understand the difference between external and internal taxes, I cannot help it; but there is a plain distinction between taxes levied for the purposes of raising a revenue, and duties imposed for the regulation of trade, for the accommodation of the subject; although, in the consequences, some revenue might incidentally arise from the latter.

The gentleman asks, when were the colonies emancipated? But I desire to know, when were they made slaves? But I dwell not upon words. When I had the honour of serving his majesty, I availed myself of the means of information which I derived from my office. I speak therefore from knowledge. My materials were good. I was at pains to collect, to digest, to consider them; and I will be bold to affirm, that the profits to Great Britain from the trade of the colonies, through all its branches, is two millions a year. This is the fund that carried you triumphantly through the last war. The estates that were rented at two thousand pounds a year, three score years ago, are at three thousand at present. Those estates sold then from fifteen to eighteen years purchase; the same may be now sold for thirty.

You owe this to America. This is the price that America pays you for her protection. And shall a miserable financier come with a boast, that he can fetch a pepper-corn into the exchequer, to the loss of a million to the nation! I dare not say, how much higher these profits may be augmented. Omitting the immense increase of people, by natural population, in the northern colonies, and the migration from every part of Europe, I am convinced the whole commercial system of America may be altered to advantage. You have prohibited where you ought to have encouraged; you have encouraged where you ought to have prohibited. Improper restraints have been laid on the continent, in favour of the islands. You have but two nations to trade with in America. Would you had twenty! Let acts of parliament in consequence of treaties remain, but let not an English minister become a custom-house officer for Spain, or for any foreign power. Much is wrong, much may be amended for the general good of the whole.

Does the gentleman complain he has been misrepresented in the public prints? It is a common misfortune . . .

The gentleman must not wonder he was not contradicted, when, as the minister, he asserted the right of parliament to tax America. I know not how it is, but there is a modesty in this house which does not choose to contradict a minister. I wish gentlemen would get the better of this modesty: Even that chair, Sir, sometimes looks towards St. James's; if they do not, perhaps the collective body may begin to abate of its respect for the representative... A great deal has been said without doors of the power, of the strength of America. It is a topic that ought to be cautiously meddled with. In a good cause, on a sound bottom, the force of this country can crush America to atoms. I know the valour of your troops. I know the skill of your officers. There is not a company of foot that has served in America out of which you may not pick a man of sufficient knowledge and experience to make a governor of a colony there. But on this ground, on the Stamp Act, which so many here will think a crying injustice, I am one who will lift up my hands against it.

In such a cause, your success would be hazardous. America, if she fell, would fall like the strong man; she would embrace the pillars of the state, and pull down the constitution along with her. Is this your boasted peace—not to sheathe the sword in its scabbard, but to sheathe it in the bowels of your countrymen? Will you quarrel with yourselves, now the whole house of Bourbon is united against you? ... The Americans have not acted in all things with prudence and temper; they have been wronged; they have been driven to madness, by injustice. Will you punish them for the madness you have occasioned? Rather let prudence and temper come first from this side.

I will undertake for America that she will follow the example. There are two lines in a ballad of Prior's, of a man's behaviour to his wife, so applicable to you and your colonies, that I cannot help repeating them:

> " Be to her faults a little blind;
> Be to her virtues very kind."

Upon the whole, I will beg leave to tell the house what is really my opinion. It is, that the Stamp Act be repealed absolutely, totally, and immediately. That the reason for the repeal be assigned because it was founded on an erroneous principle. At the same time, let the sovereign authority of this country over the colonies be asserted in as strong terms as can be devised, and be made to extend to every point of legislation whatsoever; that we may bind their trade, confine their manufactures, and exercise every power whatsoever, except that of taking money out of their pockets without their consent.

12: DEBATE ON THE CONWAY RESOLU-
TIONS. House of Lords

10 February 1766

Henry Seymour Conway, the Secretary of State for the Southern Department and therefore the minister most closely concerned with American policy, introduced five resolutions into the House of Commons on 3 February, 1766, in which the authority of Parliament was upheld and the riotous proceedings in the colonies denounced. His speech and the resolutions themselves prepared the ground for the ministry's policy of accompanying the repeal of the Stamp Act by a Declaratory Act upholding its constitutional validity.

The debate on the resolutions in the House of Lords is taken from the *Parliamentary History* XVI, pp. 161 ff.

Those taking part were Augustus Henry Fitzroy, third Duke of Grafton (1735–1811), Secretary of State for the Northern Department; William Petty, third Earl of Shelburne (1737–1805), subsequently first Marquis of Lansdowne, who became Secretary of State for the Southern Department, when Chatham formed his ministry in July; George Lyttleton, first Baron Lyttleton (1709–73), a former Chancellor of the Exchequer; Charles Pratt, Baron, later first Earl of Camden (1714–94), Chief Justice of the Common Pleas, who became Lord Chancellor in Chatham's administration; Robert Henley, Baron, later first Earl of Northington (? 1708–72), who had held the Great Seal as Lord Keeper and then Chancellor since 1757, and William Murray, Baron, later first Earl of Mansfield (1705–93), Lord Chief Justice from 1756 to 1788.

THE Debate arose upon the first of the above Resolutions, namely, " That the King's Majesty, by and with the advice and consent of the Lords spiritual and temporal and Commons of Great Britain in parliament assembled, had, hath, and of right ought to have, full power and authority to make laws and statutes, of sufficient force and validity to bind the colonies and people of America, subjects of the crown of Great Britain, in all cases whatsoever."

The Duke of *Grafton*, after lamenting the contrariety of opinion, on the first proposition, and observing that, in questions of this interesting nature, we ought to divest ourselves of all prejudice, or attachment to one man or another, declared his opinion to be, that the Americans were as liable to be taxed as any man in Great Britain. And that therefore he should not have offered the first Resolution, but that the right had been questioned, not only by the Americans, but by persons here, some of whom were eminent, and possibly the highest in the line they tread. His grace then recommended lenient measures, as thinking the Americans deluded into an opinion that England had given them up.

Lord *Shelburne* spoke next, who did not give any direct opinion on the right of parliament to tax America, though he seemed, from what I could gather of what he said, to insinuate that he was of that opinion.

His lordship said, he thought it was highly necessary never to bring constitutional points into debate but in matters of the highest consequence.

That the object of the present question seemed to him to be, whether we should, and how we should, restore tranquillity to America.

That his opinion was, that when America was acquainted of what had past in England the first day of the session, there only remained two questions for the consideration of parliament.

1st. Whether they should repeal the Act, and by that means open commerce and restore tranquillity to America; or, 2dly, Whether they should enforce it, and throw every thing into confusion. His lordship mentioned his having been lately at Antwerp, where he learnt from some of the principal persons there, that this town had refused a tax 109 times, and upon speaking on this subject afterwards in Brussels, he was informed, that it had been agitated at Vienna whether they ought to lay a tax on the Netherlands, and it had been determined it was not expedient to do it.

He applied this to the laying taxes on North America, and said, he did not choose in this situation of things to give a direct opinion on the point, but hinted at a protest if his lordship should differ in opinion with other lords.

Lord *Lyttelton* begun with observing, that he agreed with the noble lord in opinion, that this question should never have been agitated, but why? because it has been already determined by the laws of this country. It was however first agitated in America, where the right was denied.

In treating this question, I must tire your lordships with repeating many self-evident truths, but when persons of eminent knowledge and abilities dispute this point, I even doubt of my own reason.

I shall therefore take the liberty of laying before your lordships a few general maxims, not of party, but such as no statesman, no lawyer, has ever denied.

The first foundation of civil government is, that a civil society was formed by men entering into society on what may properly be called an original compact, and entrusting government with a power over their persons, liberties, and estates, for the safety of the whole. In what form or manner this power is to be exercised depends on the laws and constitutions of different countries.

There cannot be two rights existing in government at the same time, which would destroy each other; a right in government to make laws, and a right in the people, or any part, to oppose or disobey such laws. Another great principle of policy is, that in all states, democratical, aristocratical, or monarchical, or in mixed states, as Great Britain, the government must rest somewhere, and that must be fixed, or otherwise there is an end of all government. " Imperium in imperio."

But these great maxims which imply a subjection to the supreme government or legislature, do not exclude the existence of inferior legislatures with restrained powers, subject to the superior legislature. That the colonies are of this kind the many statutes made here to bind them since their first settlement plainly evince.

They went out subjects of Great Britain, and unless they can shew a new compact made between them and the parliament of Great Britain (for the king alone could not make a new compact with them) they still are subjects to all intents and purposes whatsoever. If they are subjects, they are liable to the laws of the country. Indeed, they complain that the laying internal taxes on them takes away the right of laying such taxes: this I deny; they certainly may lay such internal taxes for local purposes, and the parliament here may lay such taxes on particular occasions.

The last great maxim of this and every other free government is, that " No subject is bound by any law to which he is not actually or virtually consenting."

If the colonies are subjects of Great Britain, they are represented and consent to all statutes.

But it is said they will not submit to the Stamp Act as it lays an internal tax: if this be admitted, the same reasoning extends to all acts of parliament. The Americans will find themselves crampt by the Act of Navigation, and oppose that too.

The Americans themselves make no distinction between external and internal taxes. Mr. Otis, their champion, scouts such a distinction, and the assembly shewed they were not displeased with him, by making him their representative at the congress of the states general of America.

The only question before your lordships is, whether the American colonies are a part of the dominions of the crown of Great Britain ? If not, the parliament has no jurisdiction, if they are, as many statutes have declared them to be, they must be proper objects of our legislature: and by declaring them exempt from one statute or law, you declare them no longer subjects of Great Britain, and make them small independent communities not entitled to your protection.

If opinions of this weight are to be taken up, and argued upon through mistake or timidity, we shall have many legislators; we shall have Lycurguses, and Solons, in every coffee-house, tavern, and gin-shop in London.

The weight of taxes in England are heavy, and admit but this doctrine, many thousands who have no vote in electing representatives, will follow their brethren in America, in refusing submission to any taxes. The commons of this metropolis will with pleasure hear a doctrine propagated last week, of equality being the natural right of all.

We have a constitution which, with all its faults, is a good one, but the doctrine of equality may be carried to the destruction of this monarchy. Cromwell himself did not attempt to say that taxes were to be raised without the consent of the legislature.

Lord *Camden.*—I am very unhappy the first time of speaking in this House to differ from a lord of such superior abilities and learning, but the question before your lordships concerns the common rights of mankind; it is an abstract question, and will be judged of by your lordships gravely and deliberately, without any regard to the authority of any lord who speaks on either side of the question.

My lords; he who disputes the authority of any supreme legislature treads upon very tender ground. It is therefore necessary for me in setting out to lay in my claim to your lordships, and to desire that no inference may be drawn from any thing I shall advance. I disclaim that the consequence of my reasoning will be that the colonies can claim an independence on this country, or that they have a right to oppose acts of legislature in a rebellious manner, even though the legislature has no right to make such acts. In my own opinion, my lords, the legislature had no right to make this law.

The sovereign authority, the omnipotence of the legislature, my lords, is a favourite doctrine, but there are some things they cannot do. They cannot enact any thing against the divine law, and may forfeit their right. They cannot take away any man's private property without making him a compensation. A proof of which is the many private bills, as well as public, passed every session. They have no right to condemn any man by bill of attainder without hearing him.

But though the parliament cannot take any man's

private property, yet every subject must make contribution. And this he consents to do by his representatives; when the people consented to be taxed they reserved to themselves a power of giving and granting by their representatives.

The Resolution now proposed is in my opinion too general, as it gives the legislature an absolute power of laying any tax upon America.

Notwithstanding the King, Lords, and Commons could in ancient times tax other persons, they never could tax the clergy. I have seen a record, 17 R.2, of the Commons offering an aid to his majesty so as the clergy, who were possessed of a third part of the lands of the kingdom, would contribute a third part of the sum wanted. The clergy on that occasion said, that the parliament had no right to tax them, they might lay any part of the money wanted on the laity, and that they, the clergy, would then do what they saw just. And so late as in the year 1674 the clergy in convocation insisted on a right to tax themselves, and this right was recognized by the Commons.

At present the clergy have dropt that right; when, I cannot pretend to say, but when they did drop it they were melted down into the body of the country, and are now electors of their own representatives.

The counties palatine were little feudal governments exercising regal authority. The method was, for the crown to require them by writ to tax themselves. Tyrrel mentions some record of writs of that kind directed to Chester. It appears, however, that afterwards the legislature took to itself the power of taxation over these counties palatine, but then when they petitioned to be represented the parliament readily granted them representatives.

It is observable, that at the close of the charter erecting Lancaster into a county palatine there is a salvo of the right to the parliament a large. And the great lord Hale, in a MS. never printed, which treats of the prerogative of the crown, observes, that this was a county palatine, without the requisites of Chester and Durham, particularly as to the power of taxing and pardoning.

Wales, my lords, was not taxed till it was united to England, when it was forthwith represented.

Calais and Berwick, when they were conquered, sent members to parliament. Guernsey, Jersey, and the Isle of Man are not yet part of the realm of England, and have never yet been taxed.

Ireland was conquered originally, but was settled by the English. They tax themselves, and the parliament here has no right to tax them; lord Hale affirms this in the before-mentioned MS. where he says, that he thinks no acts here can bind the Irish in point of subsidies.

But, my lords, even supposing the Americans have no exclusive right to tax themselves, I maintain it would be good policy to give it them.—America feels she can do better without us, than we without her.

He spoke then to the expediency, and concluded that his opinion was, that the colonies had a right to tax themselves, and the parliament not.

Lord Chancellor *Northington.*—I did not think I should have troubled your lordships on the subject of this 1st Resolution, but, upon doctrines being laid down so new, so unmaintainable, and so unconstitutional, I cannot sit silent.

I have, my lords, this day heard a paradox in every law that I know of. I thought indeed, when I came into the House, that the proposition endeavoured to be supported by the noble lord, would have been rather more modified than it has been by a heated imagination, accompanied by a facility of expression and readiness of language.

The noble lord lays it down that the Americans have an exclusive right to lay taxes on themselves, and thinks that we are not to meddle with them.

What, shall it be said that one man alone could subdue all North America, and that his authority not overruling, the parliament of Great Britain cannot retain it ?

My lords, it is impossible to endeavour to prove a self evident truth.

Every government can arbitrarily impose laws on all its subjects; there must be a supreme dominion in every state; whether monarchical, aristocratical, democratical, or mixed. And all the subjects of each state are bound by the laws made by government.

But the noble lord has endeavoured to distinguish between the civil power of government, and its casuistical power. Now, my lords, there is no writer on general law but what agrees in this principle, that every legislature should make laws for the benefit and safety of the whole; but suppose they make a law contrary to this principle, a resistance to such law is at the risk of life and fortune.

As to what the noble lord says, of the clergy not having been taxed, the instruments he alludes to are commissions from the king to the laity and the clergy to tax themselves.

I do not know, my lords, that because pope Boniface had power to make the king and parliament here obey his orders in relation to the clergy taxing themselves, it is any argument for their right to do so. I do not know there ever was a period when the clergy had no right to vote in elections to parliament, and should be glad to be informed.

As to the convocation of king James, I deny the clergy taxed themselves at that period. Their orders are recited in acts of parliament, and had no legal force till they were enacted.

My lords, I seek for the liberty and constitution of this kingdom no farther back than the Revolution: there I make my stand. And in the reign of king William an act passed avowing the power of this legislature over the colonies.

As to the expediency of carrying the act into execution—if the noble lord means to suspend the execution, and advise the King on that head, I will tell his lordship the King cannot do it. He is sworn by his coronation oath to do the contrary; but if you should concur with his lordship as to the expediency of repeal, you will tell 12 millions of your subjects of Great Britain and Ireland, that you prefer the colonists who are got rich under their protection, and will have them at your doors, not making speeches, but using the *argumentum baculinum* [the argument of the big stick].

My lords, what have these favourite Americans done? They have called a meeting of their states, and then have entered into Resolutions by which, in my opinion, they have forfeited all their charters.

But, my lords, the nature of the Stamp Act seems to be mistaken. It binds all the colonies in general, but it does not controul the power each province has to lay internal taxes for local purposes.

If all the great lawyers in Westminster-hall should give an opinion that the King could grant the territory of North America, none would say, that the King could put them out of the subjection to the *summum imperium* of Great Britain.

My lords, the colonies are become too big to be governed by the laws they at first set out with. They have therefore run into confusion, and it will be the policy of this country to form a plan of laws for them.

If they withdraw allegiance you must withdraw protection; and then the little state of Genoa, or the kingdom or rather republic of Sweden, may soon overrun them.

Lord *Mansfield.*—I stand up to bring your lordships to the question before you, which is, whether the proposition made by the noble duke is, from what appears from our law and history, true or not true.

What has been wrote by those who have treated on the law of nature, or of other nations, in my opinion, is not at all applicable to the present question.

It is out of this question too, whether it is or is not expedient to repeal this act; out of this question too are the rules which are to guide the legislature in making a law. The law is made, and the question is, whether you had a right to make it.

I deny the proposition that parliament takes no man's property without his consent: it frequently takes private property without making what the owner thinks a compensation. If any lord makes objection to any part of the proposition, he ought to confine himself in his argument to the part he objects to, and not run into matters which do not relate to such objection.

I have, during the course of the debate on this great question, always wished to preserve unanimity among your lordships on every measure relating to America, and do verily believe that if every member of parlia-

116

ment had concurred in sentiments for the benefit of the whole, this great evil, as it now is, would have turned out for the advantage of the whole, and that the Americans, if they had time given them to cool, would have obeyed the law.

Your lordships must remember, upon the passing the Militia Act, how it was misrepresented, as a plot to send our subjects to America and Germany, and that the consequence of this was, that riots arose in several parts of the kingdom. A few of the rioters suffered death, but when people came to their cool senses, the act was obeyed.

I do not look upon Otis's pamphlet in a light other lords may—that it is to be totally disregarded. It may be called silly and mad, but mad people, or persons who have entertained silly and mad ideas, have led the people to rebellion, and overturned empires.

The proposition before your lordships has unhappily been attended with a difference of opinion in England. I shall therefore use my endeavours, in what I have to offer your lordships on this occasion, to quiet men's minds upon this subject.

In order to do this, I shall first lay down two propositions:

1st, That the British legislature, as to the power of making laws, represents the whole British empire, and has authority to bind every part and every subject without the least distinction, whether such subjects have a right to vote or not, or whether the law binds places within the realm or without.

2nd, That the colonists, by the condition on which they migrated, settled, and now exist, are more emphatically subjects of Great Britain than those within the realm; and that the British legislature have in

I   117

every instance exercised their right of legislation over them without any dispute or question till the 14th of January last.

As to the 1st proposition:

In every government the legislative power must be lodged somewhere, and the executive must likewise be lodged somewhere.

In Great Britain the legislative is in parliament, the executive in the crown.

The parliament first depended upon tenures. How did representation by election first arise? Why, by the favour of the crown. And the notion now taken up, that every subject must be represented by deputy, if he does not vote in parliament himself, is merely ideal.

At this day all the great companies here—the Bank, East India Company, and South Sea Company, have no representatives.

As to what has been said about the clergy—the fact is, that a demand made by them of a right to tax themselves was supported by the Pope; and the king and parliament of those times were weak enough to admit of it; but this admission is no proof of the right.

No distinction ought to be taken between the authority of parliament, over parts within or without the realm; but it is an established rule of construction, that no parts without the realm are bound unless named in the act. And this rule establishes the right of parliament; for unless they had a right to bind parts out of the realm, this distinction would never have been made.

As to the second proposition I laid out,

It must be granted that they migrated with leave as colonies, and therefore from the very meaning of the word were, are and must be subjects, and owe allegiance and subjection to their mother country.

13: LORD CAMDEN. Speech on American taxation, House of Lords

24 February 1766

This speech, in which Camden further expounded his views on
the constitutional position of Parliament with relation to the
colonies, is taken from the *Parliamentary History*, XVI, pp. 177–81.
Camden, who had achieved great popularity with the Opposition
through his decision in the Wilkes case that general warrants were
illegal, was closer to the American view of the taxation question
than most of his parliamentary associates. And, although he held
the post of Lord Chancellor from the beginning of Chatham's
ministry in July, 1766 until January, 1770, he did not approve of
the policy then adopted towards the American colonies.

MY lords; when I spoke last on this subject, I
thought I had delivered my sentiments so fully, and
supported them with such reasons, and such authorities, that I apprehended I should be under no necessity of troubling your lordships again. But I am now
compelled to rise up, and to beg your farther indulgence: I find that I have been very injuriously treated;
have been considered as the broacher of new-fangled
doctrines, contrary to the laws of this kingdom, and
subversive of the rights of parliament. My lords, this
is a heavy charge, but more so when made against one
stationed as I am in both capacities, as peer and judge,
the defender of the law and the constitution. When I
spoke last, I was indeed replied to, but not answered.

In the intermediate time, many things have been said. As I was not present, I must now beg leave to answer such as have come to my knowledge. As the affair is of the utmost importance, and in its consequences may involve the fate of kingdoms, I took the strictest review of my arguments; I re-examined all my authorities; fully determined, if I found myself mistaken, publicly to own my mistake, and give up my opinion: but my searches have more and more convinced me, that the British parliament have no right to tax the Americans. I shall not therefore consider the Declaratory Bill now lying on your table; for to what purpose, but loss of time, to consider the particulars of a Bill, the very existence of which is illegal, absolutely illegal, contrary to the fundamental laws of nature, contrary to the fundamental laws of this constitution ? A constitution grounded on the eternal and immutable laws of nature; a constitution whose foundation and centre is liberty,which sends liberty to every subject, that is or may happen to be within any part of its ample circumference. Nor my lords, is the doctrine new, it is as old as the constitution; it grew up with it; indeed it is its support; taxation and representation are inseparably, united; God hath joined them, no British parliament can separate them; to endeavour to do it, is to stab our very vitals. Nor is this the first time this doctrine has been mentioned; 70 years ago, my lords, a pamphlet was published, recommending the levying a parliamentary tax on one of the colonies; this pamphlet was answered by two others, then much read; these totally deny the power of taxing the colonies; and why ? Because the colonies had no representatives in parliament to give consent; no answer, public or private, was given to these pamphlets, no censure passed upon them; men were not startled at the doctrine as either new or illegal, or derogatory to the rights of parliament. I do not mention these pamphlets by way of authority, but to vindicate myself from the imputation of having first broached this doctrine.

My position is this—I repeat it—I will maintain it to my last hour,—taxation and representation are inseparable;—this position is founded on the laws of nature; it is more, it is itself an eternal law of nature; for whatever is a man's own, is absolutely his own; no man hath a right to take it from him without his consent, either expressed by himself or representative; whoever attempts to do it, attempts an injury; whoever does it, commits a robbery; he throws down and destroys the distinction between liberty and slavery. Taxation and representation are coeval with and essential to this constitution. I wish the maxim of Machiavel was followed, that of examining a constitution, at certain periods, according to its first principles; this would correct abuses and supply defects. I wish the times would bear it, and that men's minds were cool enough to enter upon such a task, and that the representative authority of this kingdom was more equally settled. I am sure some histories, of late published, have done great mischief; to endeavour to fix the æra when the House of Commons began in this kingdom, is a most pernicious and destructive attempt; to fix it in an Edward's or Henry's reign, is owing to the idle dreams of some whimsical, ill-judging antiquarians: but, my lords, this is a point too important to be left to such wrong-headed people. When did the House of Commons first begin? when, my lords? it began with the constitution, it grew up with the constitution; there is not a blade of grass growing in the most obscure corner of this kingdom, which is not, which was not ever, represented since the constitution began; there is not a blade of grass, which when taxed, was not taxed by the consent of the proprietor. There is a history written by one Carte, a history that most people now see through, and there is another favourite history, much read and admired. I will not name the author, your lordships must know whom I mean, and you must know from whence he pilfered his notions, concerning the first beginning of the House of Commons. My lords, I challenge any one to point out the time when any tax was laid upon any person by parliament, that person being unrepresented in parliament. My lords, the parliament laid a tax upon the palatinate of Chester, and ordered commissioners to collect it there: as commissioners were ordered to collect it in other counties; but the palatinate refused to comply; they addressed the king by petition, setting forth, that the English parliament had no right to tax them, that they had a parliament of their own, that they had always taxed themselves, and therefore desired the king to order his commissioners not to proceed. My lords, the king received the petition; he did not declare them either seditious or rebellious, but allowed their plea, and they taxed themselves. Your lordships may see both the petition and the king's answer in the records in the Tower. The clergy taxed themselves; when the parliament attempted to tax them, they stoutly refused; said they were not represented there; that they had a parliament of their own, which represented the clergy; that they would tax themselves; they did so. Much stress has been laid upon Wales, before it was united as it now is, as if the King, standing in the place of their former princes of that country, raised money by his own authority; but the real fact is otherwise; for I find that, long before Wales was subdued, the northern counties of that principality had representatives, and a parliament or assembly. As to Ireland, my lords, before that kingdom had a parliament as it now has, if your lordships will examine the old records, you will find, that when a tax was to be laid on that country, the Irish sent over here representatives; and the same records will inform your lordships, what wages those representatives received from their constituents. In short, my lords, from the whole of our history, from the earliest period, you will find that taxation and representation were always united; so true are the words of that consummate reasoner and politician Mr. Locke. I before alluded to his book; I have again consulted him; and finding what he writes so applicable to the subject in hand, and so much in favour of my sentiments, I beg your lordships' leave to read a little of this book.

" The supreme power cannot take from any man, any part of his property, without his own consent." Such are the words of this great man, and which are well worth your serious attention. His principles are drawn from the heart of our constitution, which he thoroughly understood, and will last as long as that shall last; and, to his immortal honour, I know not to what, under providence, the Revolution and all its happy effects, are more owing, than to the principles of government laid down by Mr. Locke. For these reasons, my lords, I can never give my assent to any bill for taxing the American colonies, while they remain unrepresented; for as to the distinction of virtual representation, it is so absurd as not to deserve an answer; I therefore pass it over with contempt. The forefathers of the Americans did not leave their native country, and subject themselves to every danger and distress, to be reduced to a state of slavery: they did not give up their rights; they looked for protection, and not for chains, from their mother country; by her they expected to be defended in the possession of their property, and not to be deprived of it: for, should the present power continue, there is nothing which they can call their own; or, to use the words of Mr. Locke, " What property have they in that, which another may, by right, take, when he pleases, to himself? "

14: JOHN DICKINSON. *Farmer's Letters No.* 11

November 1767

Although Dickinson's *Farmer's Letters* were the most important
and influential political writings produced by the Townshend
Acts and have been described as " upon the whole, the most
brilliant event in the literary history of the Revolution " (Tyler,
Literary History, I, p. 234), they were extremely cautious and conservative in tone; and Dickinson opposed any idea of independence. He maintained this attitude throughout the subsequent
disputes and opposed the Declaration of Independence in 1776,
losing his seat in Congress in consequence of this. He returned to
national politics later and was a member of the Constitutional
Convention in 1787.

The *Farmer's Letters* were originally published anonymously in
Philadelphia newspapers as " Letters from a Farmer in Pennsylvania to the Inhabitants of the British Colonies," in the winter of
1767–68, and reprinted in pamphlet form immediately afterwards.
They are reprinted in Dickinson's *Writings*, pp. 306–406.

THE parliament unquestionably possesses a legal
authority to regulate the trade of Great Britain and all
her colonies. Such an authority is essential to the
relation between a mother country and her colonies;
and necessary for the common good of all. He, who
considers these provinces as States distinct from the
British Empire, has very slender notions of justice or of
their interests. We are but parts of a whole; and therefore there must exist a power somewhere to preside and
preserve the connexion in due order. This power is

lodged in the Parliament; and we are as much dependent on Great Britain as a perfectly free people can be on another.

I have looked over every statute relating to these colonies, from their first settlement to this time; and I find every one of them founded on this principle till the Stamp Act administration. All before are calculated to regulate trade and preserve or promote a mutually beneficial course between the several constituent parts of the Empire; and though many of them imposed duties on trade, yet those duties were always imposed with a design to restrain the commerce of one part, that was injurious to another, and thus to promote the general welfare. The raising a revenue thereby was never intended.

15: SAMUEL ADAMS: Letters of the Massachusetts House of Representatives

January 1768

Samuel Adams (1722–1803) is more notable as a propagandist than as a political thinker in his own right. The letters drafted by him (almost certainly) for the Massachusetts Legislature helped to crystallize the opposition to the Townshend Acts and led to the adoption of the Non-Intercourse Agreements, as a method of coercing the British Government. *The Writings of Samuel Adams*, ed. H. A. Cushing. Vol. I, pp. 166–177 (New York, 1904).

(a) *To the Earl of Shelburne*, 15 *January*, 1768.

There are, my Lord, fundamental rules of the constitution, which it is humbly presumed, neither the supreme legislative nor the supreme executive can answer. In all free states, the constitution is fixed; it is from thence, that the legislative derives its authority; therefore it cannot change the constitution without destroying its own foundation. If, then, the constitution of Great Britain is the common right of all British subjects, it is humbly referred to your Lordship's judgment, whether the supreme legislative of the empire may rightly leap the bounds of it, in the exercise of power over the subjects in America, any more than over those in Britain.

(b) *To the Marquis of Rockingham*, 22 *January*, 1768.

My Lord, the superintending power of that high court [i.e., Parliament] over all his Majesty's subjects in the empire, and in all cases which can consist with the fundamental rules of the constitution, was never questioned in this province, nor, as the House conceive, in any other. But, in all free states, the constitution is fixed; it is from thence, that the supreme legislative as well as the supreme executive derives its authority. Neither, then, can break through the fundamental rules of the constitution, without destroying their own foundation.

(c) *To Lord Camden*, 29 *January*, 1768.

If in all free states, the constitution is fixed, and the supreme legislative power of the nation, from thence derives its authority; can that power overleap the bounds of the constitution, without subverting its own foundation? If the remotest subjects, are bound by the ties of allegiance, which this people and its forefathers have ever acknowledged; are they not by the rules of equity intitled to all rights of that constitution, which ascertains and limits both sovereignty and allegiance? If it is an essential unalterable right in nature, ingrafted into the British constitution as a fundamental law, and ever held sacred and irrevocable by the subjects within the realm, and that what is a man's own is absolutely his own; and that no man hath a right to take it from him without his consent; may not the subjects of this province, with a decent firmness which has always distinguished the happy subjects of Britain, plead and maintain this natural constitutional right?

16: EARL OF CHATHAM. Speech in the House of Lords

9 January 1770

Chatham had formed a ministry in succession to Rockingham in July, 1766 and had accepted a peerage in August. But his health had prevented him from taking an active part in the direction of affairs. And the Townshend Acts seem to have been passed without consulting him. He resigned office in October, 1768, and was succeeded by the Duke of Grafton. Chatham's seclusion from public affairs lasted throughout the premiership of his successor—a time during which the situation in the colonies grew considerably more critical through the spread of the Non-Importation Agreements. He did not resume his seat in the House of Lords until January, 1770, a short time before the formation of Lord North's ministry which took office on the 28th of that month.

The text from which these extracts are taken is that given in *Anecdotes and Speeches of the Earl of Chatham*. 3 v. (7th ed., 1810), II, pp. 76 ff.

THAT the situation of our foreign affairs was undoubtedly a matter of moment, and highly worthy their Lordships' consideration; but that he declared with grief, there were other matters still more important, and more urgently demanding their attention. He meant the distractions and divisions which prevailed in every part of the empire. He lamented the unhappy measure which had divided the colonies from the mother country, and which he feared had drawn them into excesses which he could not justify. He owned his natural partiality to America, and was inclined to make allowance even for those excesses. That they ought to be treated with tenderness, for in his sense they were ebullitions of liberty, which broke out upon the skin, and were a sign, if not of perfect health, at least of vigorous constitution, and must not be driven in too suddenly, lest they should strike to the heart. He professed himself entirely ignorant of the present state of America, therefore should be cautious of giving any opinion of the measures fit to be pursued with respect to that country. That it was a maxim he had observed through life, when he had lost way, to stop short, lest by proceeding without knowledge, and advancing (as he feared a noble Duke had done) from one false step to another, he should wind himself into an inextricable labyrinth, and never be able to recover the right road again. That as the House had yet no materials before them, by which they might judge of the proceedings of the colonies, he strongly objected to their passing that heavy censure upon them, which was conveyed in the word *unwarrantable*, contained in the proposed address. That it was passing a sentence without hearing the cause, or being acquainted with facts, and might expose the proceedings of the House to be received abroad with indifference or disrespect. That if *unwarrantable* meant any thing, it must mean illegal; and how could their Lordships decide that proceedings, which had not been stated to them in any shape, were contrary to law ? That what he had heard of the combinations in America, and of their success in supplying themselves with goods of their own manufacture, had indeed alarmed him much for the commercial interests of the mother country; but he could not conceive in what sense they could be called illegal, much less how a declaration of that House could remove the evil. That they were *dangerous* indeed, and he greatly wished to have that word substituted for unwarrantable. That we must look for other remedies. That the discontent of two millions of people deserved consideration; and the foundation of it ought to be removed. That this was the true way of putting a stop to combinations and manufactures in that country; but that he reserved himself to give his opinion more particularly upon this subject, when authentic information of the state of America should be laid before the House; declaring only for the present, that we should be cautious how we invade the liberties of any part of our fellow subjects, however remote in situation, or unable to make resistance. That liberty was a plant that deserved to be cherished; that he loved the tree, and wished well to every branch of it. That, like the vine in the Scripture, it had spread from east to west, had embraced whole nations with its branches, and sheltered them under its leaves. That the Americans had purchased their liberty at a dear rate, since they had quitted their native country, and gone in search of freedom to a desert.

17: THOMAS HUTCHINSON. Speech to the Massachusetts Assembly

6 January 1773

Thomas Hutchinson (1711–80) was a prominent native of Massachusetts and held many public offices, becoming Deputy-Governor in 1758. His support for Grenville's policy led to his house being sacked in the troubles in Boston in August, 1765. After Bernard's recall in 1769, he acted as governor and was formally appointed in 1771. He was thus the chief executive of the colony during the mounting tension signalized by the affray between British troops and the citizens of Boston, known as the " Boston Massacre ", in March, 1770 and the establishment in December, 1772, of the Boston Committee of Correspondence, the great instrument of agitation devised by Samuel Adams.

In an endeavour to stop what he called the attempted measures of " the grand incendiary " to " bring the Province into an open declaration of independency", Hutchinson convened the legislature on 6 January, 1773, and expounded his views on the constitutional position. The leaders of the legislature headed by Samuel Adams drafted a reply which was delivered to Hutchinson on the 26th; Hutchinson restated his position in a further speech of 16 February and the Council replied on the 25th. All four documents are printed in J. K. Hosmer, *The Life of Thomas Hutchinson* (Boston 1896), pp. 363–428.

Later in the year, after Franklin had disclosed the contents of some of Hutchinson's correspondence which had come into his hands, and which the colonists regarded as indicating that he was plotting against their liberties, the legislature petitioned for his recall. He was replaced by General Gage in May, 1774, just after the receipt of the news of the penal measures taken against Boston by the British Parliament in reply to the " Tea Party " of the previous December.

WHEN our predecessors first took possession of this plantation or colony, under a grant and charter from the Crown of England, it was their sense and it was the sense of the kingdom, that they were to remain subject to the supreme authority of Parliament. This appears from the charter itself and from other irresistible evidence. . . .

So much, however, of the spirit of liberty breathes through all parts of the English constitution, that although from the nature of government, there must be one supreme authority over the whole, yet this constitution will admit of subordinate powers with Legislative and Executive authority, greater or less according to local and other circumstances. Thus we see a variety of corporations formed within this kingdom, with powers to make and execute such bylaws as are for their immediate use and benefit, the members of such corporations still remaining subject to the general laws of the kingdom. We see also governments established in the plantations, which, from their separate and remote situation, require more general and extensive powers of legislation within themselves, than those formed within the kingdom, but subject, nevertheless, to all such laws of the kingdom as immediately respect them, or are designed to extend to them; and accordingly, we, in this province have, from the first settlement of it, been left to the exercise of our Legislative and Executive powers, Parliament, occasionally, though rarely, interposing, as its wisdom has been judged necessary . . .

K

I know of no line that can be drawn between the supreme authority of Parliament and the total independence of the colonies: it is impossible there should be two independent Legislatures in one and the same state; for although there may be one head, the King, yet the two legislative bodies will make two governments as distinct as the kingdoms of England and Scotland before the Union.

18. EDMUND BURKE: Speech on American Taxation, House of Commons

19 April 1774

Edmund Burke (1729–97) had become private secretary to Rockingham in 1765, and a member of Parliament in the same year. He strongly opposed the Administrations of Chatham and Grafton, particularly on American questions, and provided the main driving force behind the Whig opposition to Lord North. In 1771, he acquired a direct connection with American affairs through being given the post of agent for New York. The policy which Burke advocated in the early years of North's ministry was that of returning to the old position before the Stamp Act, and the abandonment of North's Tea Act, the unhappy survival of the Townshend duties. Instead of this the Coercive Acts were passed into law between March and June, 1774.

The speech from which extracts are given here was delivered in the course of a debate on the tea duty. It was published in 1775 and appears in Burke's *Works* (ed. in 16 vols.), (London, 1808), II, pp. 347 ff.

PERMIT me then, Sir, to lead your attention very far back; back to the act of navigation; the corner stone of the policy of this country with regard to its colonies. Sir, that policy was, from the beginning, purely commercial; and the commercial system was wholly restrictive. It was the system of a monopoly. No trade was let loose from that constraint, but merely to enable the colonists to dispose of what, in the course of your trade, you could not take; or to enable them to dispose of such articles as we forced upon them, and for which, without some degree of liberty, they could not pay. Hence all your specifick and detailed enumerations: hence the innumerable checks and counterchecks: hence that infinite variety of paper chains by which you bind together this complicated system of the colonies. This principle of commercial monopoly runs through no less than twenty-nine acts of parliament, from the year 1660 to the unfortunate period of 1764.

In all those acts the system of commerce is established, as, that, from whence alone you proposed to make the colonies contribute (I mean directly and by the operation of your superintending legislative power) to the strength of the empire. I venture to say, that during that whole period, a parliamentary revenue from thence was never once in contemplation. Accordingly, in all the number of laws passed with regard to the plantations, the words which distinguish revenue laws, specifically as such, were, I think, premeditately avoided. I do not say, Sir, that a form of words alters the nature of the law, or abridges the power of the lawgiver. It certainly does not. However, titles and formal preambles are not always idle words; and the lawyers frequently argue from them. I state these facts to shew, not what was your right, but what has been your settled policy. Our revenue laws have usually a *title*, purporting their being *grants*; and the words *give and grant* usually precede the enacting parts. Although duties were imposed on America in acts of King Charles the Second, and in acts of King William, no one title of giving " an aid to his majesty," or any other of the usual titles to revenue acts, was to be found in any of them till 1764; nor were the words " give and

136

grant " in any preamble until the 6th of George the Second. However the title of this act of George the Second, notwithstanding the words of donation, considers it merely as a regulation of trade, " an act for the better securing of the trade " of his majesty's sugar colonies in America." This act was made on a compromise of all, and at the express desire of a part, of the colonies themselves. It was therefore in some measure with their consent; and having a title directly purporting only a *commercial regulation*, and being in truth nothing more, the words were passed by, at a time when no jealousy was entertained, and things were little scrutinized.

[*Only in* 1764, *had Parliament, for the first time, avowedly attempted to raise a revenue in America.*]

Whatever the right might have been, this mode of using it was absolutely new in policy and practice.

Sir, they who are friends to the schemes of American revenue say, that the commercial restraint is full as hard a law for America to live under. I think so too. I think it, if uncompensated, to be a condition of as rigorous servitude as men can be subject to. But America bore it from the fundamental act of navigation until 1764.—Why ? because men do bear the inevitable constitution of their original nature with all its infirmities. The act of navigation attended the colonies from their infancy, grew with their growth, and strengthened with their strength. They were confirmed in obedience to it, even more by usage than by law. They scarcely remembered a time when they were not subject to such restraint. Besides, they were indemnified for it by pecuniary compensation. Their

137

monopolist happened to be one of the richest men in the world. By his immense capital (primarily employed, not for their benefit, but his own) they were enabled to proceed with their fisheries, their agriculture, their ship-building (and their trade too within the limits), in such a manner as got far the start of the slow languid operations of unassisted nature. This capital was a hot-bed to them. Nothing in the history of mankind is like their progress. For my part, I never cast an eye on their flourishing commerce, and their cultivated and commodious life, but they seem to me rather antient nations grown to perfection through a long series of fortunate events, and a train of successful industry, accumulating wealth in many centuries, than the colonies of yesterday; than a set of miserable out-casts, a few years ago, not so much sent as thrown out, on the bleak and barren shore of a desolate wilderness three thousand miles from all civilized intercourse.

All this was done by England, whilst England pursued trade, and forgot revenue. You not only acquired commerce, but you actually created the very objects of trade in America; and by that creation you raised the trade of this kingdom at least four-fold. America had the compensation of your capital, which made her bear her servitude. She had another compensation, which you are now going to take away from her. She had, except the commercial restraint, every characteristick mark of a free people, in all her internal concerns. She had the image of the British constitution. She had the substance. She was taxed by her own magistrates. She paid them all. She had in effect the sole disposal of her own internal government. This whole state of commercial servitude and civil liberty, taken together, is certainly not perfect freedom; but comparing it with the ordinary circumstances of human nature, it was an happy and a liberal condition.

[*The existence of smuggling did not prove that her right to control trade was disputed.*]

Whether you were right or wrong in establishing the colonies on the principles of commercial monopoly, rather than on that of revenue, is at this day a problem of mere speculation. You cannot have both by the same authority. To join together the restraints of an universal internal and external monopoly, with an universal internal and external taxation, is an unnatural union; perfect uncompensated slavery. You have long since decided for yourself and them; and you and they have prospered exceedingly under that decision.

This nation, Sir, never thought of departing from that choice until the period immediately on the close of the last war. Then a scheme of government new in many things seemed to have been adopted. I saw, or thought I saw, several symptoms of a great change, whilst I sat in your gallery, a good while before I had the honour of a seat in this house. At that period the necessity was established of keeping up no less than twenty new regiments, with twenty colonels capable of seats in this house. This scheme was adopted with very general applause from all sides, at the very time that, by your conquests in America, your danger from foreign attempts in that part of the world was much lessened, or indeed rather quite over. When this huge increase of military establishment was resolved on, a revenue was to be found to support so great a burthen. Country gentlemen, the great patrons of economy, and the great resisters of a standing armed force, would not have entered with much alacrity into the vote for so large and so expensive an army, if they had been very sure that they were to continue to pay for it. But hopes of another kind were held out to them; and in particular, I well remember, that Mr. Townshend, in a brilliant harangue on this subject, did dazzle them, by playing before their eyes the image of a revenue to be raised in America.

Here began to dawn the first glimmerings of this new·colony system.

Mr. Grenville thought better of the wisdom and power of human legislation than in truth it deserves. He conceived, and many conceived along with him, that the flourishing trade of this country was greatly owing to law and institution, and not quite so much to liberty; for but too many are apt to believe regulation to be commerce, and taxes to be revenue. Among regulations, that which stood first in reputation was his idol. I mean the act of navigation.

[*Growth of American trade during and after the Seven Years' War: hence smuggling and tightening up of administration.*]

The bonds of the act of navigation were straitened so much, that America was on the point of having no trade, either contraband or legitimate. They found, under the construction and execution then used, the act no longer tying but actually strangling them. All

140

this coming with new enumerations of commodities; with regulations which in a manner put a stop to the mutual coasting intercourse of the colonies; with the appointment of courts of admiralty under various improper circumstances; with a sudden extinction of the paper currencies; with a compulsory provision for the quartering of soldiers; the people of America thought themselves proceeded against as delinquents, or at best as people under suspicion of delinquency; and in such a manner, as they imagined, their recent services in the war did not at all merit. Any of these innumerable regulations, perhaps, would not have alarmed alone; some might be thought reasonable; the multitude struck them with terrour.

But the grand manœuvre in that business of new regulating the colonies, was the 15th act of the fourth of George III; which, besides containing several of the matters to which I have just alluded, opened a new principle; and here properly began the second period of the policy of this country with regard to the colonies; by which the scheme of a regular plantation parliamentary revenue was adopted in theory, and settled in practice. A revenue not substituted in the place of, but superadded to, a monopoly; which monopoly was enforced at the same time with additional strictness, and the execution put into military hands.

This act, Sir, had for the first time the title of " granting duties in the colonies and plantations of America; " and for the first time it was asserted in the preamble, " that is was *just* and *necessary* that a revenue should be raised there." Then came the technical words of " giving and granting," and thus a complete American revenue act was made in all the forms, and with a full avowal of the right, equity, policy, and even necessity of taxing the colonies, without any formal consent of theirs. There are contained also in the preamble to that act these very remarkable words—the commons, &c.—" being desirous to make *some* provision in the *present* session of parliament *towards* raising the said revenue." By these words it appeared to the colonies, that this act was but a beginning of sorrows; that every session was to produce something of the same kind; that we were to go on from day to day, in charging them with such taxes as we pleased, for such a military force as we should think proper. Had this plan been pursued, it was evident that the provincial assemblies, in which the Americans felt all their portion of importance, and beheld their sole image of freedom, were *ipso facto* annihilated. This ill prospect before them seemed to be boundless in extent, and endless in duration. Sir, they were not mistaken. The ministry valued themselves when this act passed, and when they gave notice of the stamp act, that both of the duties came very short of their ideas of American taxation. Great was the applause of this measure here. In England we cried out for new taxes on America, whilst they cried out that they were nearly crushed with those which the war and their own grants had brought upon them.

Sir, it has been said in the debate, that when the first American revenue act [the act in 1764, imposing the port duties] passed, the Americans did not object to the principle. It is true they touched it but very tenderly. It was not a direct attack. They were, it is true, as yet novices; as yet unaccustomed to direct attacks upon any of the rights of parliament. The duties were port duties, like those that they had been accustomed to bear; with this difference, that the title was not the same, the preamble not the same, and the spirit altogether unlike. But of what service is this observation to the cause of those that make it ? It is a full refutation of the pretence for their present cruelty to America; for it shews, out of their own mouths, that our colonies were backward to enter into the present vexatious and ruinous controversy.

There is also another circulation abroad, (spread with a malignant intention, which I cannot attribute to those who say the same thing in this house) that Mr. Grenville gave the colony agents an option for their assemblies to tax themselves, which they had refused. I find that much stress is laid on this, as a fact. However, it happens neither to be true nor possible. I will observe first, that Mr. Grenville never thought fit to make this apology for himself in the innumerable debates that were had upon the subject. He might have proposed to the colony agents, that they should agree in some mode of taxation as the ground of an act of parliament. But he never could have proposed that they should tax themselves on requisition, which is the assertion of the day. Indeed, Mr. Grenville well knew, that the colony agents could have no general powers to consent to it; and they had no time to consult their assemblies for particular powers, before he passed his first revenue act. If you compare dates, you will find it impossible. Burthened as the agents knew the colonies were at that time, they could not give the least hope of such grants.

Mr. Grenville could not have made this proposition to the agents, for another reason. He was of opinion which he has declared in this house an hundred times, that the colonies could not legally grant any revenue to the crown; and that infinite mischiefs would be the consequence of such a power. When Mr. Grenville had passed the first revenue act, and in the same session had made this house come to a resolution for laying a stamp-duty on America, between that time and the passing the stamp-act into a law, he told a considerable and most respectable merchant, a member of this house, whom I am truly sorry I do not now see in his place, when he represented against this proceeding, that if the stamp-duty was disliked, he was willing to exchange it for any other equally productive; but that, if he objected to the Americans being taxed by parliament, he might save himself the trouble of the discussion, as he was determined on the measure. This is the fact, and, if you please, I will mention a very unquestionable authority for it.

Thus, Sir, I have disposed of this falsehood. But falsehood has a perennial spring. It is said, that no conjecture could be made of the dislike of the colonies to the principle. This is as untrue as the other. After the resolution of the house, and before the passing of the stamp-act, the colonies of Massachusetts Bay and New York did send remonstrances, objecting to this mode of parliamentary taxation. What was the consequence? They were suppressed; they were put under the table; notwithstanding an order of council to the contrary, by the ministry which composed the very council that had made the order; and thus the house proceeded to its business of taxing without the least regular knowledge of the objections which were made to it. But to give that house its due, it was not over desirous to receive information, or to hear remonstrance. On the 13th of February, 1765, whilst the stamp-act was under deliberation, they refused with scorn even so much as to receive four petitions presented from so respectable colonies as Connecticut, Rhode Island, Virginia, and Carolina; besides one from the traders of Jamaica. As to the colonies, they had no alternative left to them, but to disobey; or to pay the taxes imposed by that parliament which was not suffered, or did not suffer itself, even to hear them remonstrate upon the subject.

[*After a defence of the repeal of the Stamp Act and of the passage of the Declaratory Act, Burke described the genesis of the Townshend duties and argued for total repeal:*]

Your ministers, in their own and his majesty's name, have already adopted the American distinction of internal duties. It is a distinction, whatever merit it may have, that was originally moved by the Americans themselves; and I think they will acquiesce in it, if they are not pushed with too much logick and too little sense, in all the consequences. That is, if external taxation be understood, as they and you understand it, when you please, to be not a distinction of geography, but of policy; that it is a power for regulating trade, and not for supporting establishments. The distinction, which is as nothing with regard to right, is of most weighty consideration in practice. Recover your old ground, and your old tranquillity—try it—I am persuaded the Americans will compromise with you . . .

Again, and again, revert to your old principles—
seek peace and ensue it—leave America, if she has
taxable matter in her, to tax herself. I am not here
going into the distinctions of rights, nor attempting to
mark their boundaries. I do not enter into these metaphysical distinctions; I hate the very sound of them.
Leave the Americans as they anciently stood, and these
distinctions, born of our unhappy contest, will die
along with it. They and we, and their and our ancestors, have been happy under that system. Let the
memory of all actions, in contradiction to that good
old mode, on both sides, be extinguished for ever. Be
content to bind America by laws of trade; you have
always done it. Let this be your reason for binding
their trade. Do not burthen them by taxes; you were
not used to do so from the beginning. Let this be your
reason for not taxing. These are the arguments of
states and kingdoms. Leave the rest to the schools; for
there only they may be discussed with safety. But if,
intemperately, unwisely, fatally, you sophisticate and
poison the very source of government, by urging subtle
deductions, and consequences odious to those you
govern, from the unlimited and illimitable nature of
supreme sovereignty, you will teach them by these
means to call that sovereignty itself in question. When
you drive him hard, the boar will surely turn upon the
hunters. If that sovereignty and their freedom cannot
be reconciled, which will they take? They will cast
your sovereignty in your face. Nobody will be argued
into slavery. Sir, let the gentlemen on the other side
call forth all their ability; let the best of them get up,
and tell me, what one character of liberty the Americans have, and what one brand of slavery they are
free from, if they are bound in their property and

industry, by all the restraints you can imagine on commerce, and at the same time are made pack-horses of
every tax you choose to impose, without the least share
in granting them. When they bear the burthens of
unlimited monopoly, will you bring them to bear the
burthens of unlimited revenue too? The Englishman
in America will feel that this is slavery—that it is *legal*
slavery, will be no compensation, either to his feelings
or his understanding.

A noble lord [*Lord Carmarthen*] has said, that the
Americans are our children, and how can they revolt
against their parent? He says, that if they are not
free in their present state, England is not free; because
Manchester, and other considerable places, are not
represented. So then, because some towns in England
are not represented, America is to have no representative at all. They are " our children; " but when children ask for bread, we are not to give a stone. It is
because the natural resistance of things, and the various mutations of time, hinders our government, or
any scheme of government, from being any more than
a sort of approximation to the right, is it therefore that
the colonies are to recede from it infinitely? When
this child of ours wishes to assimilate to its parent, and
to reflect with a true filial resemblance the beauteous
countenance of British liberty; are we to turn to them
the shameful parts of our constitution? are we to give
them our weakness for their strength? our opprobrium
for their glory; and the slough of slavery, which we are
not able to work off, to serve them for their freedom?

If this be the case, ask yourselves this question, Will
they be content in such a state of slavery? If not, look
to the consequences. Reflect how you are to govern a
people, who think they ought to be free, and think they

are not. Your scheme yields no revenue; it yields nothing but discontent, disorder, disobedience; and such is the state of America, that after wading up to your eyes in blood, you could only end just where you begun; that is, to tax where no revenue is to be found, to—my voice fails me; my inclination indeed carries me no further—all is confusion beyond it.

Well, Sir, I have recovered a little, and before I sit down I must say something to another point with which gentlemen urge us. What is to become of the declaratory act asserting the entireness of British legislative authority, if we abandon the practice of taxation?

For my part I look upon the rights stated in that act, exactly in the manner in which I viewed them on its very first proposition, and which I have often taken the liberty, with great humility, to lay before you. I look, I say, on the imperial rights of Great Britain, and the privileges which the colonists ought to enjoy under these rights, to be just the most reconcileable things in the world. The parliament of Great Britain fits at the head of her extensive empire in two capacities: one as the local legislature of this island, providing for all things at home, immediately, and by no other instrument than the executive power.—The other, and I think her nobler capacity, is what I call her *imperial character*; in which, as from the throne of heaven, she superintends all the several inferiour legislatures, and guides, and controuls them all without annihilating any. As all these provincial legislatures are only co-ordinate to each other, they ought all to be subordinate to her; else they can neither preserve mutual peace, nor hope for mutual justice, nor effectually afford mutual assistance. It is necessary to

148

coerce the negligent, to restrain the violent, and to aid the weak and deficient, by the over-ruling plenitude of her power. She is never to intrude into the place of the others, whilst they are equal to the common ends of their institution. But in order to enable parliament to answer all these ends of provident and beneficent superintendance, her powers must be boundless. The gentlemen who think the powers of parliament limited, may please themselves to talk of requisitions. But suppose the requisitions are not obeyed? What! Shall there be no reserved power in the empire, to supply a deficiency which may weaken, divide, and dissipate the whole? We are engaged in war—the Secretary of State calls upon the colonies to contribute—some would do it, I think most would chearfully furnish whatever is demanded—one or two, suppose, hang back, and, easing themselves, let the stress of the draft lie on the others—surely it is proper, that some authority might legally say—" Tax yourselves for the common supply, or parliament will do it for you." This backwardness was, as I am told, actually the case of Pennsylvania for some short time towards the beginning of the last war, owing to some internal dissentions in the colony. But, whether the fact were so, or otherwise, the case is equally to be provided for by a competent sovereign power. But then this ought to be no ordinary power; nor ever used in the first instance. This is what I meant, when I have said at various times, that I consider the power of taxing in parliament as an instrument of empire, and not as a means of supply.

Such, Sir, is my idea of the constitution of the British empire, as distinguished from the constitution of Britain; and on these grounds I think subordination and liberty may be sufficiently reconciled through the whole; whether to serve a refining speculatist, or a factious demagogue, I know not; but enough surely for the ease and happiness of man.

19: EARL OF CHATHAM. Speech in the House of Lords

26 May 1774

One of the measures taken to assist Lord Gage in his task of carrying out the coercive designs of Parliament against Massachusetts, was the passage of a bill authorizing the quartering of soldiers on the inhabitants of the colonies—a measure similar to that passed in the spring of 1765 and known to be supremely obnoxious to the Americans. Chatham's speech (*Chatham Anecdotes*, II, pp. 246–52) was made on the third reading of this Bill, but it provided an occasion for repeating his general belief in the unconstitutionality of all Parliamentary taxation of the colonies— a belief which distinguished Chatham's position from that of Burke.

MY Lords, the unfavourable state of health under which I have long labored could not prevent me from laying before your Lordships my thoughts on the bill now upon the table, and on the American affairs in general.

If we take a transient view of those motives which induced the ancestors of our fellow-subjects in America to leave their native country, to encounter the innumerable difficulties of the unexplored regions of the western world, our astonishment at the present conduct of their descendants will naturally subside. There was no corner of the world into which men of their free and enterprising spirit would not fly with alacrity, rather than submit to the slavish and tyrannical principles, which prevailed at that period in their native country. And shall we wonder, my Lords, if the descendants of such illustrious characters spurn, with contempt, the hand of unconstitutional power, that would snatch from them such dear-bought privileges as they now contend for? Had the British Colonies been planted by any other kingdom than our own, the inhabitants would have carried with them the chains of slavery, and spirit of despotism; but as they are, they ought to be remembered as great instances to instruct the world, what great exertions mankind will naturally make, when they are left to the free exercise of their own powers. And, my Lords, notwithstanding my intention to give my hearty negative to the question now before you, I cannot help condemning, in the severest manner, the late turbulent and unwarrantable conduct of the Americans in some instances, particularly in the late riots of Boston. But, my Lords, the mode which has been pursued to bring them back to a sense of their duty to their parent state has been so diametrically opposite to the fundamental principles of sound policy, that individuals, possessed of common understanding, must be astonished at such proceedings. By blocking up the harbour of Boston, you have involved the innocent trader in the same punishment with the guilty profligates who destroyed your merchandize; and instead of making a well-concerted effort to secure the real offenders, you clap a naval and military extinguisher over their harbour, and punish the crime of a few lawless depredators and their abettors upon the whole body of the inhabitants.

My Lords, this country is little obliged to the framers and promoters of this tea-tax. The Americans had almost forgot, in their excess of gratitude for the repeal of the stamp act, any interest but that of the mother country; there seemed an emulation among the different provinces, who should be most dutiful and forward in their expressions of loyalty to their real benefactor; as you will readily perceive by the following letter from Governor *Bernard* to a noble Lord then in office.

" The House of Representatives, (says he) from the time of opening the session to this day, has shewn a disposition to avoid all dispute with me; every thing having passed with as much good humour as I could desire. They have acted, in all things, with temper and moderation; they have avoided some subjects of dispute, and have laid a foundation for removing some causes of former altercation."

This, my Lords, was the temper of the Americans; and would have continued so, had it not been interrupted by your fruitless endeavours to tax them without their consent; but the moment they perceived your intention was renewed to tax them, under a pretence of serving the East India Company, their resentment got the ascendant of their moderation, and hurried them into actions contrary to law, which, in their cooler hours, they would have thought on with horror; for I sincerely believe, the destroying of the tea was the effect of despair.

But, my Lords, from the complexion of the whole of the proceedings, I think that Administration has purposely irritated them into those late violent acts, for which they now so severely smart; purposely to be revenged on them for the victory they gained by the repeal of the stamp act; a measure to which they seemingly acquiesced, but at the bottom they were its real enemies. For what other motive could induce them to dress taxation, that father of American sedition, in the robes of an East India Director, but to break in upon that mutual peace and harmony, which then so happily subsisted between them and the mother country.

My Lords, I am an old man, and would advise the noble Lords in office to adopt a more gentle mode of governing America; for the day is not far distant, when America may vie with these kingdoms, not only in arms, but in arts also. It is an established fact, that the principal towns in America are learned and polite, and understand the constitution of the empire as well as the noble Lords who are now in office; and consequently, they will have a watchful eye over their liberties, to prevent the least encroachment on their hereditary rights.

This observation is so recently exemplified in an excellent pamphlet, which comes from the pen of an American gentleman, that I shall take the liberty of reading to your Lordships his thoughts on the competency of the British Parliament to tax America, which, in my opinion, puts this interesting matter in the clearest view.

" The High Court of Parliament (says he) is the supreme legislative power over the whole empire; in all free states the constitution is fixed; and as the supreme legislature derives its power and authority from the constitution, it cannot overleap the bounds of it, without destroying its own foundation. The constitution ascertains and limits both sovereignty and allegiance: and therefore his Majesty's American subjects, who acknowledge themselves bound by the ties of allegiance, have an equitable claim to the full enjoyment of the fundamental rules of the English constitution; and that it is an essential unalterable right in nature, ingrafted into the British constitution as a fundamental law, and ever held sacred and irrevocable by the subjects within this realm—that what a man has honestly acquired, is absolutely his own; which he may freely give, but which cannot be taken from him without his consent."

This, my Lords, though no new doctrine, has always been my received and unalterable opinion, and I will carry it to my grave, *that this country had no right under heaven to tax America.* It is contrary to all the principles of justice and civil policy, which neither the exigencies of the state, nor even an acquiescence in the taxes, could justify upon any occasion whatever. Such proceedings will never meet their wished-for success; and, instead of adding to their miseries, as the bill now before you most undoubtedly does, adopt some lenient measures, which may lure them to their duty; proceed like a kind and affectionate parent over a child whom he tenderly loves; and, instead of those harsh and severe proceedings, pass an amnesty on all their youthful errors; clasp them once more in your fond and affectionate arms; and I will venture to affirm you will find them children worthy of their sire. But should their turbulence exist after your proffered terms of forgiveness, which I hope and expect this house will immediately adopt, I will be among the foremost of your Lordships to move for such measures as will effectually prevent a future relapse, and make them feel what it is to provoke a fond and forgiving parent! a parent, my Lords, whose welfare has ever been my greatest and most pleasing consolation. This declaration may seem unnecessary; but I will venture to declare, the period is not far distant, when she will want the assistance of her most distant friends: but should the all-disposing hand of Providence prevent me from affording her my poor assistance, my prayers shall be ever for her welfare—" *Length of days be in her right hand, and in her left riches and honour; may her ways be the ways of pleasantness, and all her paths be peace!* "

20: JAMES WILSON: *Considerations on the Authority of Parliament*

Philadelphia, August, 1774

James Wilson (1742–98) emigrated from Scotland at the age of twenty-three and rapidly rose to prominence as a leader of the Pennsylvanian bar. He later played an important part in the Continental Congress, 1775–77 and 1785–86, and in the Constitutional Convention in 1787. He served as an Associate Justice of the United States Supreme Court from its establishment in 1789 until his death.

The pamphlet from which these extracts are taken was the first exposition of the historical and legal case for the view that the colonies were only linked to Great Britain by their allegiance to the Crown and hence that the British Parliament was a body alien to their constitutions.

It is reprinted in Wilson's *Works*, ed. J. De Witt Andrews, 2 v. (Chicago, 1896), II, pp. 504–43.

BUT from what source does this mighty, this uncontrolled authority of the House of Commons flow ? from the collective body of the commons of Great Britain. This authority must therefore, originally reside in them; for whatever they convey to their representatives must ultimately be in themselves. And have those, whom we have hitherto been accustomed to consider as our fellow-subjects, an absolute and unlimited power over us ? Have they a natural right to make laws, by which we may be deprived of our properties, of our liberties, of our lives? By what title do they claim to be our masters? What act of ours has rendered us subject to those, to whom we were formerly equal? Is British freedom denominated from the soil or from the people of Britain? If from the latter, do they lose it by quitting the soil? Do those who embark freemen in Great Britain, disembark slaves in America?

If . . . by a dependence of the colonies on Great Britain, it is meant that they are obliged to obey the laws of Great Britain, reason, as well as the unanimous voice of the Americans, teaches us to disown it. . . . There is another and much more reasonable meaning, which may be intended by the dependence of the colonies on Great Britain. The phrase may be used to denote the obedience and loyalty which the colonists owe to the kings of Great Britain. . . . It is a dependence which they have acknowledged hitherto; which they acknowledge now; and, which if it is reasonable to judge of the future by the past and the present, they will continue to acknowledge hereafter.

21: **THOMAS JEFFERSON.** A Summary View of
the Rights of British America

Williamsburg, Virginia, August 1774

Thomas Jefferson (1743–1826), subsequently third President of
the United States, who had by 1774 already achieved local
prominence in Virginian politics, drafted this document as suggested instructions for Virginia's delegates to the first Continental
Congress which met at Philadelphia in September, 1774. The
views expressed—which were very close to those held at the time
by James Wilson—were too advanced for the delegates to adopt
officially, but published in pamphlet form, they secured considerable attention and helped to make Jefferson's reputation a
national one.

The text here is that given in *The Complete Jefferson* (ed. S. K.
Padover, New York, 1943). Cf. *The Papers of Thomas Jefferson,*
ed. J. P. Boyd. Vol. I. (Princeton, 1950).

[*The delegates are to point out the failure of past petitions
for redress and to express the hope that this address will
" receive a more respectful acceptance from the King . . ."*]
when he reflects that he is no more than the chief
officer of the people, appointed by the laws, and circumscribed with definite powers, to assist in working
the great machine of government erected for their use
and consequently, subject to their superintendence.

[*The deputies are to set forth to the King the rights of the
colonies and of the invasions of them from the time of their
first settlement and . . .*]

159

To remind him that our ancestors, before their emigration to America, were the free inhabitants of the British dominions in Europe, and possessed a right, which nature has given to all men, of departing from the country in which chance, not choice, has placed them, of going in quest of new habitations, and of there establishing new societies, under such laws and regulations as, to them, shall seem most likely to promote public happiness. That their Saxon ancestors had, under this universal law, in like manner, left their native wilds and woods in the North of Europe, had possessed themselves of the Island of Britain, then less charged with inhabitants, and had established there that system of laws which has so long been the glory and protection of that country. Nor was ever any claim of superiority or dependence asserted over them, by that mother country from which they had migrated: and were such a claim made, it is believed his Majesty's subjects in Great Britain have too firm a feeling of the rights derived to them from their ancestors, to bow down the sovereignty of their state before such visionary pretensions. And it is thought that no circumstance has occurred to distinguish, materially, the British from the Saxon emigration. America was conquered, and her settlements made and firmly established, at the expense of individuals, and not of the British public. Their own blood was spilt in acquiring lands for their settlement, their own fortunes expended in making that settlement effectual. For themselves they fought, for themselves they conquered, and for themselves alone they have right to hold. No shilling was ever issued from the public treasures of his Majesty, or his ancestors, for their assistance, till of very late times, after the colonies had become established on a firm and permanent footing. That then, indeed, having become valuable to Great Britain for her commercial purposes, his Parliament was pleased to lend them assistance against an enemy who would fain have drawn to herself the benefits of their commerce, to the great aggrandisement of herself, and danger of Great Britain. Such assistance, and in such circumstances, they had often before given to Portugal and other allied states, with whom they carry on a commercial intercourse. Yet these states never supposed, that by calling in her aid, they thereby submitted themselves to her sovereignty. Had such terms been proposed, they would have rejected them with disdain, and trusted for better, to the moderation of their enemies, or to a vigorous exertion of their own force. We do not, however, mean to underrate those aids, which, to us, were doubtless valuable, on whatever principles granted: but we would shew that they cannot give a title to that authority which the British Parliament would arrogate over us; and that may amply be repaid by our giving to the inhabitants of Great Britain such exclusive privileges in trade as may be advantageous to them, and, at the same time, not too restrictive to ourselves. That settlement having been thus effected in the wilds of America, the emigrants thought proper to adopt that system of laws, under which they had hitherto lived in the mother country, and to continue their union with her, by submitting themselves to the same common sovereign, who was thereby made the central link, connecting the several parts of the empire thus newly multiplied.

But that not long were they permitted, however far they thought themselves removed from the hand of oppression, to hold undisturbed the rights thus acquired at the hazard of their lives and loss of their fortunes. A family of Princes was then on the British throne, whose treasonable crimes against their people, brought on them, afterwards, the exertion of those sacred and sovereign rights of punishment, reserved in the hands of the people for cases of extreme necessity, and judged by the constitution unsafe to be delegated to any other judicature. While every day brought forth some new and unjustifiable exertion of power over their subjects on that side of the water, it was not to be expected that those here, much less able at that time to oppose the designs of despotism, should be exempted from injury. Accordingly, this country which had been acquired by the lives, the labors, and fortunes of individual adventurers, was by these Princes, several times, parted out and distributed among the favorites and followers of their fortunes; and, by an assumed right of the Crown alone, were erected into distinct and independent governments; a measure, which it is believed, his Majesty's prudence and understanding would prevent him from imitating at this day; as no exercise of such power, of dividing and dismembering a country, has ever occurred in his Majesty's realm of England, though now of very ancient standing; nor could it be justified or acquiesced under there, or in any part of his Majesty's empire.

That the exercise of a free trade with all parts of the world, possessed by the American colonists, as of natural right, and which no law of their own had taken away or abridged, was next the object of unjust encroachment. Some of the colonies having thought proper to continue the administration of their government in the name and under the authority of his Majesty, King Charles the first, whom, notwithstanding his late deposition by the Commonwealth of England, they continued in the sovereignty of their State, the Parliament, for the Commonwealth, took the same in high offence, and assumed upon themselves the power of prohibiting their trade with all other parts of the world, except the island of Great Britain. This arbitrary act, however, they soon recalled, and by solemn treaty entered into on the 12th day of March, 1651, between the said Commonwealth, by their Commissioners, and the colony of Virginia by their House of Burgesses, it was expressly stipulated by the eighth article of the said treaty, that they should have " free trade as the people of England do enjoy to all places and with all nations, according to the laws of that Commonwealth." But that, upon the restoration of his Majesty, King Charles the second, their rights of free commerce fell once more a victim to arbitrary power; and by several acts of his reign, as well as some of his successors, the trade of the colonies was laid under such restrictions, as show what hopes they might form from the justice of a British Parliament, were its uncontrolled power admitted over these States. History has informed us, that bodies of men as well as of individuals, are susceptible of the spirit of tyranny. A view of these acts of Parliament for regulation, as it has been affectedly called, of the American trade, if all other evidences were removed out of the case, would undeniably evince the truth of this observation. Besides the duties they impose on our articles of export and import, they prohibit our going to any markets Northward of Cape Finisterra, in the kingdom of Spain, for the sale of commodities which Great Britain will not take from us, and for the purchase of others, with which she cannot supply us; and that, for no other than the arbitrary purpose of purchasing for themselves, by a sacrifice of our rights and interests certain privileges in their commerce with an allied state, who, in confidence, that their exclusive trade with America will be continued, while the principles and power of the British Parliament be the same, have indulged themselves in every exorbitance which their avarice could dictate or our necessity extort: have raised their commodities called for in America, to the double and treble of what they sold for, before such exclusive privileges were given them, and of what better commodities of the same kind would cost us elsewhere; and, at the same time, give us much less for what we carry thither, than might be had at more convenient ports. That these acts prohibit us from carrying, in quest of other purchasers, the surplus of our tobaccos, remaining after the consumption of Great Britain is supplied: so that we must leave them with the British merchant, for whatever he will please to allow us, to be by him re-shipped to foreign markets, where he will reap the benefits of making sale of them for full value. That, to heighten still the idea of Parliamentary justice, and to show with what moderation they are like to exercise power, where themselves are to feel no part of its weight, we take leave to mention to his Majesty, certain other acts of the British Parliament, by which they would prohibit us from manufacturing, for our own use, the articles we raise on our own lands, with our own labor. By an act passed in the fifth year of the reign of his late Majesty, King George the second, an American subject is forbidden to make a hat for himself, of the fur which he has taken, perhaps, on his own soil; an instance of despotism, to which no parallel can be produced in the most arbitrary ages of

British history. By one other act, passed in the twenty-third year of the same reign, the iron which we make, we are forbidden to manufacture; and, heavy as that article is, and necessary in every branch of husbandry, besides commission and insurance, we are to pay freight for it to Great Britain, and freight for it back again, for the purpose of supporting, not men, but machines, in the island of Great Britain. In the same spirit of equal and impartial legislation, is to be viewed the act of Parliament, passed in the fifth year of the same reign, by which American lands are made subject to the demands of British creditors, while their own lands were still continued unanswerable for their debts; from which, one of these conclusions must necessarily follow, either that justice is not the same thing in America as in Britain, or else, that the British Parliament pay less regard to it here than there. But, that we do not point out to his Majesty the injustice of these acts, with intent to rest on that principle the cause of their nullity; but to show that experience confirms the propriety of those political principles, which exempt us from the jurisdiction of the British Parliament. The true ground on which we declare these acts void, is, that the British Parliament has no right to exercise authority over us.

That these exercises of usurped power have not been confined to instances alone, in which themselves were interested; but they have also intermeddled with the regulation of the internal affairs of the colonies. The act of the 9th of Anne for establishing a post office in America, seems to have had little connection with British convenience, except that of accommodating his Majesty's ministers and favorites with the sale of a lucrative and easy office.

M   165

That thus have we hastened through the reigns which preceded his Majesty's, during which the violation of our rights were less alarming, because repeated at more distant intervals, than that rapid and bold succession of injuries, which is likely to distinguish the present from all other periods of American story. Scarcely have our minds been able to emerge from the astonishment into which one stroke of Parliamentary thunder has involved us, before another more heavy and more alarming is fallen on us. Single acts of tyranny may be ascribed to the accidental opinion of the day; but a series of oppressions, begun at a distinguished period, and pursued unalterably through every change of ministers, too plainly prove a deliberate, systematical plan of reducing us to slavery.

[*After enumerating the Acts of Parliament objected to, Jefferson continues:*]

One free and independent legislature, hereby takes upon itself to suspend the powers of another, free and independent as itself. Thus exhibiting a phenomenon unknown in nature, the creator, and creature of its own power. Not only the principles of common sense, but the common feelings of human nature must be surrendered up, before his Majesty's subjects here, can be persuaded to believe, that they hold their political existence at the will of a British Parliament. Shall these governments be dissolved, their property annihilated, and their people reduced to a state of nature, at the imperious breath of a body of men whom they never saw, in whom they never confided and over whom they have no powers of punishment or removal, let their crimes against the American public be ever so great? Can any one reason be assigned, why one hundred and sixty thousand electors in the island of Great Britain, should give law to four millions in the States of America, every individual of whom is equal to every individual of them in virtue, in understanding, and in bodily strength? Were this to be admitted, instead of being a free people, as we have hitherto supposed, and mean to continue ourselves, we should suddenly be found the slaves, not of one, but of one hundred and sixty thousand tyrants; distinguished, too, from all others, by this singular circumstance, that they are removed from the reach of fear, the only restraining motive which may hold the hand of a tyrant.

[*Jefferson then describes the 'Boston tea-party' and its sequel in Parliament, and continues:*]

That these are the acts of power, assumed by a body of men foreign to our constitutions, and unacknowledged by our laws; against which we do, on behalf of the inhabitants of British America, enter this, our solemn and determined protest. And we do earnestly intreat his Majesty, as yet the only mediatory power between the several States of the British empire, to recommend to his Parliament of Great Britain, the total revocation of these acts, which, however nugatory they may be, may yet prove the cause of further discontents and jealousies among us.

That we next proceed to consider the conduct of his Majesty, as holding the Executive powers of the laws of these States, and mark out his deviations from the line of duty. By the Constitution of Great Britain, as well as of the several American States, his Majesty possesses the power of refusing to pass into a law, any bill which has already passed the other two branches of the legislature. His Majesty, however, and his ancestors, conscious of the impropriety of opposing their single opinion to the united wisdom of two Houses of Parliament, while their proceedings were unbiassed by interested principles, for several ages past, have modestly declined the exercise of this power, in that part of his empire called Great Britain. But, by change of circumstances, other principles than those of justice simply, have obtained an influence on their determinations. The addition of new States to the British empire has produced an addition of new, and sometimes, opposite interests. It is now, therefore, the great office of his Majesty to resume the exercise of his negative power, and to prevent the passage of laws by any one legislature of the empire, which might bear injuriously on the rights and interests of another. Yet this will not excuse the wanton exercise of this power, which we have seen his Majesty practice on the laws of the American legislature. For the most trifling reasons, and, sometimes for no conceivable reason at all, his Majesty has rejected laws of the most salutary tendency. The abolition of domestic slavery is the great object of desire in those colonies, where it was, unhappily, introduced in their infant state. But previous to the enfranchisement of the slaves we have, it is necessary to exclude all further importations from Africa. Yet our repeated attempts to effect this by prohibitions, and by imposing duties which might amount to a prohibition, having been hitherto defeated by his Majesty's negative: thus prefering the immediate advantages of a few British corsairs, to the lasting

168

interests of the American States, and to the rights of human nature, deeply wounded by this infamous practice. Nay, the single interposition of an interested individual against a law was scarcely ever known to fail of success, though, in the opposite scale, were placed the interests of a whole country. That this is so shameful an abuse of a power, trusted with his Majesty for other purposes, as if, not reformed, would call for some legal restrictions.

With equal inattention to the necessities of his people here has his Majesty permitted our laws to lie neglected, in England, for years neither confirming them by his assent, nor annulling them by his negative: so, that such of them as have no suspending clause, we hold on the most precarious of all tenures, his Majesty's will; and such of them as suspend themselves till his Majesty's assent be obtained, we have feared might be called into existence at some future and distant period, when time and change of circumstances shall have rendered them destructive to his people here. And, to render this grievance still more oppressive, his Majesty, by his instructions, has laid his Governors under such restrictions, that they can pass no law, of any moment, unless it have such suspending clause: so that, however immediate may be the call for legislative interposition, the law cannot be executed, till it has twice crossed the Atlantic, by which time the evil may have spent its whole force.

But in what terms reconcilable to Majesty, and at the same time to truth, shall we speak of a late instruction to his Majesty's Governor of the colony of Virginia, by which he is forbidden to assent to any law for the division of a county, unless the new county will consent to have no representative in Assembly ? That

169

colony has as yet affixed no boundary to the Westward. Their Western counties, therefore, are of an indefinite extent. Some of them are actually seated many hundred miles from their Eastern limits. Is it possible, then, that his Majesty can have bestowed a single thought on the situation of those people, who in order to obtain justice for injuries, however great or small, must, by the laws of that colony, attend their county court at such a distance, with all their witnesses, monthly, till their litigation be determined ? Or does his Majesty seriously wish, and publish it to the world, that his subjects should give up the glorious right of representation, with all the benefits derived from that, and submit themselves the absolute slaves of his sovereign will ? Or is it rather meant to confine the legislative body to their present numbers, that they may be the cheaper bargain, whenever they shall become worth a purchase ?

One of the articles of impeachment against Tresilian and the other Judges of Westminster Hall, in the reign of Richard the Second, for which they suffered death, as traitors to their country, was, that they had advised the King, that he might dissolve his Parliament at any time; and succeeding kings have adopted the opinion of these unjust Judges. Since the establishment, however, of the British constitution, at the glorious Revolution, on its free and ancient principles, neither his Majesty, nor his ancestors, have exercised such a power of dissolution in the island of Great Britain; and when his Majesty was petitioned, by the united voice of his people there, to dissolve the present Parliament, who had become obnoxious to them, his Ministers were heard to declare, in open Parliament, that his Majesty possessed no such power by the constitution. But how different their language, and his practice here! To declare, as their duty required, the known rights of their country, to oppose the usurpation of every foreign judicature, to disregard the imperious mandates of a Minister or Governor, have been the avowed causes of dissolving Houses of Representatives in America. But if such powers be really vested in his Majesty, can he suppose they are there placed to awe the members from such purposes as these ? When the representative body have lost the confidence of their constituents, when they have notoriously made sale of their most valuable rights, when they have assumed to themselves powers which the people never put into their hands, then, indeed, their continuing in office becomes dangerous to the State, and calls for an exercise of the power of dissolution. Such being the cause for which the representative body should, and should not, be dissolved, will it not appear strange, to an unbiassed observer, that that of Great Britain was not dissolved, while those of the colonies have repeatedly incurred that sentence?

But your Majesty, or your Governors, have carried this power beyond every limit known or provided for by the laws. After dissolving one House of Representatives, they have refused to call another, so that, for a great length of time, the legislature provided by the laws, has been out of existence. From the nature of things, every society must, at all times, possess within itself the sovereign powers of legislation. The feelings of human nature revolt against the supposition of a State so situated, as that it may not, in any emergency, provide against dangers which, perhaps, threaten immediate ruin. While those bodies are in existence to whom the people have delegated the powers of legislation, they alone possess, and may exercise, those powers. But when they are dissolved, by the lopping off one or more of their branches, the power reverts to the people, who may use it to unlimited extent, either assembling together in person, sending deputies, or in any other way they may think proper. We forbear to trace consequences further; the dangers are conspicuous with which this practice is replete.

That we shall, at this time also, take notice of an error in the nature of our land holdings, which crept in at a very early period of our settlement. The introduction of the feudal tenures into the kingdom of England, though ancient, is well enough understood to set this matter in a proper light. In the earlier ages of the Saxon settlement, feudal holdings were certainly altogether unknown, and very few, if any, had been introduced at the time of the Norman conquest. Our Saxon ancestors held their lands, as they did their personal property, in absolute dominion, disencumbered with any superior, answering nearly to the nature of those possessions which the feudalists term Allodial. William the Norman, first introduced that system generally. The lands which had belonged to those who fell in the battle of Hastings, and in the subsequent insurrections of his reign, formed a considerable proportion of the lands of the whole kingdom. These he granted out, subject to feudal duties, as did he also those of a great number of his new subjects, who, by persuasions or threats, were induced to surrender them for that purpose. But still, much was left in the hands of his Saxon subjects, held of no superior, and not subject to feudal conditions. These, therefore, by express laws, enacted to render uniform the system of military defence, were made liable to the same military duties as if they had been feuds; and the Norman lawyers

soon found means to saddle them, also, with the other
feudal burthens. But still they had not been surrendered to the King, they were not derived from his
grant, and therefore they were not holden of him. A
general principle was introduced, that " all lands in
England were held either mediately or immediately
of the Crown "; but this was borrowed from those
holdings which were truly feudal, and only applied to
others for the purposes of illustration. Feudal holdings
were, therefore, but exceptions out of the Saxon laws
of possession, under which all lands were held in absolute right. These, therefore, still form the basis or
groundwork of the Common law, to prevail whereso-
ever the exceptions have not taken place. America
was not conquered by William the Norman, nor its
lands surrendered to him or any of his successors.
Possessions there are, undoubtedly, of the Allodial
nature. Our ancestors, however, who migrated hither,
were laborers, not lawyers. The fictitious principle,
that all lands belong originally to the King, they were
early persuaded to believe real, and accordingly took
grants of their own lands from the Crown. And while
the Crown continued to grant for small sums and on
reasonable rents, there was no inducement to arrest
the error, and lay it open to public view. But his
Majesty has lately taken on him to advance the terms
of purchase and of holding, to the double of what they
were; by which means, the acquisition of lands being
rendered difficult, the population of our country is
likely to be checked. It is time, therefore, for us to
lay this matter before his Majesty, and to declare,
that he has no right to grant lands of himself. From the
nature and purpose of civil institutions, all the lands
within the limits, which any particular party has

circumscribed around itself, are assumed by that society, and subject to their allotment; this may be done by themselves assembled collectively, or by their legislature, to whom they may have delegated sovereign authority; and, if they are allotted in neither of these ways, each individual of the society may appropriate to himself such lands as he finds vacant, and occupancy will give him title.

That, in order to enforce the arbitrary measures before complained of, his Majesty has, from time to time, sent among us large bodies of armed forces, not made up of the people here, nor raised by the authority of our laws. Did his Majesty possess such a right as this, it might swallow up all our other rights, whenever he should think proper. But his Majesty has no right to land a single armed man on our shores; and those whom he sends here are liable to our laws, for the suppression and punishment of riots, routs, and unlawful assemblies, or are hostile bodies invading us in defiance of law. When, in the course of the late war, it became expedient that a body of Hanoverian troops should be brought over for the defence of Great Britain, his Majesty's grandfather, our late sovereign, did not pretend to introduce them under any authority he possessed. Such a measure would have given just alarm to his subjects of Great Britain, whose liberties would not be safe if armed men of another country, and of another spirit, might be brought into the realm at any time, without the consent of their legislature. He, therefore, applied to Parliament, who passed an act for that purpose, limiting the number to be brought in, and the time they were to continue. In like manner is his Majesty restrained in every part of the empire. He possesses indeed the executive power of the laws in every State; but they are the laws of the particular State, which he is to administer within that State, and not those of any one within the limits of another. Every State must judge for itself, the number of armed men which they may safely trust among them, of whom they are to consist, and under what restrictions they are to be laid. To render these proceedings still more criminal against our laws, instead of subjecting the military to the civil power, his majesty has expressly made the civil subordinate to the military. But can his Majesty thus put down all law under his feet? Can he erect a power superior to that which erected himself? He has done it indeed by force; but let him remember that force cannot give right.

That these are our grievances, which we have thus laid before his Majesty, with that freedom of language and sentiment which becomes a free people, claiming their rights as derived from the laws of nature, and not as the gift of their Chief Magistrate. Let those flatter, who fear: it is not an American art. To give praise where it is not due might be well from the venal, but would ill beseem those who are asserting the rights of human nature. They know, and will, therefore, say, that Kings are the servants, not the proprietors of the people. Open your breast, Sire, to liberal and expanded thought. Let not the name of George the third, be a blot on the page of history. You are surrounded by British counsellors, but remember that they are parties. You have no ministers for American affairs, because you have none taken from among us, nor amenable to the laws on which they are to give you advice. It behooves you, therefore, to think and to act for yourself and your people. The great principles of right and wrong are legible to every reader;

to pursue them, requires not the aid of many counsellors. The whole art of government consists in the
art of being honest. Only aim to do your duty, and
mankind will give you credit where you fail. No longer
persevere in sacrificing the rights of one part of the
empire to the inordinate desires of another; but deal
out to all, equal and impartial right. Let no act be
passed by any one legislature, which may infringe on
the rights and liberties of another. This is the important post in which fortune has placed you, holding the
balance of a great, if a well-poised empire. This, Sire,
is the advice of your great American council, on the
observance of which may perhaps depend your felicity
and future fame, and the preservation of that harmony
which alone can continue, both to Great Britain and
America, the reciprocal advantages of their connection. It is neither our wish nor our interest to separate
from her. We are willing, on our part, to sacrifice
everything which reason can ask, to the restoration of
that tranquillity for which all must wish. On their
part, let them be ready to establish union on a generous plan. Let them name their terms, but let them be
just. Accept of every commercial preference it is in
our power to give, for such things as we can raise for
their use, or they make for ours. But let them not
think to exclude us from going to other markets to dispose of those commodities which they cannot use, nor
to supply those wants which they cannot supply. Still
less, let it be proposed, that our properties, within our
own territories, shall be taxed or regulated by any
power on earth, but our own. The God who gave us
life, gave us liberty at the same time: the hand of force
may destroy, but cannot disjoin them. This, Sire, is
our last, our determined resolution. And that you will

176

be pleased to interpose, with that efficacy which your earnest endeavors may insure, to procure redress of these our great grievances, to quiet the minds of your subjects in British America against any apprehensions of future encroachment, to establish fraternal love and harmony through the whole empire, and that that may continue to the latest ages of time, is the fervent prayer of all British America.

22: JAMES WILSON. Speech in the Pennsylvania Convention

January 1775

When the Pennsylvania Convention met in January, 1775, its purpose was to force the hand of the conservatively-minded legislature by drawing up strong instructions for the province's delegation to the meeting of the Second Continental Congress which took place in the following May. Wilson took the lead in the Convention in supporting the right of Massachusetts to resist changes in its charter, and in denying the authority of Parliament in the colonies.

The extract here is taken from the text given in *Works*, II, pp. 547–65.

THE government of Britain, sir, was never an arbitrary government: our ancestors were never inconsiderate enough to trust those rights, which God and nature had given them, unreservedly into the hands of their princes. However difficult it may be in other states, to prove an original contract, subsisting in any other manner, and on any other conditions, than are naturally and necessarily implied in the very idea of the first institution of a state; it is the easiest thing imaginable to prove it in our constitution and to ascertain some of the material articles of which it consists. It has been often appealed to: it has been often broken at least on one part: it has been often reviewed: it has been often confirmed: it still subsists in its full force:

" it binds the king as much as the meanest subject ". The measures of his power and the limits beyond which he cannot extend it, are circumscribed and regulated by the same authority, and with the same processes, as the limits of the subject's obedience; and the limits beyond which he is under no obligation to practise it, are fixed and ascertained. Liberty is by the constitution, of equal stability and of equal authority with prerogative. The duties of the king and those of the subject are plainly reciprocal; and they can be violated on neither side, unless they be performed on the other. The law is the common standard by which the excesses of prerogative as well as the excesses of liberty are to be regulated and reformed.

Of this great compact between the king and his people, one essential article to be performed on his part is—that, in those cases where provision is expressly made, and limitations set by the laws, his government shall be conducted according to those limitations—that, in those cases, which are not expressly provided for by the laws, it shall be conducted by the best rules of discretion, agreeably to the general spirit of the laws and subservient to their ultimate end —the interest and happiness of his subjects—that, in no case it shall be conducted contrary to the express or to the implied principles of the constitution.

23: DANIEL LEONARD. *Massachusettensis* No. V

Boston 9 January 1775

Daniel Leonard (1740–1829) was the author of a series of seventeen letters, signed " Massachusettensis ", and addressed to " The Inhabitants of the Province of the Massachusetts-Bay ", which appeared in a loyalist Boston newspaper between mid-December, 1774 and mid-April, 1775. Leonard, whose authorship was for long successfully concealed, was a prominent lawyer and a member of a wealthy family long established in the colony. By general admission, the *Massachusettensis* letters, subsequently republished in pamphlet form, were the best expression of the Tory view that the colonists' grievances were largely without foundation. His views made it necessary for Leonard to leave Massachusetts when the British troops evacuated Boston in March, 1776, and his loyalty was eventually rewarded with the post of Chief Justice of Bermuda.

. . . . .

The extract here is taken from the London reprint of the second edition, dated 1776.

T HE security of the people from internal rapacity and violence and from foreign invasion, is the end and design of government. The simple forms of government are monarchy, aristocracy and democracy; that is, where the authority of the state is vested in one, a few, or many. Each of these species of government has advantages peculiar to itself, and would answer the ends of government, were the persons entrusted with the authority of the state, always guided themselves,

180

by unerring wisdom and public virtue; but rulers are
not always exempt from the weaknesses and depravity
which make government necessary to society. Thus
monarchy is apt to rush headlong into tyranny, aristocracy to beget faction, and multiplied usurpation
and democracy, to degenerate into tumult, violence
and anarchy. A government formed upon these three
principles in due proportion is the best calculated to
answer the ends of government and to endure. Such
a government is the British Constitution, consisting
of kings, lords and commons, which at once includes
the principal excellencies and excludes the principal
defects of the other kinds of government. It is allowed
both by Englishmen and foreigners to be the most perfect system that the wisdom of ages has produced. The
distributions of power are so just, and the proportions
so exact as at once to support and controul each other.
An Englishman glories in being subject to, and protected by such a government. The colonies are part of
the British Empire. The best writers upon the law of
nations, tell us that when a nation takes possession of a
distant country and settles there, that country, though
separated from the principal establishments or mother
country, naturally becomes a part of the state, equal
with its ancient possessions. Two systems of independent authority cannot exist within the same state. It
would be what is called *imperium in imperio*, the height
of political absurdity. The analogy between the political and the human body is great. Two independent
authorities in a state would be like two distinct principles of volition and action in the human body, dissenting, opposing and destroying each other. If then,
we are part of the British Empire, we must be subject
to the supreme power of the state, which is vested with

the estates of parliament, notwithstanding each of the colonies have legislatures and executives of their own, delegated or granted to them for the purpose of regulating their own internal police, which are subordinate to, and must necessarily be subject to, the checks, controul and regulation of the supreme authority.

This doctrine is not new, but the denial of it is. It is beyond a doubt that it was the sense, both of the parent country and our ancestors, that they were to remain subject to parliament. It is evident from the charter (*of Massachusetts*) itself, and this authority has been exercised by parliament from time to time almost ever since the first settlement of the country, and has been expressly acknowledged by our provincial legislature. It is not less our interest than our duty to continue subject to the authority of parliament, which will be more fully considered hereafter. The principal argument against the authority of parliament is this; the Americans are entitled to all the privileges of an Englishman; it is the privilege of an Englishman to be exempt from all laws that he does not consent to in person, or by representative. The Americans are not represented in Parliament, and therefore are exempt from acts of parliament, or in other words not subject to its authority. This appears specious; but leads to such absurdities as demonstrates its fallacy. If the colonies are not subject to the authority of Parliament, Great Britain and the colonies must be distinct states, as completely so as England and Scotland were before the union, or as Great Britain and Hanover are now. The colonies in that case will owe no allegiance to the imperial crown, and perhaps not to the person of the king, as the title to the crown is derived from an act of parliament, made since the settlement of this

province, which act respects the imperial crown only.
Let us waive this difference, and suppose allegiance
due from the colonies to the person of the king of Great
Britain. He then appears in a new capacity of king of
America, or rather in several new capacities, of king
of Massachusetts, king of Rhode Island, king of Connecticut, etc., etc. For if our connexion with Great
Britain by the parliament is dissolved, we shall have
none among ourselves, but each colony becomes as
distinct from the others as England was from Scotland
before the Union. Some have supposed that each state
having one and the same person for its king, is a sufficient connexion. Were he an absolute monarch, it might
be but in a mixed government it is no union at all. For
as the king must govern each state by its parliament,
those several parliaments will pursue the particular interests of its own state; and however well disposed the
king might be to pursue a line of interest that was common to all, the checks and control that he would meet
with would render it impossible. If the king of Great
Britain has really these new capacities, they ought to be
added to his titles; and another difficulty will arise; the
prerogatives of these new crowns have never been de-
fined or limited. Is the monarchical part of the several
provincial constitutions to be nearer or more remote
from absolute monarchy, in an inverted ratio, to each
one's approaching to or receding from a republic?
But let us suppose the same prerogatives inherent in
the several American crowns, as are in the imperial
crown of Great Britain, where shall we find the British
constitution that we all agree we are entitled to? We
shall seek for it in vain in our provincial assemblies.
They are but faint sketches of the estates of parliament.
The house of representatives, or Burgesses, have not

all the powers of the house of commons; in the charter government they have no more than what is granted by their several charters. The first charters granted to this province (Massachusetts) did not empower the assembly to tax the people at all. Our council boards are as destitute of the constitutional authority of the House of Lords as their several members are of the noble independence and splendid appendages of peerage. The house of peers is the bulwark of the British constitution, and through successive ages, has withstood the shocks of monarchy and the sapping of democracy, and the constitution gained strength by the conflict. Thus the supposition of our being independent states, or exempt from the authority of parliament, destroys the very idea of our having a British constitution. The provincial courts, considered as subordinate, are generally well adapted to those purposes of government, for which they were intended; that is to regulate the internal police of the several colonies; but have no principles of stability within themselves; they may support themselves in moderate times but would be merged by the violence of the turbulent ones, and the several colonies become wholly monarchical, or wholly republican, were it not for the checks, controuls, regulations and supports of the supreme authority of the empire. Thus the argument that is drawn from their first principle of our being entitled to English liberties, destroys the principle itself, it deprives us of the bill of rights, and all the benefits resulting from the revolution of English laws, and the British constitution.

Our patriots have been so intent upon building **up** American rights, that they have overlooked the rights of Great Britain and our own interest. Instead of proving that we were entitled to privileges that our fathers knew our situation would not admit us to enjoy, they have been arguing away our most essential rights. If there be any grievance it does not consist in our being subject to the authority of parliament, but in our not having an equal representation in it. Were it possible for the colonies to have an equal representation in parliament, and were refused it upon proper application, I confess I should think it a grievance, but at present, it seems to be allowed by all parties, to be impracticable.

The major must rule the minor. After many more centuries shall have rolled away, long after we, who are now bustling on the stage of life, shall have been received to the bosom of mother earth, and our names are forgotten, the colonies may be so far increased as to have the balance of wealth, numbers and power in their favor, the good of the empire makes it necessary to fix the seat of government here, and some future George, equally the friend of mankind, with him that now sways the British sceptre, may cross the Atlantic and rule Great Britain, by an American parliament.

24: JOHN ADAMS: *Novanglus* Nos. VII and VIII

Boston January 1775

John Adams (1735–1826) subsequently second President of the United States, had already made a reputation for himself as a speaker and writer for the Massachusetts Opposition, when, after his return from the first Continental Congress, he found the colony much impressed by the essays of 'Massachusettensis.' His reply took the form of a series of essays published in the *Boston Gazette* between January and April, 1775, when they were brought to an end by the outbreak of hostilities. They were republished in pamphlet form on both sides of the Atlantic.

The extracts are taken from the reprint in John Adams' *Works* (ed. C. F. Adams), (10 v., Boston, 1856), IV, pp. 11–177.

VII

I AGREE, that "two supreme and independent authorities cannot exist in the same state," any more than two supreme beings in one universe; and, therefore, I contend, that our provincial legislatures are the only supreme authorities in our colonies. . . .

I say we are not a part of the British empire; because the British government is not an empire. The governments of France, Spain, etc., are not empires, but monarchies, supposed to be governed by fixed fundamental laws, though not really. The British government is still less entitled to the style of *an empire*. It is

a limited monarchy. If Aristotle, Livy and Harrington, knew what a republic was, the British constitution
is much more like a republic than an empire. They
define a republic to be a *government of laws, and not of
men.* If this definition be just, the British constitution
is nothing more than a republic in which the king is
first magistrate. This office being hereditary, and
being possessed of such ample and splendid prerogatives, is no objection to the government's being a
republic, as long as it is bound by fixed laws, which the
people have a voice in making and a right to defend. . . .

Distinct states may be united under one king. And
those states may be further united and cemented together by a treaty of commerce. This is the case. We
have, by our own express consent, contracted to observe the Navigation Act, and by our implied consent,
by long usage and uninterrupted acquiescence, have
submitted to the other acts of trade, however grievous
some of them may be. This may be compared to a
treaty of commerce by which those distinct states are
cemented together in perpetual league and amity.

There is no avoiding all inconveniences in human
affairs. The greatest possible, or conceivable, would
arise from ceding to parliament power over us without
a representation in it. The next greatest would accrue
from any plan that can be devised for a representation
there. The least of all would arise from going on as we
began, and fared well for one hundred and fifty years,
by letting parliament regulate trade, and our own
assemblies all other matters. . . .

We are part of the British dominions, that is of the King of Great Britain, and it is our interest and duty to continue so. It is equally our interest and duty to continue subject to the authority of parliament in the regulation of our trade, as long as she shall leave us to govern our internal policy, and to give and grant our own money and no longer.

This letter (Massachusettensis, No. 5) concludes with an agreeable flight of fancy. The time may not be so far off, however, as this writer imagines, when the colonies may have the balance of numbers and wealth in their favour. But when that shall happen, if we should attempt to rule her (i.e., Great Britain) by an American parliament, without an adequate representation in it, she will infallibly resist us by her arms.

VIII

How then do we New Englandmen derive our laws? I say not from parliament, not from common law, but from the law of nature and the compact made with the king in our charters. Our ancestors were entitled to the common law of England when they emigrated, that is, to just so much of it as they pleased to adopt and no more. They were not bound or obliged to submit to it unless they chose it.

25: EARL OF CHATHAM. Speech in the House of Lords

20 January 1775

Chatham's speech was made in support of a motion which he proposed for withdrawing General Gage's troops from Boston, in order to prevent any possibility of an armed clash there precipitating a crisis. He reiterated his view that the Imperial Parliament had the right of commercial regulation but not of taxation, thus separating himself from the Rockingham Whigs. The news from several parts of America showed indeed that the colonists were preparing resistance and that Chatham's fears were not idle ones. Nevertheless only eighteen peers supported Chatham's motion, while sixty-eight voted against it.

The extracts here are taken from the text given in *Chatham Anecdotes*, II, pp. 255 ff.

WHEN I state the importance of the Colonies to this country, and the magnitude of danger hanging over this country, from the present plan of misadministration practised against them, I desire not to be understood to argue for a reciprocity of indulgence between England and America. I contend not for indulgence, but justice to America; and I shall ever contend, that the Americans justly owe obedience to us in a limited degree—they owe obedience to our ordinances of trade and navigation; but let the line be skilfully drawn between the objects of those ordinances, and their private, internal property; let the sacredness of their property remain inviolate; let it be taxable only by their own consent, given in their provincial assemblies, else *it will cease to be property*. As to the metaphysical refinements, attempting to shew that the Americans are equally free from obedience and commercial restraints, as from taxation for revenue, as being unrepresented here, I pronounce them futile, frivolous, and groundless.

When I urge this measure of recalling the troops from Boston, I urge it on this pressing principle, that it is necessarily preparatory to the restoration of your peace, and the establishment of your prosperity. It will then appear that you are disposed to treat amicably and equitably and to consider, revise, and repeal, if it should be found necessary, as I affirm it will, those violent acts and declarations which have disseminated confusion throughout your empire.

Resistance to your acts was necessary as it was just; and your vain declarations of the omnipotence of Parliament, and your imperious doctrines of the necessity of submission, will be found equally impotent to convince, or to enslave your fellow-subjects in America, who feel that tyranny, whether *ambitioned* by an individual part of the legislature, or the bodies who compose it, is equally intolerable to British subjects.

But his Majesty is advised, that the union in America cannot last. Ministers have more eyes than I, and should have more ears; but with all the information I have been able to procure, I can pronounce it—an union, solid, permanent, and effectual. Ministers may satisfy themselves, and delude the public, with the report of what they call commercial bodies in America. They are not *commercial*; they are your packers and factors: they live upon nothing—for I call commission nothing. I mean the ministerial *authority* for this American intelligence; the runners for government, who are paid for their intelligence. But these are not the men, nor this the influence, to be considered in America, when we estimate the firmness of their union. Even to extend the question, and to take in the really mercantile circle, will be totally inadequate to the consideration. Trade indeed increases the wealth and glory of a country; but its real strength and stamina are to be looked for among the cultivators of the land; in their simplicity of life is found the simpleness of virtue—the integrity and courage of freedom. These true genuine sons of the earth are invincible: and they surround and hem in the mercantile bodies; even if these bodies, which supposition I totally disclaim, could be supposed disaffected to the cause of liberty. Of this general spirit existing in the British nation; (for so I wish to distinguish the real and genuine Americans from the pseudo-traders I have described) —of this spirit of independance, animating the *nation* of America, I have the most authentic information. It is not new among them; it is, and has ever been, their established principle, their confirmed persuasion: it is their nature, and their doctrine.

I remember some years ago, when the repeal of the stamp act was in agitation, conversing in a friendly confidence with a person of undoubted respect and authenticity, on that subject; and he assured me with a certainty which his judgment and opportunity gave him, that these were the prevalent and steady principles of America—That you might destroy their towns, and cut them off from the superfluities, perhaps the conveniences of life; but that they were prepared to despise your power, and would not lament their loss, whilst they have—what, my Lords ?—their *woods* and their *liberty*. The name of my authority, if I am called upon, will authenticate the opinion irrefragably.

If illegal violences have been, as it is said, committed in America; prepare the way, open the door of possibility, for acknowledgment and satisfaction: but proceed not to such coercion, such proscription; cease your indiscriminate inflictions; amerce not thirty thousand; oppress not three millions, for the fault of forty or fifty individuals. Such severity of injustice must for ever render incurable the wounds you have already given your colonies; you irritate them to unappeasable rancour. What though you march from town to town, and from province to province; though you should be able to enforce a temporary and local submission, which I only suppose, not admit—how shall you be able to secure the obedience of the country you leave behind you in your progress, to grasp the dominion of eighteen hundred miles of continent, populous in numbers, possessing valour, liberty and resistance ?

This resistance to your arbitrary system of taxation might have been foreseen: it was obvious from the nature of things, and of mankind; and above all, from the Whiggish spirit flourishing in that country. The spirit which now resists your taxation in America, is the same which formerly opposed loans, benevolences, and ship-money, in England: the same spirit which called all England *on its legs*, and by the Bill of Rights vindicated the English constitution: the same spirit which established the great fundamental essential maxim of your liberties, *that no subject of England shall be taxed but by his own consent.*

This glorious spirit of Whiggism animates three

millions in America; who prefer poverty with liberty, to gilded chains and sordid affluence; and who will die in defence of their rights as men, as freemen. What shall oppose this spirit, aided by the congenial flame glowing in the breasts of every Whig in England, to the amount, I hope, of double the American numbers? Ireland they have to a man. In that country, joined as it is with the cause of Colonies, and placed at their head, the distinction I contend for is and must be observed. This country superintends and controuls their trade and navigation; but they *tax themselves.* And this distinction between external and internal controul is sacred and insurmountable; it is involved in the abstract nature of things; Property is private, individual, absolute. Trade is an extended and complicated consideration: it reaches as far as ships can sail or winds can blow: it is a great and various machine. To regulate the numberless movements of its several parts, and combine them into effect, for the good of the whole, requires the superintending wisdom and energy of the supreme power in the empire. But this supreme power has no effect towards internal taxation; for it does not exist in that relation; there is no such thing, *no such idea in this constitution, as a supreme power operating upon property.* Let this distinction then remain for ever ascertained; taxation is theirs, commercial regulation is ours. As an American I would recognize to England her supreme right of regulating commerce and navigation: as an Englishman by birth and principle, I recognize to the Americans their supreme unalienable right in their property; a right which they are justified in the defence of to the last extremity. To maintain this principle is the common cause of the Whigs on the other side of the Atlantic

193

and on this. " 'Tis liberty to liberty engaged," that they will defend themselves, their families, and their country. In this great cause they are immoveably allied: it is the alliance of God and nature—immutable, eternal—fixed as the firmament of heaven.

Then your Lordships look at the papers transmitted us from America; when you consider their decency, firmness, and wisdom, you cannot but respect their cause, and wish to make it your own. For myself, I must declare and avow, that in all my reading and observation—and it has been my favourite study—I have read Thucidydes, and have studied and admired the master-states of the world—that for solidity of reasoning, force of sagacity, and wisdom of conclusion, under such a complication of difficult circumstances, no nation, or body of men, can stand in preference to the general Congress at Philadelphia. I trust it is obvious to your Lordships that all attempts to impose servitude upon such men, to establish despotism over such a mighty continental *nation*, must be vain, must be fatal. We shall be *forced ultimately to retract*; let us retract while we can, not when we must.

26: EARL OF CHATHAM. Bill for Settling the Troubles in America

1 February 1775

Benjamin Franklin's last months in London, which he left for good in March, 1775, were spent in a final effort at finding a peaceful solution. Chatham, who had been seeking information about American opinion from many sources, took part in the negotiations and they were encouraged by Lord Dartmouth, the Secretary of State for the American Colonies, who had succeeded Lord Hillsborough, the first holder of the office, in August, 1772. The bill introduced by Chatham on 1 February was the fruit of these negotiations. But although it strongly asserted the rights of Parliament in all matters of Imperial concern and refused to accept the new claim that troops should not be sent to the colonies without the consent of their legislatures, it limited this supremacy with regard to taxation and to the use of troops for coercion. The bill was rejected by sixty-one votes to thirty-two.

The text given here is that in *Chatham Anecdotes*, II, pp. 275–83.

The suggestion in the Bill that the Continental Congress should become an official body and make a free grant of money for Imperial purposes reappeared in a different form in the measure of conciliation which North himself introduced on 20 February and carried with the support of the Crown. Under this any colony would have been able to free itself of Imperial taxation by making a contribution to Imperial defence and due provision for the support of the civil government. (Text in Morison, *Sources and Documents*, p. 138, ff.)

WHEREAS by an act 6 Geo. III it is declared, that Parliament has full power and authority to make laws and statutes to bind the people of the Colonies, in all cases whatsoever; and whereas reiterated complaints and most dangerous disorders have grown, touching the right of taxation claimed and exercised over America, to the disturbance of peace and good order there, and to the actual interruption of the due intercourse from Great Britain and Ireland to the Colonies, deeply affecting the navigation, trade, and manufactures of this kingdom and of Ireland, and announcing farther an interruption of all exports from the said Colonies to Great Britain, Ireland, and the British Islands in America: Now, for prevention of these ruinous mischiefs, and in order to an equitable, honourable, and lasting settlement of claims not sufficiently ascertained and curcumscribed, May it please your most Excellent Majesty, that it may be declared, and be it declared by the King's most Excellent Majesty, by and with the advice and consent of the Lords Spiritual and Temporal and Commons in this present Parliament assembled, and by the authority of the same, that the Colonies of America have been, are, and of right ought to be, dependent upon the Imperial Crown of Great-Britain, and subordinate unto the British Parliament, and that the King's most Excellent Majesty, by and with the advice and consent of the Lords Spiritual and Temporal and Commons in Parliament assembled, had, hath, and of right ought to have, full power and authority to make laws and statutes of sufficient force and validity to bind the people of the British Colonies in America, in all matters touching the general weal of the whole dominion of the Imperial Crown of Great Britain, and beyond the competency of the local representative of a distinct colony; and most especially an indubitable and indispensable right to make and ordain laws for regulating navigation and trade throughout the complicated system of British commerce; the deep policy of such prudent acts upholding the guardian navy of the whole British empire; and that all subjects in the Colonies are bound in duty and allegiance duly to recognize and obey (and they are hereby required so to do) the supreme legislative authority and superintending power of the Parliament of Great Britain, as aforesaid. And whereas, in a petition from America to his Majesty, it has been represented, that the keeping a standing army within any of the Colonies, in time of peace, without consent of the respective Provincial Assembly there, is against law: Be it declared by the King's most Excellent Majesty, by and with the consent of the Lords Spiritual and Temporal and Commons in this present Parliament assembled, that the Declaration of Right, at the ever-glorious Revolution, namely, " That the raising and keeping a standing army within the kingdom, in time of peace, unless it be by the consent of Parliament, is against law," having reference only to the consent of the Parliament of Great Britain, the legal, constitutional, and hitherto unquestioned prerogative of the Crown, to send any part of such army, so lawfully kept, to any of the British dominions and possessions, whether in America or elsewhere, as his Majesty, in due care of his subjects, may judge necessary for the security and protection of the same, cannot be rendered dependent upon the consent of a Provincial Assembly in the Colonies, without a most dangerous innovation, and derogation from the dignity of the Imperial Crown of Great Britain. Nevertheless, in order to quiet and dispel groundless jealousies and fears, be it hereby declared, That no military force, however raised, and kept according to law, can ever be lawfully employed to violate and destroy the just rights of the people. Moreover, in order to remove for ever all causes of pernicious discord, and in due contemplation of the vast increase of possessions and population in the Colonies; and having a heart to render the condition of so great a body of industrious subjects there more and more happy, by the sacredness of property and of personal liberty, of more extensive and lasting utility to the parent kingdom, by indissoluble ties of mutual affection, confidence, trade and reciprocal benefits, Be it declared and enacted, by the King's most Excellent Majesty, by and with the advice and consent of the Lords Spiritual and Temporal and Commons in this present Parliament assembled, and it is hereby declared and enacted by the authority of the same, That no tallage, tax, or other charge for his Majesty's revenue, shall be commanded or levied, from British freemen in America, without common consent, by act of Provincial Assembly there, duly convened for that purpose. And it is hereby further declared and enacted, by the King's most Excellent Majesty, by and with the advice and consent of the Lords Spiritual and Temporal and Commons in this present Parliament asembled, and by the authority of the same, That it shall and may be lawful for delegates from the respective provinces, lately assembled at Philadelphia, to meet in general Congress at the said city of Philadelphia, on the 9th day of May next ensuing, in order then and there to take into consideration the making due recognition of the supreme legislative authority and superintending power of Parliament over the Colonies as aforesaid. And moreover, may it please your most Excellent Majesty, that the said Delegates, to be in Congress assembled in manner aforesaid, may be required, and the same are hereby required, by the King's Majesty sitting in his Parliament, to take into consideration (over and above the usual charge for support of civil government in the respective Colonies) the making a free grant to the King, his heirs, and successors, of a certain perpetual revenue, subject to the disposition of the British Parliament, to be by them appropriated as they in their wisdom shall judge fit, to the alleviation of the national debt: no doubt being had but this just, free aid, will be in such honourable proportion as may seem meet and becoming from great and flourishing colonies towards a parent country labouring under the heaviest burdens, which, in no inconsiderable part, have been willingly taken upon ourselves and posterity, for the defence, extension, and prosperity of the Colonies. And to this great end, be it farther hereby declared and enacted, that the general Congress (to meet at Philadelphia as aforesaid) shall be, and is hereby authorized and empowered (the Delegates composing the same being first sufficiently furnished with powers from their respective provinces for this purpose) to adjust and fix the proportions and quotas of the several charges to be borne by each province respectively, towards the general contributory supply; and this in such fair and equitable measure, as may best suit the abilities and due convenience of all: Provided always, that the powers for fixing the said quotas, hereby given to the delegates from the old provinces composing the Congress, shall not extend to the new provinces of East and West Florida, Georgia, Nova Scotia, St. John's, and Canada; the circumstances and abilities of the said provinces being reserved for the wisdom of Parliament in their due time. And in order to afford necessary time for mature deliberation in America, be it hereby declared, That the provisions for ascertaining and fixing the exercise of the right of taxation in the Colonies, as agreed and expressed by this present act, shall not be in force, or have any operation, until the delegates to be in Congress assembled, sufficiently authorized and empowered by their respective provinces to this end, shall, as an indispensable condition, have duly recognised the supreme legislative authority and superintending power of the Parliament of Great Britain over the Colonies aforesaid: Always understood, That the free grant of an aid, as heretofore required and expected from the Colonies, is not to be considered as a condition of redress, but as a just testimony of their affection. And whereas, divers acts of Parliament have been humbly represented, in a petition to his Majesty from America, to have been found grievous, in whole or in part, to the subjects of the Colonies, be it hereby declared by the King's most Excellent Majesty, by and with the advice and consent of the Lords Spiritual and Temporal and Commons in this present Parliament assembled, and by the authority of the same, That the powers of Admiralty and Vice-Admiralty Courts in America shall be restrained within their ancient limits, and the Trial by Jury, in all civil cases, where the same may be abolished, restored: And that no subject in America shall, in capital cases, be liable to be indicted and tried for the same, in any place out of the province wherein such offence shall be alleged to have been committed, nor be deprived of a trial by his peers of the vicinage; nor shall it be lawful to send persons indicted for murder in any province of America, to another colony, or to Great Britain, for trial. And be it hereby declared and enacted, by the authority aforesaid, That all and every the said acts, or so much thereof as are represented to have been found grievous, namely, the several acts of the 4th Geo. III. ch. 15. and ch. 34.–5th Geo. III. ch. 25.–6th Geo. III ch. 52–7th Geo. III ch. 41. and ch. 46.–8th Geo III ch. 22–12th Geo. III ch. 24.—with the three acts for stopping the port and blocking up the harbour of Boston; for altering the charter and government of Massachusetts Bay; and that entitled, An act for the better administration of justice, &c., also the act for regulating the government of Quebec, and the act passed in the same session relating to the quarters of soldiers, shall be, and are hereby suspended, and not to have effect or execution, from the date of this act. And be it moreover hereby declared and enacted, by the authority aforesaid, That all and every the before-recited acts, or the parts thereof complained of, shall be and are, in virtue of this present act, finally repealed and annulled, from the day that the new recognition of the supreme legislative authority and superintending power of Parliament over the Colonies shall have been made on the part of the said Colonies.

And for the better securing due and impartial administration of justice in the Colonies, be it declared and enacted by the King's most Excellent Majesty, by and with the advice and consent of the Lords Spiritual and Temporal and Commons in this present Parliament assembled, That his Majesty's Judges in Courts of Law in the Colonies of America, to be appointed with salaries by the Crown, shall hold their offices and salaries as his Majesty's Judges in England, *quamdiu se bene gesserint*. And it is hereby further declared, by the authority aforesaid, that the Colonies in America are justly entitled to the privileges, franchises, and immunities granted by their several Charters or Constitutions: and that the said Charters or Constitutions ought not to be invaded or resumed, unless for misuser, or some legal ground of forfeiture. So shall true reconcilement avert impending calamities, and this solemn national accord between Great Britain and her colonies stand an everlasting monument of clemency and magnanimity in the benignant father of his people, of wisdom and moderation in this great nation, famed for humanity as for valour, and of fidelity and grateful affection from brave and loyal Colonies to their parent kingdom, which will ever protect and cherish them.

27: BENJAMIN FRANKLIN. Letter to Joseph Galloway

25 February 1775

Benjamin Franklin (1706–90) had already had a long career of public service, when he returned to London in 1764 for a second spell as agent for Pennsylvania. The interests of New Jersey, Georgia and Massachusetts were also committed to his care. His interest in the problem of colonial government dated back at least to 1754 when he had propounded a plan for colonial union at the Albany Convention.

Joseph Galloway, one of the leaders of the Pennsylvania conservatives, was actively concerned in the first Continental Congress, in devising some scheme to prevent the dissolution of the Imperial connection, and to this end propounded on September 28, 1774 "A Plan of a proposed Union between Great Britain and her Colonies", similar in some respects to Franklin's Albany Plan, and providing for an All-American Executive and Legislature intermediate between Parliament and the separate colonial governments, but essentially subordinate to the former. Galloway's scheme (given in Morison, *Sources and Documents*, pp. 116–8) found favour neither with Congress, nor, as can be seen, with Franklin whose letter also condemned the North proposal. (See J. P. Boyd: *Anglo-American Union: Joseph Galloway's plans to preserve the British Empire*, 1774–88. Philadelphia, 1941.)

The full text of Franklin's letter is in his *Complete Works* (ed. J. Bigelow), (10 v., New York 1887–88), V, pp. 435–9.

I HAVE not heard what objections were made to the plan in the Congress, nor would I make more than this one, that, when I consider the extreme corruption prevalent among all orders of men in this old rotten state, and the glorious public virtue so predominant in our rising country, I cannot but apprehend more mischief than benefit from a closer union. I fear they will drag us after them in all the plundering wars which their desperate circumstances, injustice, and rapacity may prompt them to undertake; and their wide-wasting prodigality and profusion is a gulf that will swallow up every aid we may distress ourselves to afford them.

Here numberless and needless places, enormous salaries, pensions, perquisites, bribes, groundless quarrels, foolish expeditions, false accounts or no accounts, contracts and jobs, devour all revenue, and produce continual necessity in the midst of natural plenty. I apprehend, therefore, that to unite us intimately will only be to corrupt and poison us also. . . . However I would try anything and bear anything that can be borne with safety to our just liberties, rather than engage in a war with such relations, unless compelled to it by dire necessity in our own defence.

28: EDMUND BURKE. Speech on Conciliation with America

House of Commons, 22 March 1775

A bill for restraining the trade of New England was introduced into Parliament early in February, 1775, and its provisions were later extended to the southern colonies. Reports of American readiness to submit were weakening the opposition to the Government when Burke introduced his proposals for conciliation. He could do this with the more appropriateness and effect since the election of 1774 had seen his return as one of the members for Bristol. The fortunes of this great port were largely bound up with the American trade. But neither this scheme, nor another which Burke produced in November and which went still further in the direction of renouncing Parliament's authority, were acceptable to the Parliament. Nor is it clear that the colonists could have been brought to agree to any proposals which left the Declaratory Act on the statute-book.

The speech made by Burke on 22 March, was later published and the extracts here are from this version. *Works*, III, pp. 23–132.

IN this character of the Americans, a love of freedom is the predominating feature which marks and distinguishes the whole: and as an ardent is always a jealous affection, your colonies become suspicious, restive, and untractable, whenever they see the least attempt to wrest from them by force, or shuffle from them by chicane, what they think the only advantage worth living for. This fierce spirit of liberty is stronger in the English colonies probably than in any other people of the earth; and this from a great variety of powerful causes which, to understand the true temper of their minds, and the direction which this spirit takes, it will not be amiss to lay open somewhat more largely.

First, the people of the colonies are descendants of Englishmen. England, Sir, is a nation, which still I hope respects, and formerly adored, her freedom. The colonists emigrated from you, when this part of your character was most predominant; and they took this bias and direction the moment they parted from your hands. They are therefore not only devoted to liberty, but to liberty according to English ideas, and on English principles. Abstract liberty, like other mere abstractions, is not to be found. Liberty inheres in some sensible object; and every nation has formed to itself some favourite point, which by way of eminence becomes the criterion of their happiness. It happened, you know, Sir, that the great contests for freedom in this country were from the earliest times chiefly upon the question of taxing. Most of the contests in the ancient commonwealths turned primarily on the right of election of magistrates; or on the balance among the several orders of the state. The question of money was not with them so immediate. But in England it was otherwise. On this point of taxes the ablest pens, and most eloquent tongues, have been exercised; the greatest spirits have acted and suffered. In order to give the fullest satisfaction concerning the importance of this point, it was not only necessary for those who in argument defended the excellence of the English constitution, to insist on this privilege of granting money as a dry point of fact, and to prove, that the right had been acknowledged in ancient parchments, and blind usages, to reside in a certain body called an house of commons. They went much further; they attempted to prove, and they succeeded, that in theory it ought to be so, from the particular nature of a house of commons, as an immediate representative of the people; whether the old records had delivered this oracle or not. They took infinite pains to inculcate, as a fundamental principle, that, in all monarchies, the people must in effect themselves mediately or immediately possess the power of granting their own money, or no shadow of liberty could subsist. The colonies draw from you, as with their life-blood, these ideas and principles. Their love of liberty, as with you, fixed and attached on this specifick point of taxing. Liberty might be safe, or might be endangered in twenty other particulars, without their being much pleased or alarmed. Here they felt its pulse; and as they found that beat, they thought themselves sick or sound. I do not say whether they were right or wrong in applying your general arguments to their own case. It is not easy indeed to make a monopoly of theorems and corollaries. The fact is, that they did thus apply those general arguments; and your mode of governing them, whether through lenity or indolence, through wisdom or mistake, confirmed them in the imagination, that they, as well as you, had an interest in these common principles.

They were further confirmed in this pleasing errour, by the form of their provincial legislative assemblies. Their governments are popular in an high degree; some are merely popular; in all, the popular representative is the most weighty; and this share of the people in their ordinary government never fails to inspire them with lofty sentiments, and with a strong aversion from whatever tends to deprive them of their chief importance.

If any thing were wanting to this necessary operation of the form of government, religion would have given it a complete effect. Religion, always a principle of energy, in this new people, is no way worn out or impaired; and their mode of professing it is also one main cause of this free spirit. The people are protestants; and of that kind, which is the most adverse to all implicit submission of mind and opinion. This is a persuasion not only favourable to liberty, but built upon it. I do not think, Sir, that the reason of this averseness in the dissenting churches from all that looks like absolute government is so much to be sought in their religious tenets, as in their history. Every one knows that the Roman Catholick religion is at least coeval with most of the governments where it prevails; that it has generally gone hand in hand with them; and received great favour and every kind of support from authority. The church of England too was formed from her cradle under the nursing care of regular government. But the dissenting interests have sprung up in direct opposition to all the ordinary powers of the world; and could justify that opposition only on a strong claim to natural liberty. Their very existence depended on the powerful and unremitted assertion of that claim. All protestantism, even the most cold and passive, is a sort of dissent. But the religion most prevalent in our northern colonies is a refinement on the principle of resistance; it is the dissidence of dissent; and the protestantism of the protestant religion. This religion, under a variety of denominations, agreeing in nothing but in the communion of the spirit of liberty, is predominant in most of the northern provinces; where the church of England, notwithstanding its legal rights, is in reality no more than a sort of

208

private sect, not composing most probably the tenth of the people. The colonists left England when this spirit was high; and in the emigrants was the highest of all: and even that stream of foreigners, which has been constantly flowing into these colonies, has, for the greatest part, been composed of dissenters from the establishments of their several countries, and have brought with them a temper and character far from alien to that of the people with whom they mixed.

Sir, I can perceive by their manner, that some gentlemen object to the latitude of this description; because in the southern colonies the church of England forms a large body, and has a regular establishment. It is certainly true. There is however a circumstance attending these colonies, which, in my opinion, fully counterbalances this difference, and makes the spirit of liberty still more high and haughty than in those to the northward. It is that in Virginia and the Carolinas, they have a vast multitude of slaves. Where this is the case in any part of the world, those who are free, are by far the most proud and jealous of their freedom. Freedom is to them not only an enjoyment, but a kind of rank and privilege. Not seeing there, that freedom, as in countries where it is a common blessing, and as broad and general as the air, may be united with much abject toil, with great misery, with all the exterior of servitude, liberty looks, amongst them, like something that is more noble and liberal. I do not mean, Sir, to commend the superior morality of this sentiment, which has at least as much pride as virtue in it; but I cannot alter the nature of man. The fact is so; and these people of the southern colonies are much more strongly, and with an higher and more stubborn spirit, attached to liberty than those to the northward. Such were all the ancient commonwealths; such were our Gothick ancestors; such in our days were the Poles; and such will be all masters of slaves, who are not slaves themselves. In such a people the haughtiness of domination combines with the spirit of freedom, fortifies it, and renders it invincible.

Permit me, Sir, to add another circumstance in our colonies, which contributes no mean part towards the growth and effect of this untractable spirit. I mean their education. In no country perhaps in the world is the law so general a study. The profession itself is numerous and powerful; and in most provinces it takes the lead. The greater number of the deputies sent to the congress were lawyers. But all who read, and most do read, endeavour to obtain some smattering in that science. I have been told by an eminent bookseller, that in no branch of his business, after tracts of popular devotion, were so many books as those on the law exported to the plantations. The colonists have now fallen into the way of printing them for their own use. I hear that they have sold nearly as many of Blackstone's Commentaries in America as in England. General Gage marks out this disposition very particularly in a letter on your table. He states, that all the people in his government are lawyers, or smatterers in law; and that in Boston they have been enabled, by successful chicane, wholly to evade many parts of one of your capital penal constitutions. The smartness of debate will say, that this knowledge ought to teach them more clearly the rights of legislature, their obligations to obedience, and the penalties of rebellion. All this is mighty well. But my honourable and learned friend on the floor, who condescends to mark what I say for animadversion, will disdain that ground. He has heard, as well as I, that when great honours and great emoluments do not win over this knowledge to the service of the state, it is a formidable adversary to government. If the spirit be not tamed and broken by these happy methods, it is stubborn and litigious. *Abeunt studia in mores.* This study renders men acute, inquisitive, dexterous, prompt in attack, ready in defence, full of resources. In other countries, the people, more simple, and of a less mercurial cast, judge of an ill principle in government only by an actual grievance; here they anticipate the evil, and judge of the pressure of the grievance by the badness of the principle. They augur misgovernment at a distance; and snuff the approach of tyranny in every tainted breeze.

The last cause of this disobedient spirit in the colonies is hardly less powerful than the rest, as it is not merely moral, but laid deep in the natural constitution of things. Three thousand miles of ocean lie between you and them. No contrivance can prevent the effect of this distance, in weakening government. Seas roll, and months pass, between the order and the execution: and the want of a speedy explanation of a single point, is enough to defeat a whole system. You have, indeed, winged ministers of vengeance, who carry their bolts in their pounces to the remotest verge of the sea. But there a power steps in, that limits the arrogance of raging passions and furious elements, and says, " So far shalt thou go, and no farther." Who are you, that should fret and rage, and bite the chains of nature ?—Nothing worse happens to you, than does to all nations, who have extensive empire; and it happens in all the forms into which empire can be thrown.

Then, Sir, from these six capital sources; of descent; of form of government; of religion in the northern provinces; of manners in the southern; of education; of the remoteness of situation from the first mover of government; from all these causes a fierce spirit of liberty has grown up. It has grown with the growth of the people in your colonies, and increased with the increase of their wealth; a spirit, that unhappily meeting with an exercise of power in England, which, however lawful, is not reconcileable to any ideas of liberty, much less with theirs, has kindled this flame, that is ready to consume us.

I do not mean to commend either the spirit in this excess, or the moral causes which produce it. Perhaps a more smooth and accommodating spirit of freedom in them would be more acceptable to us. Perhaps ideas of liberty might be desired, more reconcileable with an arbitrary and boundless authority. Perhaps we might wish the colonists to be persuaded, that their liberty is more secure when held in trust for them by us (as their guardians during a perpetual minority) than with any part of it in their own hands. But the question is, not whether their spirit deserves praise or blame; —what, in the name of God, shall we do with it? You have before you the object; such as it is, with all its glories with all its imperfections on its head. You see the magnitude; the importance; the temper; the habits; the disorders. By all these considerations, we are strongly urged to determine something concerning it. We are called upon to fix some rule and line for our future conduct, which may give a little stability to our politicks, and prevent the return of such unhappy deliberations as the present. Every such return will bring the matter before us in a still more untractable form. For,

what astonishing and incredible things have we not
seen already ? What monsters have not been generated from this unnatural contention ? Whilst every
principle of authority and resistance has been pushed,
upon both sides, as far as it would go, there is nothing
so solid and certain, either in reasoning or in practice,
that has not been shaken. Until very lately, all authority in America seemed to be nothing but an emanation
from yours. Even the popular part of the colony constitution derived all its activity, and its first vital movement, from the pleasure of the crown. We thought,
Sir, that the utmost which the discontented colonists
could do, was to disturb authority; we never dreamt
they could of themselves supply it; knowing in general
what an operose business it is, to establish a government absolutely new. But having, for our purposes in
this contention, resolved, that none but an obedient
assembly should fit, the humours of the people there,
finding all passage through the legal channel stopped,
with great violence broke out another way. Some
provinces have tried their experiment, as we have tried
ours; and theirs has succeeded. They have formed a
government sufficient for its purposes, without the
bustle of a revolution, or the troublesome formality of
an election. Evident necessity and tacit consent, have
done the business in an instant. So well they have done
it, that Lord Dunmore (the account is among the
fragments on your table) tells you, that the new institution is infinitely better obeyed than the ancient government ever was in its most fortunate periods. Obedience is what makes government, and not the names
by which it is called; not the name of governour, as
formerly, or committee, as at present. This new government has originated directly from the people; and

was not transmitted through any of the ordinary artificial media of a positive constitution. It was not a
manufacture ready formed, and transmitted to them
in that condition from England. The evil arising
from hence is this; that the colonists having once found
the possibility of enjoying the advantages of order, in
the midst of a struggle for liberty, such struggles will
not henceforward seem so terrible to the settled and
sober part of mankind, as they had appeared before
the trial.

Pursuing the same plan of punishing by the denial
of the exercise of government to still greater lengths,
we wholly abrogated the ancient government of Mas-
sachuset. We were confident, that the first feeling, if not
the very prospect of anarchy, would instantly enforce
a complete submission. The experiment was tried. A
new, strange, unexpected face of things appeared.
Anarchy is found tolerable. A vast province has now
subsisted, and subsisted in a considerable degree of
health and vigour, for near a twelvemonth, without
governour, without publick council, without judges,
without executive magistrates. How long it will continue in this state, or what may arise out of this unheard-of situation, how can the wisest of us conjecture ?
Our late experience has taught us, that many of those
fundamental principles, formerly believed unfallible,
are either not of the importance they were imagined
to be; or that we have not at all adverted to some
other far more important, and far more powerful
principles, which entirely over-rule those we had considered as omnipotent. I am much against any further
experiments, which tend to put to the proof any more
of these allowed opinions, which contribute so much
to the publick tranquillity. In effect, we suffer as much

at home, by this loosening of all ties, and this concus-
sion of all established opinions, as we do abroad. For,
in order to prove that the Americans have no right to
their liberties, we are every day endeavouring to sub-
vert the maxims which preserve the whole spirit of our
own. To prove that the Americans ought not to be
free, we are obliged to depreciate the value of freedom
itself; and we never seem to gain a paltry advantage
over them in debate, without attacking some of those
principles, or deriding some of those feelings, for which
our ancestors have shed their blood.

The temper and character, which prevail in our
colonies, are I am afraid, unalterable by any human
art. We cannot, I fear, falsify the pedigree of this
fierce people, and persuade them that they are not
sprung from a nation, in whose veins the blood of
freedom circulates. The language in which they would
hear you tell them this tale, would detect the imposition; your speech would betray you. An Englishman
is the unfittest person on earth to argue another
Englishman into slavery.

If then, Sir, it seems almost desperate to think of any
alterative course, for changing the moral causes (and
not quite easy to remove the natural) which produce
prejudices irreconcileable to the late exercise of our
authority; but that the spirit infallibly will continue;
and, continuing, will produce such effects, as now em-
barrass us; the second mode under consideration is, to
prosecute that spirit in its overt acts, as *criminal*.

At this proposition, I must pause a moment. The thing seems a great deal too big for my ideas of jurisprudence. It should seem, to my way of conceiving such matters, that there is a very wide difference in reason and policy, between the mode of proceeding on the irregular conduct of scattered individuals, or even of bands of men, who disturb order within the state, and the civil dissentions which may, from time to time, on great questions, agitate the several communities which compose a great empire. It looks to me to be narrow and pedantick, to apply the ordinary ideas of criminal justice to this great publick contest. I do not know the method of drawing up an indictment against an whole people. I cannot insult and ridicule the feelings of millions of my fellow creatures, as Sir Edward Coke insulted one excellent individual (Sir Walter Raleigh) at the bar. I am not ripe to pass sentence on the gravest publick bodies, entrusted with magistracies of great authority and dignity, and charged with the safety of their fellow citizens, upon the very same title that I am. I really think, that for wise men this is not judicious; for sober men, not decent; for minds tinctured with humanity, not mild and merciful.

Perhaps, Sir, I am mistaken in my idea of an empire, as distinguished from a single state or kingdom. But my idea of it is this; that an empire is the aggregate of many states, under one common head; whether this head be a monarch, or a presiding republick. It does, in such constitutions, frequently happen (and nothing but the dismal, cold, dead uniformity of servitude can prevent its happening) that the subordinate parts have many local privileges and immunities. Between these privileges and the supreme common authority, the line may be extremely nice. Of course disputes, often too, very bitter disputes, and much ill blood, will arise. But though every privilege is an exemption (in the case) from the ordinary exercise of the supreme authority, it is no denial of it. The claim of a privilege seems rather *ex vi termini*, to imply a superiour power. For to talk of the privileges of a state or of a person, who has no superiour, is hardly any better than speaking nonsense. Now, in such unfortunate quarrels, among the component parts of a great political union of communities, I can scarcely conceive any thing more completely imprudent, than for the head of the empire to insist, that, if any privilege is pleaded against his will, or his acts, that his whole authority is denied; instantly to proclaim rebellion, to beat to arms, and to put the offending provinces under the ban. Will not this, Sir, very soon teach the provinces to make no distinctions on their part? Will it not teach them that the government, against which a claim of liberty is tantamount to high treason, is a government to which submission is equivalent to slavery? It may not always be quite convenient to impress dependent communities with such an idea.

If then the removal of the causes of this spirit of American liberty be, for the greater part, or rather entirely, impracticable; if the ideas of criminal process be inapplicable, or, if applicable, are in the highest degree inexpedient, what way yet remains? No way is open, but the third and last—to comply with the American spirit as necessary; or, if you please to submit to it, as a necessary evil.

If we adopt this mode; if we mean to conciliate and concede; let us see of what nature the concession ought to be; to ascertain the nature of our concession, we must look at their complaint. The colonies complain, that they have not the characteristick mark and seal of British freedom. They complain, that they are taxed in a parliament, in which they are not represented. If you mean to satisfy them at all, you must satisfy them with regard to this complaint. If you mean to please any people, you must give them the boon which they ask; not what you may think better for them, but of a kind totally different. Such an act may be a wise regulation, but it is no concession; whereas our present theme is the mode of giving satisfaction.

Sir, I think you must perceive, that I am resolved this day to have nothing at all to do with the question of the right of taxation. Some gentlemen startle—but it is true: I put it totally out of the question. It is less than nothing in my consideration. I do not indeed wonder, nor will you, Sir, that gentlemen of profound learning are fond of displaying it on this profound subject. But my consideration is narrow, confined, and wholly limited to the policy of the question. I do not examine, whether the giving away a man's money be a power excepted and reserved out of the general trust of government; and how far all mankind, in all forms of polity, are entitled to an exercise of that right by the charter of nature. Or whether, on the contrary, a right of taxation is necessarily involved in the general principle of legislation, and inseparable from the ordinary supreme power. These are deep questions, where great names militate against each other; where reason is perplexed; and an appeal to authorities only thickens the confusion. For high and reverend authorities lift up their heads on both sides; and there is no sure footing in the middle. This point is the *great Serbonian bog, betwixt Damiata and Mount Casius old, where armies whole have sunk.* I do not intend to be overwhelmed in that bog, though in such respectable company. The question with me is not whether you have a right to render your people miserable; but whether it is not your interest to make them happy. It is not, what a lawyer tells me, I *may* do; but what humanity, reason, and justice, tell me, I ought to do. Is a politick act the worse for being a generous one? Is no concession proper, but that which is made from your want of right to keep what you grant? or does it lessen the grace or dignity of relaxing in the exercise of an odious claim, because you have your evidence-room full of titles, and your magazines stuffed with arms to enforce them? What signify all those titles, and all those arms? Of what avail are they, when the reason of the thing tells me, that the assertion of my title is the loss of my suit; and that I could do nothing but wound myself by the use of my own weapons?

Such is stedfastly my opinion of the absolute necessity of keeping up the concord of this empire by a unity of spirit, though in diversity of operations, that, if I were sure the colonists had, at their leaving this country, sealed a regular compact of servitude; that they had solemnly abjured all the rights of citizens; that they had made a vow to renounce all ideas of liberty for them and their posterity, to all generations, yet I should hold myself obliged to conform to the temper I found universally prevalent in my own day, and to govern two million of men, impatient of servitude, on the principles of freedom. I am not determining a point of law; I am restoring tranquillity; and the general character and situation of a people must determine what sort of government is fitted for them. That point nothing else can or ought to determine.

My idea therefore, without considering whether we yield as matter of right, or grant as matter of favour, is *to admit the people of our colonies into an interest in the constitution*; and, by recording that admission in the journals of parliament, to give them as strong an assurance as the nature of the thing will admit, that we mean for ever to adhere to that solemn declaration of systematick indulgence.

The more moderate among the opposers of parliamentary concession freely confess, that they hope no good from taxation; but they apprehend the colonists have further views; and if this point were conceded, they would instantly attack the trade laws. These gentlemen are convinced, that this was the intention from the beginning; and the quarrel of the Americans with taxation was no more than a cloke and cover to this design.

[*the trade laws are useful, continued Burke,*]

But my perfect conviction of this, does not help me in the least to discern how the revenue laws form any security whatsoever to the commercial regulations; or that these commercial regulations are the true ground of the quarrel; or, that the giving way in any one instance of authority, is to lose all that may remain unconceded.

One fact is clear and indisputable. The publick and avowed origin of this quarrel, was on taxation. This quarrel has indeed brought on new disputes on new questions; but certainly the least bitter, and the fewest of all, on the trade laws. To judge which of the two be the real radical cause of quarrel, we have to see whether the commercial dispute did, in order of time, precede the dispute on taxation? There is not a shadow of evidence for it. Next, to enable us to judge whether at this moment a dislike to the trade laws be the real cause of quarrel, it is absolutely necessary to put the taxes out of the question by a repeal. See how the Americans act in this position, and then you will be able to discern correctly what is the true object of the controversy, or whether any controversy at all will remain? Unless you consent to remove this cause of difference, it is impossible, with decency, to assert that the dispute is not upon what it is avowed to be.

But, Sir, I am sure that I shall not be misled, when, in a case of constitutional difficulty, I consult the genius of the English constitution. Consulting at that oracle (it was with all due humility and piety) I found four capital examples in a similar case before me: those of Ireland, Wales, Chester, and Durham.

[*Burke discusses the extension of the franchise to Ireland, Wales, Chester and Durham: Why not apply this example?*]

But your legislative authority is perfect with regard to America; was it less perfect in Wales, Chester, and Durham? But America is virtually represented. What! does the electrick force of virtual representation more easily pass over the Atlantick, than pervade Wales, which lies in your neighbourhood; or than Chester and Durham, surrounded by abundance of representation that is actual and palpable? But, Sir, your ancestors thought this sort of virtual representation, however ample, to be totally insufficient for the freedom of the inhabitants of territories that are so near, and comparatively so inconsiderable. How then can I think it sufficient for those which are infinitely greater, and infinitely more remote?

You will now, Sir, perhaps imagine, that I am on the point of proposing to you a scheme for a representation of the colonies in parliament. Perhaps I might be inclined to entertain some such thought; but a great flood stops me in my course. *Opposuit natura*—I cannot remove the eternal barriers of the creation. The thing in that mode, I do not know to be possible. As I meddle with no theory, I do not absolutely assert the impracticability of such a representation. But I do not see my way to it; and those who have been more confident, have not been more successful. However, the arm of publick benevolence is not shortened; and there are often several means to the same end. What nature has disjoined in one way, wisdom may unite in another. When we cannot give the benefit as we would wish, let us not refuse it altogether. If we cannot give the principal, let us find a substitute. But how? Where? What substitute?

Fortunately I am not obliged for the ways and means of this substitute to tax my own unproductive invention. I am not even obliged to go to the rich treasury of the fertile framers of imaginary commonwealths; not to the Republick of Plato, not to the Utopia of More; not to the Oceana of Harrington. It is before me—It is at my feet, *and the rude swain treads daily on it with his clouted shoon.* I only wish you to recognize, for the theory, the ancient constitutional policy of this kingdom with regard to representation, as that policy has been declared in acts of parliament; and, as to the practice, to return to that mode which an uniform experience has marked out to you, as best; and in which you walked with security, advantage, and honour, until the year 1763.

My resolutions therefore mean to establish the equity, and justice of a taxation of America, by *grant*, and not by *imposition*. To mark the *legal competency* of the colony assemblies for the support of their government in peace, and for publick aids in time of war. To acknowledge that this legal competency has had *a dutiful and beneficial exercise*; and that experience has shewn the benefit of their grants, and the *futility of parliamentary taxation as a method of supply*.

I do not know, that the colonies have, in any general way, or in any cool hour, gone much beyond the demand of immunity in relation to taxes. It is not fair to judge of the temper or dispositions of any man, or any set of men, when they are composed and at rest, from their conduct, or their expressions, in a state of disturbance and irritation. It is besides a very great mistake to imagine, that mankind follow up practically any speculative principle, either of government or of freedom, as far as it will go in argument and logical illation. We Englishmen stop very short of the principles upon which we support any given part of our constitution; or even the whole of it together. I could easily, if I had not already tired you, give you very striking and convincing instances of it. This is nothing but what is natural and proper. All government, indeed every human benefit and enjoyment, every virtue, and every prudent act, is founded on compromise and barter. We balance inconveniences; we give and take; we remit some rights, that we may enjoy others; and, we choose rather to be happy citizens, than subtle disputants. As we must give away some natural liberty, to enjoy civil advantages; so we must sacrifice some civil liberties, for the advantages to be derived from the communion and fellowship of a great empire. But in all fair dealings the thing bought, must bear some proportion to the purchase paid. None will barter away the immediate jewel of his soul. Though a great house is apt to make slaves haughty, yet it is purchasing a part of the artificial importance of a great empire too dear, to pay for it all essential rights, and all the intrinsick dignity of human nature. None of us who would not risk his life, rather than fall under a government purely arbitrary. But, although there are some amongst us who think our constitution wants many improvements, to make it a complete system of liberty, perhaps none who are of that opinion would think it right to aim at such improvement, by disturbing his country, and risking every thing that is dear to him. In every arduous enterprise, we consider what we are to lose, as well as what we are to gain; and the more and better stake of liberty every people possess, the less they will hazard in a vain attempt to make it more. These are *the cords of man.*

Man acts from adequate motives relative to his interest; and not on metaphysical speculations. Aristotle, the great master of reasoning, cautions us, and with great weight and propriety, against this species of delusive geometrical accuracy in moral arguments, as the most fallacious of all sophistry.

The Americans will have no interest contrary to the

grandeur and glory of England, when they are not oppressed by the weight of it; and they will rather be inclined to respect the acts of a superintending legislature; when they see them the acts of that power, which is itself the security, not the rival, of their secondary importance. In this assurance, my mind most perfectly acquiesces; and I confess, I feel not the least alarm, from the discontents which are to arise, from putting people at their ease; nor do I apprehend the destruction of this empire, from giving, by an act of free grace and indulgence to two millions of my fellow citizens, some share of those rights, upon which I have always been taught to value myself.

It is said, indeed, that this power of granting, vested in American assemblies, would dissolve the unity of the empire; which was preserved, entire, although Wales, and Chester, and Durham, were added to it. Truly, Mr. Speaker, I do not know, what this unity means; nor has it ever been heard of, that I know, in the constitutional policy of this country. The very idea of subordination of parts, excludes this notion of simple and undivided unity. England is the head; but she is not the head and the members too. Ireland has ever had from the beginning a separate, but not an independent legislature; which, far from distracting, promoted the union of the whole. Every thing was sweetly and harmoniously disposed through both islands for the conservation of English dominion, and the communication of English liberties. I do not see that the same principles might not be carried into twenty islands, and with the same good effect. This is my model with regard to America, as far as the internal circumstances of the two countries are the same. I know no other unity of this empire, than I can draw from its example during these periods, when it seemed to my poor understanding more united than it is now, or than it is likely to be by the present methods.

[*No revenue will ever be drawn to Britain from the colonies: let them reserve their resources for service in time of war.*]

For that service, for all service, whether of revenue, trade, or empire, my trust is in her interest in the British constitution. My hold of the colonies is in the close affection which grows from common names, from kindred blood, from similar privileges, and equal protection. These are ties, which, though light as air, are as strong as links of iron. Let the colonies always keep the idea of their civil rights associated with your government;—they will cling and grapple to you; and no force under heaven will be of power to tear them from their allegiance. But let it be once understood, that your government may be one thing, and their privileges another; that these two things may exist without any mutual relation; the cement is gone; the cohesion is loosened; and every thing hastens to decay and dissolution. As long as you have the wisdom to keep the sovereign authority of this country as the sanctuary of liberty, the sacred temple consecrated to our common faith, wherever the chosen race and sons of England worship freedom, they will turn their faces towards you. The more they multiply, the more friends you will have; the more ardently they love liberty, the more perfect will be their obedience. Slavery they can have any where. It is a weed that grows in every soil. They may have it from Spain, they may have it from Prussia. But until you become lost to all feeling of your true interest and your natural dignity, freedom

they can have from none but you. This is the com-
modity of price, of which you have the monopoly. This
is the true act of navigation, which binds to you the
commerce of the colonies, and through them secures to
you the wealth of the world. Deny them this participation of freedom, and you break that sole bond, which
originally made, and must still preserve, the unity of
the empire. Do not entertain so weak an imagination,
as that your registers and your bonds, your affidavits
and your sufferances, your cockets and your clear-
ances, are what form the great securities of your commerce. Do not dream that your letters of office, and
your instructions, and your suspending clauses, are the
things that hold together the great contexture of this
mysterious whole. These things do not make your
government. Dead instruments, passive tools as they
are, it is the spirit of the English communion, that gives
all their life and efficacy to them. It is the spirit of the
English constitution, which, infused through the mighty
mass, pervades, feeds, unites, invigorates, vivifies, every
part of the empire, even down to the minutest member.

Is it not the same virtue which does every thing for
us here in England ? Do you imagine then, that it is
the land tax act which raises your revenue ? that it is
the annual vote in the committee of supply, which
gives you your army ? or that it is the mutiny bill
which inspires it with bravery and discipline ? No!
surely no! It is the love of the people; it is their attachment to their government from the sense of the deep
stake they have in such a glorious institution, which
gives you your army and your navy, and infuses into
both that liberal obedience, without which your army
would be a base rabble, and your navy nothing but
rotten timber.

227

All this, I know well enough, will sound wild and chimerical to the profane herd of those vulgar and mechanical politicians, who have no place among us; a sort of people who think that nothing exists but what is gross and material; and who therefore, far from being qualified to be directors of the great movement of empire, are not fit to turn a wheel in the machine. But to men truly initiated and rightly taught, these ruling and master principles, which, in the opinion of such men as I have mentioned, have no substantial existence, are in truth every thing, and all in all. Magnanimity in politicks is not seldom the truest wisdom; and a great empire and little minds go ill together. If we are conscious of our situation, and glow with zeal to fill our places as becomes our station and ourselves, we ought to auspicate all our publick proceedings on America, with the old warnings of the church, *Sursum corda*! We ought to elevate our minds to the greatness of that trust to which the order of Providence has called us. By adverting to the dignity of this high calling, our ancestors have turned a savage wilderness into a glorious empire; and have made the most extensive, and the only honourable conquests; not by destroying, but by promoting, the wealth, the number, the happiness of the human race. Let us get an American revenue as we have got an American empire. English privileges have made it all that it is; English privileges alone will make it all it can be.

29: THOMAS PAINE. *Common Sense*

Philadelphia 9 January 1776

Thomas Paine (1737–1809) had been dismissed in 1774 from his post in the excise as a penalty for leading an agitation in favour of an increase in the pay of excisemen, and had shortly afterwards, left for America with an introduction from Franklin. This brought him into radical politics and for eighteen months he edited the *Pennsylvania Magazine*.

Paine had originally hoped for a peaceful solution of the problem of American relations with Britain, but after the events of 1775—the outbreak of fighting in New England, the meeting of the Second Continental Congress, Washington's appointment as Commander-in-Chief and the American invasion of Canada—his views altered. His new position was set out in the pamphlet *Common Sense* which has been called " the first open and unqualified argument in championship of the doctrine of American independence ". (Tyler, op. cit. I, p. 458.)

The instantaneous success of Paine's pamphlet, which owed as much to his forthright and simple style as to the novelty of his argument, proved that the idea of independence was now congenial to large numbers of politically-minded Americans and this helped to pave the way for the decision taken by Congress in July.

It took some time for the authorship of *Common Sense* to become known but when it did so, it helped to consolidate Paine's position as a leading political figure and from 1777 to 1779 he served as Secretary to the Congress's Committee on Foreign Affairs. He left for Europe in 1787 and did not return to America until 1802.

INTRODUCTION

PERHAPS the sentiments contained in the following pages are not yet sufficiently fashionable to procure them general favor; a long habit of not thinking a thing wrong, gives it a superficial appearance of being right, and raises at first a formidable outcry in defence of custom. But the tumult soon subsides. Time makes more converts than reason.

As a long and violent abuse of power, is generally the means of calling the right of it in question, (and in matters too which might never have been thought of, had not the sufferers been aggravated into the enquiry) and as the King of England hath undertaken in his own right, to support the parliament in what he calls theirs, and as the good people of this country are grievously oppressed by the combination they have an undoubted privilege to enquire into the pretensions of both, and equally to reject the usurpation of either.

In the following sheets the author hath studiously avoided every thing which is personal among ourselves. Compliments as well as censure to individuals make no part thereof. The wise, and the worthy, need not the triumph of a pamphlet; and those whose sentiments are injudicious, or unfriendly, will cease of themselves, unless too much pains are bestowed upon their conversion.

The cause of America is in a great measure the cause of all mankind. Many circumstances have arisen, and will arise, which are not local, but universal, and through which the principles of all lovers of mankind are affected, and in the event of which their affections are interested. The laying a country desolate with fire and sword, declaring war against the natural rights of

230

all mankind, and extirpating the defenders thereof from the face of the earth, is the concern of every man to whom nature hath given the power of feeling; of which class, regardless of party censure, is the author.

COMMON SENSE

OF THE ORIGIN AND DESIGN OF GOVERNMENT IN GENERAL.
WITH CONCISE REMARKS ON THE ENGLISH CONSTITUTION.

SOME writers have so confounded society with government, as to leave little or no distinction between them; whereas they are not only different, but have different origins. Society is produced by our wants and government by our wickedness; the former promotes our happiness *positively* by uniting our affections, the latter *negatively* by restraining our vices. The one encourages intercourse, the other creates distinctions. The first is a patron, the last a punisher.

Society in every state is a blessing, but government even in its best state is but a necessary evil; in its worst state an intolerable one; for when we suffer, or are exposed to the same miseries *by a government*, which we might expect in a country *without government*, our calamity is heightened by reflecting that we furnish the means by which we suffer. Government, like dress, is the badge of lost innocence; the palaces of kings are built on the ruins of the bowers of paradise. For were the impulses of conscience clear, uniform, and irresistably obeyed, man would need no other lawgiver; but that not being the case, he finds it necessary to surrender up a part of his property to furnish means for the protection of the rest; and this he is induced to do by the same prudence which in every other case, advises him out of two evils to choose the least. *Wherefore* security being the true design and end of government, it unanswerably follows, that whatever *form* thereof appears most likely to insure it to us, with the least expence and greatest benefit, is preferable to all others.

In order to gain a clear and just idea of the design and end of government, let us suppose a small number of persons settled in some sequestred part of the earth, unconnected with the rest: they will then represent the first peopling of any country, or of the world. In this state of natural liberty, society will be their first thought. A thousand motives will excite them thereto, the strength of one man is so unequal to his wants, and his mind so unfitted for perpetual solitude, that he is soon obliged to seek assistance and relief of another, who in his turn requires the same. Four or five united would be able to raise a tolerable dwelling in the midst of a wilderness; but *one* man might labour out the common period of life without accomplishing any thing; when he has felled his timber he could not remove it, nor erect it after it was removed; hunger in the mean time would urge him from his work, and every different want call him a different way. Disease, nay even misfortune would be death: for tho' neither might be mortal, yet either would disable him from living, and reduce him to a state in which he might rather be said to perish than to die.

Thus necessity, like a gravitating power, would soon form our newly-arrived emigrants into society, the reciprocal blessings of which, would supersede, and render the obligations of law and government unnecessary while they remained perfectly just to each other. But, as nothing but heaven is impregnable to vice, it will unavoidably happen, that in proportion

232

as they surmount the first difficulties of emigration, which bound them together in a common cause, they will begin to relax in their duty and attachment to each other; and this remissness will point out the necessity of establishing some form of government to supply the defect of moral virtue.

Some convenient tree will afford them a State-House, under the branches of which, the whole colony may assemble to deliberate on public matters. It is more than probable that their first laws will have the title only of REGULATIONS, and be inforced by no other penalty than public disesteem. In this first parliament every man, by natural right, will have a seat.

But as the colony increases, the public concerns will increase likewise, and the distance at which the members may be separated, will render it too inconvenient for all of them to meet on every occasion as at first, when their number was small, their habitations near, and the public concerns few and trifling. This will point out the convenience of their consenting to leave the legislative part to be managed by a select number chosen from the whole body, who are supposed to have the same concerns at stake which those have who appointed them, and who will act in the same manner as the whole body would act, were they present. If the colony continue increasing, it will become necessary to augment the number of the representatives, and that the interest of every part of the colony may be attended to, it will be found best to divide the whole into convenient parts, each part sending its proper number; and that the *elected* might never form to themselves an interest separate from the *electors*, prudence will point out the necessity of having elections often; because as the *elected* might by that means return and mix again with the general body of the *electors* in a few months, their fidelity to the public will be secured by the prudent reflection of not making a rod for themselves. And as this frequent interchange will establish a common interest with every part of the community, they will mutually and naturally support each other, and on this (not on the unmeaning name of king) depends the *strength of government and the happiness of the governed*.

Here then is the origin and rise of government; namely, a mode rendered necessary by the inability of moral virtue to govern the world; here too is the design and end of government, viz. freedom and security. And however our eyes may be dazzled with show, or our ears deceived by sound; however prejudice may warp our wills, or interest darken our understanding; the simple voice of nature and of reason will say, it is right.

I draw my idea of the form of government from a principle in nature, which no art can overturn, viz. that the more simple any thing is, the less liable it is to be disordered, and the easier repaired when disordered; and with this maxim in view, I offer a few remarks on the so much boasted constitution of England. That it was noble for the dark and slavish times in which it was erected, is granted. When the world was over-run with tyranny, the least remove therefrom was a glorious rescue. But that it is imperfect, subject to convulsions, and incapable of producing what it seems to promise, is easily demonstrated.

Absolute governments, (tho' the disgrace of human nature) have this advantage with them, that they are simple; if the people suffer, they know the head from which their suffering springs, know likewise the remedy and are not bewildered by a variety of causes and cures. But the constitution of England is so exceedingly complex, that the nation may suffer for years together without being able to discover in which part the fault lies; some will say in one and some in another, and every political physician will advise a different medicine.

I know it is difficult to get over local or long standing prejudices, yet if we will suffer ourselves to examine the component parts of the English constitution, we shall find them to be the base remains of two ancient tyrannies, compounded with some new republican materials.

First. The remains of monarchical tyranny in the person of the king.

Secondly. The remains of aristocratical tyranny in the persons of the peers.

Thirdly. The new republican materials in the persons of the commons, on whose virtue depends the freedom of England.

The two first, by being hereditary, are independent of the people; wherefore in a *constitutional sense* they contribute nothing towards the freedom of the state.

To say that the constitution of England is a *union* of three powers reciprocally *checking* each other, is farcical, either the words have no meaning, or they are flat contradictions.

To say that the commons are a check upon the king, presupposes two things:

First. That the king is not to be trusted without being looked after, or in other words, that a thirst for absolute power is the natural disease of monarchy.

Secondly. That the commons, by being appointed for that purpose, are either wiser or more worthy of confidence than the crown.

But as the same constitution which gives the commons a power to check the king by withholding the supplies, gives afterwards the king a power to check the commons by empowering him to reject their other bills; it again supposes that the king is wiser than those whom it has already supposed to be wiser than him. A mere absurdity.

There is something exceedingly ridiculous in the composition of monarchy; it first excludes a man from the means of information, yet empowers him to act in cases where the highest judgment is required. The state of a king shuts him from the world, yet the business of a king requires him to know it thoroughly; wherefore the different parts, by unnaturally opposing and destroying each other, prove the whole character to be absurd and useless.

Some writers have explained the English constitution thus: The king, say they, is one, the people another; the peers are an house in behalf of the king, the commons in behalf of the people. But this hath all the distinctions of an house divided against itself; and though the expressions be pleasantly arranged, yet when examined, they appear idle and ambiguous; and it will always happen, that the nicest construction that words are capable of when applied to the description of something which either cannot exist, or is too incomprehensible to be within the compass of description, will be words of sound only, and tho' they may amuse the ear, they cannot inform the mind, for this explanation includes a previous question, viz. *How came the king by a power which the people are afraid to trust, and always obliged to check* Such a power could not be the gift of a wise people, neither can any power, which *needs checking*, be from God; yet the provision, which the constitution makes, supposes such a power to exist.

But the provision is unequal to the task; the means either cannot or will not accomplish the end, and the whole affair is a *felo de se*; for as the greater weight will always carry up the less, and as all the wheels of a machine are put in motion by one, it only remains to know which power in the constitution has the most weight, for that will govern; and tho' the others, or a part of them, may clog, or, as the phrase is, check the rapidity of its motion, yet so long as they cannot stop it, their endeavours will be ineffectual; the first moving power will at last have its way, and what it wants in speed, is supplied by time.

That the crown is this overbearing part in the English constitution, needs not be mentioned, and that it derives its whole consequence merely from being the giver of places and pensions, is self-evident; wherefore, though we have been wise enough to shut and lock a door against absolute monarchy, we at the same time have been foolish enough to put the crown in possession of the key.

The prejudice of Englishmen in favour of their own government by kings, lords and commons, arises as much or more from national pride than reason. Individuals are undoubtedly safer in England than in some other countries, but the *will* of the king is as much the *law* of the land in Britain as in France, with this difference, that instead of proceeding directly from his mouth, it is handed to the people under the more formidable shape of an act of parliament. For the fate of Charles the First hath only made kings more subtle—not more just.

Wherefore, laying aside all national pride and prejudice in favour of modes and forms, the plain truth is, that *it is wholly owing to the constitution of the people, and not to the constitution of the government*, that the crown is not as oppressive in England as in Turkey.

An inquiry into the *constitutional errors* in the English form of government is at this time highly necessary; for as we are never in a proper condition of doing justice to others, while we continue under the influence of some leading partiality, so neither are we capable of doing it to ourselves while we remain fettered by any obstinate prejudice. And as a man, who is attached to a prostitute, is unfitted to choose or judge of a wife, so any prepossession in favour of a rotten constitution of government will disable us from discerning a good one.

OF MONARCHY AND HEREDITARY SUCCESSION

Mankind being originally equals in the order of creation, the equality could only be destroyed by some subsequent circumstances; the distinction of rich and poor may in a great measure be accounted for, and that without having recourse to the harsh, ill-founding names of oppression and avarice. Oppression is often the *consequence*, but seldom or never the *means* of riches; and though avarice will preserve a man from being necessitously poor, it generally makes him too timorous to become wealthy.

But there is another and greater distinction, for which no truly natural or religious reason can be assigned, and that is, the distinction of men into KINGS and SUBJECTS. Male and female are the distinctions of nature, good and bad the distinction of heaven; but how a race of men came into the world so exalted above the rest, and distinguished like some new species, is worth enquiring into, and whether they are the means of happiness or of misery to mankind.

In the early ages of the world, according to the scripture chronology, there were no kings; the consequence of which was, there were no wars; it is the pride of kings which throws mankind into confusion. Holland without a king hath enjoyed more peace for this last century than any of the monarchical governments in Europe. Antiquity favours the same remark; for the quiet and rural lives of the first patriarchs hath a happy something in them, which vanishes away when we come to the history of Jewish royalty.

[*Paine goes on to discuss various scriptural references to monarchy which bear out its essentially oppressive nature.*]

These portions of scripture are direct and positive. They admit of no equivocal construction. That the Almighty hath here entered his protest against monarchial government, is true, or the scripture is false. And a man hath good reason to believe that there is as much of king-craft, as priest-craft, in withholding the scripture from the public in Popish countries. For monarchy in every instance is the Popery of government.

To the evil of monarchy we have added that of hereditary succession; and as the first is a degradation and lessening of ourselves, so the second, claimed as a matter of right, is an insult and an imposition on posterity. For all men being originally equals, no *one* by *birth* could have a right to set up his own family in perpetual preference to all others for ever, and though himself might deserve *some* decent degree of honours of his contemporaries, yet his descendants might be far too unworthy to inherit them. One of the strongest *natural* proofs of the folly of hereditary right in kings, is, that nature disapproves it, otherwise she would not so frequently turn it into ridicule by giving mankind an *Ass for a Lion.*

Secondly, as no man at first could possess any other public honors than were bestowed upon him, so the givers of those honors could have no right to give away the right of posterity. And though they might say, " We choose you for *our* head," they could not, without manifest injustice to their children, say " that your children, and your children's children shall reign over *ours* for ever." Because such an unwise, unjust, unnatural compact might (perhaps) in the next succession put them under the government of a rogue or a fool. Most wise men, in the private sentiments, have ever treated hereditary right with contempt; yet it is one of those evils which, when once established, is not easily removed; many submit from fear, others from superstition, and the more powerful part shares with the king the plunder of the rest.

This is supposing the present race of kings in the world to have had an honourable origin; whereas it is more than probable, that could we take off the dark covering of antiquity, and trace them to first rise, that we should find the first of them nothing better than the principal ruffians of some restless gang, whose savage manners, or pre-eminence in subtility obtained him the title of chief among plunderers; and who by increasing in power, and extending his depredations, over-awed the quiet and defenceless to purchase their safety by frequent contributions. Yet his electors could have no idea of giving hereditary right to his descendants, because such a perpetual exclusion of themselves was incompatible with the free and unrestrained

principles they professed to live by. Wherefore hereditary succession in the early ages of monarchy could not
take place as a matter of claim, but as something casual
or complimental; but as few or no records were extant
in those days, and traditionary history stuffed with
fables, it was very easy, after the lapse of a few generations, to trump up some superstitious tale, conven-
iently timed, Mahomet like, to cram hereditary rights
down the throats of the vulgar. Perhaps the disorders
which threatened, or seemed to threaten, on the de-
cease of a leader, and the choice of a new one (for elections among ruffians could not be very orderly) induced many at first to favor hereditary pretensions; by
which means it happened, as it hath happened since,
that what at first was submitted to as a convenience,
was afterwards claimed as a right.

England, since the conquest, hath known some few
good monarchs, but groaned beneath a much larger
number of bad ones; yet no man in his senses can say
that their claim under William the Conqueror is a
very honourable one. A French bastard landing with
an armed banditti, and establishing himself king of
England against the consent of the natives, is in plain
terms a very paltry rascally original. It certainly hath
no divinity in it. However, it is needless to spend much
time in exposing the folly of hereditary right; if there
are any so weak as to believe it, let them promiscuously
worship the ass and the lion, and welcome. I shall
neither copy their humility, nor disturb their devotion.

Yet I should be glad to ask how they suppose kings
came at first? The question admits but of three
answers, viz. either by lot, by election, or by usurpation. If the first king was taken by lot, it establishes

241

a precedent for the next, which excludes hereditary succession. Saul was by lot, yet the succession was not hereditary, neither does it appear from that transaction there was any intention it ever should. If the first king of any country was by election, that likewise establishes a precedent for the next; for to say that the *right* of all future generations is taken away, by the act of the first electors, in their choice not only of a king, but of a family of kings for ever, hath no parallel in or out of Scripture but the doctrine of original sin, which supposes the free will of all men lost in Adam; and from such comparison, and it will admit of no other, hereditary succession can derive no glory. For as in Adam all sinned, and as in the first electors all men obeyed; as in the one all mankind were subjected to Satan, and in the other to sovereignty; as our innocence was lost in the first, and our authority in the last; and as both disable us from re-assuming some former state and privilege, it unanswerably follows, that original sin and hereditary succession are parallels. Dishonourable rank! Inglorious connexion! Yet the most subtile sophist cannot produce a juster simile.

As to usurpation, no man will be so hardy as to defend it; and that William the conqueror was an usurper, is a fact not to be contradicted. The plain truth is, that the antiquity of English monarchy will not bear looking into.

But is is not so much the absurdity as the evil of hereditary succession which concerns mankind. Did it ensure a race of good and wise men, it would have the seal of divine authority, but as it opens a door to the *foolish*, the *wicked*, and the *improper*, it hath in it the nature of oppression. Men who look upon themselves

242

born to reign, and others to obey, soon grow insolent; selected from the rest of mankind their minds are early poisoned by importance; and the world they act in differs so materially from the world at large, that they have but little opportunity of knowing its true interests, and when they succeed to the government, are frequently the most ignorant and unfit of any throughout the dominions.

Another evil which attends hereditary succession is, that the throne is subject to be possessed by a minor at any age; all which time the regency, acting under the cover of a king, have every opportunity and inducement to betray their trust. The same national misfortune happens, when a king, worn out with age and infirmity, enters the last stage of human weakness. In both these cases, the public becomes a prey to every miscreant, who can tamper successfully with the follies either of age or infancy.

The most plausible plea which hath ever been offered in favour of hereditary succession, is, that it preserves a nation from civil wars; and were this true, it would be weighty; whereas, it is the most barefaced falsity ever imposed upon mankind. The whole history of England disowns the fact. Thirty kings and two minors have reigned in that distracted kingdom since the conquest, in which time there have been (including the revolution) no less than eight civil wars and nineteen rebellions. Wherefore instead of making for peace, it makes against it, and destroys the very foundation it seems to stand on.

[*After referring to the Wars of the Roses, Paine asks his next question: what is the business of a king? In absolute monarchies he has the whole business of the State to perform. But:*]

The nearer any government approaches to a republic the less business there is for a king. It is somewhat difficult to find a proper name for the government of England. Sir William Meredith calls it a republic; but in its present state it is unworthy of the name, because the corrupt influence of the crown, by having all the places in its disposal, hath so effectually swallowed up the power, and eaten out the virtue of the house of commons (the republican part in the constitution) that the government of England is nearly as monarchical as that of France or Spain. Men fall out with names without understanding them. For it is the republican and not the monarchical part of the constitution of England which Englishmen glory in, viz. the liberty of choosing an house of commons from out of their own body—and it is easy to see that when republican virtue fails, slavery ensues. Why is the constitution of England sickly, but because monarchy hath poisoned the republic, the crown hath engrossed the commons?

In England a king hath little more to do than to make war and give away places; which in plain terms, is to impoverish the nation, and set it together by the ears. A pretty business indeed for a man to be allowed eight hundred thousand sterling a year for, and worshipped into the bargain! Of more worth is one honest man to society, and in the fight of God, than all the crowned ruffians that ever lived.

THOUGHTS ON THE PRESENT STATE OF AMERICAN AFFAIRS.

In the following pages I offer nothing more than
simple facts, plain arguments, and common sense; and
have no other preliminaries to settle with the reader,
than that he will divest himself of prejudice and prepossession, and suffer his reason and his feelings to
determine for themselves; that he will put *on*, or rather
that he will not put *off* the true character of a man, and
generously enlarge his views beyond the present day.

Volumes have been written on the subject of the
struggle between England and America. Men of all
ranks have embarked in the controversy, from different
motives and with various designs; but all have been
ineffectual, and the period of debate is closed. Arms,
as the last resource, decide the contest; the appeal was
the choice of the king, and the continent hath accepted
the challenge.

It hath been reported of the late Mr. Pelham (who
tho' an able minister was not without his faults) that
on his being attacked in the house of commons, on the
score, that his measures were only of a temporary kind,
replied " *they will last my time.*" Should a thought so
fatal and unmanly possess the colonies in the present
contest, the name of ancestors will be remembered by
future generations with detestation.

The sun never shone on a cause of greater worth.
'Tis not the affair of a city, a county, a province, or a
kingdom, but of a continent—of at least one eighth
part of the habitable globe. 'Tis not the concern of a
day, a year, or an age; posterity are virtually involved
in the contest, and will be more or less affected, even
to the end of time, by the proceedings now. Now is
the seed-time of continental union, faith and honor.

The least fracture now will be like a name engraved with the point of a pin on the tender rind of a young oak; the wound will enlarge with the tree, and posterity read it in full grown characters.

By referring the matter from argument to arms, a new era for politicks is struck; a new method of thinking hath arisen. All plans, proposals, &c. prior to the nineteenth of April, i.e. to the commencement of hostilities, are like the almanacks of the last year; which though proper then are superseded and useless now. Whatever was advanced by the advocates on either side of the question then, terminated in one and the same point, viz., a union with Great Britain; the only difference between the parties was the method of effecting it; the one proposing force, the other friendship; but it hath so far happened that the first hath failed, and the second hath withdrawn her influence.

As much hath been said of the advantages of reconciliation, which, like an agreeable dream, hath passed away and left us as we were, it is but right, that we should examine the contrary side of the argument, and enquire into some of the many material injuries which these colonies sustain, and always will sustain, by being connected with, and dependant on Great Britain. To examine that connexion and dependence, on the principles of nature and common sense, to see what we have to trust to, if separated, and what we are to expect, if dependant.

I have heard it asserted by some, that as America hath flourished under her former connexion with Great Britain, that the same connexion is necessary towards her future happiness, and will always have the same effect. Nothing can be more fallacious than this kind of argument. We may as well assert that because

246

a child has thriven upon milk, that it is never to have meat, or that the first twenty years of our lives is to become a precedent for the next twenty. But even this is admitting more than is true, for I answer roundly, that America would have flourished as much, and probably much more, had no European power had any thing to do with her. The commerce by which she hath inriched herself, are the necessaries of life, and will always have a market while eating is the custom of Europe.

But she has protected us, say some. That she has engrossed us is true, and defended the continent at our expence as well as her own, is admitted, and she would have defended Turkey from the same motive, viz. the sake of trade and dominion.

Alas, we have been long led away by ancient prejudices; and made large sacrifices to superstition. We have boasted the protection of Great Britain, without considering that her motive was *interest* not *attachment*; that she did not protect us from our *enemies* on *our account*, but from *her enemies* on *her own account*, from those who had no quarrel with us on any *other account*, and who will always be our enemies on the *same account*. Let Britain waive her pretensions to the continent, or the continent throw off the dependance, and we should be at peace with France and Spain were they at war with Britain. The miseries of Hanover last war ought to warn us against connexions.

It has lately been asserted in parliament, that the colonies have no relation to each other but through the parent country, i.e. that Pennsylvania and the Jerseys, and so on for the rest, are sister colonies by the way of England; this is certainly a very roundabout way of proving enemyship if I may so call it. France and Spain never were, nor perhaps ever will be our enemies as

Americans, but as our being the *subjects of Great Britain*.

But Britain is the parent country, say some. Then the more shame upon her conduct. Even brutes do not devour their young, nor savages make war upon their families; wherefore the assertion, if true, turns to her reproach; but it happens not to be true, or only partly so, and the phrase *parent* or *mother country* hath been jesuitically adopted by the king and his parasites with a low papistical design of gaining an unfair bias on the credulous weakness of our minds. Europe, and not England, is the parent country of America. This new world hath been the asylum for the persecuted lovers of civil and religious liberty from *every part* of Europe. Hither have they fled, not from the tender embraces of the mother, but from the cruelty of the monster; and it is so far true of England, that the same tyranny which drove the first emigrants from home, pursues their descendants still.

In this extensive quarter of the globe, we forget the narrow limits of three hundred and sixty miles (the extent of England) and carry our friendship on a larger scale; we claim brotherhood with every European Christian, and triumph in the generosity of the sentiment.

It is pleasant to observe by what regular gradations we surmount the force of local prejudice, as we enlarge our acquaintance with the world. A man born in any town in England divided into parishes, will naturally associate most with his fellow-parishioners (because their interests in many cases will be common) and distinguish him by the name of *neighbour*; if he meet him but a few miles from home, he drops the narrow idea of a street, and salutes him by the name of *townsman*; if he travel out of the county, and meet him in any other, he forgets the minor divisions of street and town, and calls him *countryman*, i.e., *countyman*; but if in their foreign excursions they should associate in France, or any other part of *Europe*, their local remembrance would be enlarged into that of *Englishmen*. And by a just parity of reasoning, all Europeans meeting in America, or any other quarter of the globe, are *countrymen*. For England, Holland, Germany, or Sweden, when compared with the whole, stand in the same places on the larger scale, which the divisions of street, town, and county do on the smaller ones; distinctions too limited for continental minds. Not one-third of the inhabitants, even of this province, are of English descent. Wherefore I reprobate the phrase of parent or mother country applied to England only as being false, selfish, narrow, and ungenerous.

But admitting, that we were all of English descent, what does it amount to ? Nothing. Britain being now an open enemy, extinguishes every other name and title: And to say that reconciliation is our duty, is truly farcical. The first king of England, of the present line (William the Conqueror) was a Frenchman, and half the Peers of England are descendants from the same country; wherefore, by the same method of reasoning, England ought to be governed by France.

Much hath been said of the united strength of Britain and the colonies, that in conjunction they might bid defiance to the world. But this is mere presumption; the fate of war is uncertain, neither do the expressions mean any thing; for this continent would never suffer itself to be drained of inhabitants, to support the British arms in either Asia, Africa, or Europe.

Besides what have we to do with setting the world at defiance ? Our plan is commerce, and that, well attended to, will secure us the peace and friendship of all Europe; because, it is the interest of all Europe to have America a *free port*. Her trade will always be a protection, and her barrenness of gold and silver secure her from invaders.

I challenge the warmest advocate for reconciliation, to shew, a single advantage that this continent can reap, by being connected with Great Britain. I repeat the challenge, not a single advantage is derived. Our corn will fetch its price in any market in Europe, and our imported goods must be paid for buy them where we will.

But the injuries and disadvantages we sustain by that connexion, are without number; and our duty to mankind at large, as well as to ourselves, instruct us to renounce the alliance: Because, any submission to, or dependance on Great Britain, tends directly to involve this continent in European wars and quarrels; and set us at variance with nations, who would otherwise seek our friendship, and against whom we have neither anger nor complaint. As Europe is our market for trade, we ought to form no partial connexion with any part of it. It is the true interest of America to steer clear of European contentions, which she never can do, while by her dependance on Britain, she is made the make-weight in the scale of British politicks.

Europe is too thickly planted with kingdoms to be long at peace, and whenever a war breaks out between England and any foreign power, the trade of America goes to ruin, *because of her connexion with Britain.* The next war may not turn out like the last, and should it not, the advocates for reconciliation now, will be wishing for separation then, because, neutrality in that case, would be a safer convoy than a man of war.

Every thing that is right or natural pleads for separation. The blood of the slain, the weeping voice of
nature cries, 'TIS TIME TO PART. Even the distance at
which the Almighty hath placed England and America, is a strong and natural proof, that the authority of
the one, over the other, was never the design of Heaven. The time likewise at which the continent was
discovered, adds weight to the argument, and the
manner in which it was peopled increases the force of
it. The reformation was preceded by the discovery of
America, as if the Almighty graciously meant to open
a sanctuary to the persecuted in future years, when
home should afford neither friendship nor safety.

The authority of Great Britain over this continent,
is a form of government, which sooner or later must
have an end: and a serious mind can draw no true
pleasure by looking forward, under the painful and
positive conviction, that what is called " the present
constitution " is merely temporary. As parents, we
can have no joy, knowing that *this government* is not
sufficiently lasting to ensure any thing which we may
bequeath to posterity: And by a plain method of argument, as we are running the next generation into debt,
we ought to do the work of it, otherwise we use them
meanly and pitifully. In order to discover the line of
our duty rightly, we should take our children in our
hand, and fix our station a few years farther into life;
that eminence will present a prospect, which a few
present fears and prejudices conceal from our sight.

Though I would carefully avoid giving unnecessary
offence, yet I am inclined to believe, that all those who
espouse the doctrine of reconciliation, may be included
within the following descriptions. Interested men,
who are not to be trusted; weak men, who *cannot* see;

prejudiced men, who *will not* see; and a certain set of moderate men, who think better of the European world than it deserves; and this last class, by an ill-judged deliberation, will be the cause of more calamities to this continent, than all the other three.

[*Moderation in feeling is due to distance from the struggle; the inhabitants of Boston have felt its full weight, says Paine, giving a rather heightened version of their sufferings from the fire and sword of Britain.*]

It is repugnant to reason, to the universal order of things, to all examples from former ages, to suppose, that this continent can longer remain subject to any external power. The most sanguine in Britain does not think so. The utmost stretch of human wisdom cannot, at this time, compass a plan short of separation, which can promise the continent even a year's security. Reconciliation is *now* a fallacious dream. Nature hath deserted the connexion, and art cannot supply her place.

[*Efforts for peace only harden the obstinacy of the oppressor:*]

Wherefore, since nothing but blows will do, for God's sake, let us come to a final separation, and not leave the next generation to be cutting throats, under the violated unmeaning names of parent and child.

To say, they will never attempt it again is idle and visionary, we thought so at the repeal of the Stamp-Act, yet a year or two undeceived us; as well may we suppose that nations, which have been once defeated, will never renew the quarrel.

As to government matters, it i. not in the power

of Britain to do this continent justice: The business of it will soon be too weighty, and intricate, to be managed with any tolerable degree of convenience, by a power so distant from us, and so very ignorant of us; for if they cannot conquer us, they cannot govern us. To be always running three or four thousand miles with a tale or a petition, waiting four or five months for an answer, which when obtained requires five or six more to explain it in, will in a few years be looked upon as folly and childishness—There was a time when it was proper, and there is a proper time for it to cease.

Small islands, not capable of protecting themselves, are the proper objects for kingdoms to take under their care; but there is something very absurd in supposing a continent to be perpetually governed by an island. In no instance hath nature made the satellite larger than its primary planet, and as England and America, with respect to each other, reverse the common order of nature, it is evident they belong to different systems; England to Europe, America to itself.

I am induced by motives of pride, party, or resentment to espouse the doctrine of separation and independance; I am clearly, positively, and conscientiously persuaded, that it is the true interest of this continent to be so; that everything short of *that* is mere patchwork, that it can afford no lasting felicity,—that it is leaving the sword to our children, and shrinking back at a time, when, a little more, a little farther, would have rendered this continent the glory of the earth.

As Britain hath not manifested the least inclination towards a compromise, we may be assured that no terms can be obtained worthy the acceptance of the continent, or anyways equal to the expence of blood and treasure we have been already put to.

[*Now that the struggle has begun, the outcome must be worthy of the sacrifices made; the removal of the present government is insufficient. Since independence is ultimately inevitable, reconciliation now would be absurd.*]

But admitting that matters were not made up, what would be the event? I answer, the ruin of the continent.—And that for several reasons.

First, The powers of governing still remaining in the hands of the king, he will have a negative over the whole legislation of this continent.

[*This is more baneful in America than in England whose interests are preferred.*]

Secondly, That as even the best terms which we can expect to obtain, can amount to no more than a temporary expedient, or a kind of government by guardianship, which can last no longer than 'til the colonies come of age, so the general face and state of things in the interim, will be unsettled and unpromising. Emigrants of property will not choose to come to a country whose form of government hangs but by a thread, and who is every day tottering on the brink of commotion and disturbance; and numbers of the present inhabitants would lay hold of the interval, to dispose of their effects, and quit the continent.

But the most powerful of all arguments, is, that nothing but independance, i.e. a continental form of government, can keep the peace of the continent and preserve it inviolate from civil wars. I dread the event of a reconciliation with Britain now, as it is more than probable, that it will be followed by a revolt somewhere or other, the consequences of which may be far more fatal than all the malice of Britain.

[*Therefore it is necessary to have permanent arrangements for the colonies to govern themselves. A conference representing them all should be called.*]

The conferring members being met, let their business be to frame a CONTINENTAL CHARTER, or Charter of the United Colonies; (answering to what is called the Magna Charta of England) fixing the number and manner of choosing members of Congress, members of Assembly, with their date of sitting, and drawing the line of business and jurisdiction between them: (Always remembering, that our strength is continental, not provincial:) Securing freedom and property to all men, and above all things, the free exercise of religion, according to the dictates of conscience: with such other matter as is necessary for a charter to contain. Immediately after which the said Conference to dissolve, and the bodies which shall be chosen conformable to the said charter, to be the legislators and governors of this continent for the time being: Whose peace and happiness may God preserve.

Amen.

But where; say some, is the King of America? I'll tell you, Friend, he reigns above, and doth not make havoc of mankind like the royal brute of Britain. Yet that we may not appear to be defective even in earthly honours, let a day be solemnly set apart for proclaiming the charter; let it be brought forth placed on the divine law, the word of God; let a crown be placed thereon, by which the world may know that so far we approve of monarchy, that in America THE LAW IS KING. For as in absolute governments the King is law, so in free countries the law *ought* to be King; and there ought to be no other. But lest any ill use should afterwards arise, let the crown, at the conclusion of the ceremony, be demolished, and scattered among the people whose right it is.

A government of our own is our natural right: And when a man seriously reflects on the precariousness of human affairs, he will become convinced, that it is infinitely wiser and safer, to form a constitution of our own in a cool deliberate manner, while we have it in our power, than to trust such an interesting event to time and chance. If we omit it now, some Massanello[1] may hereafter arise, who laying hold of popular disquietudes, may collect together the desperate and the discontented, and by assuming to themselves the powers of government, may sweep away the liberties of the continent like a deluge. Should the government of America return again into the hands of Britain, the tottering situation of things will be a temptation for some desperate adventurer to try his fortune; and in such a case, what relief can Britain give? Ere she could hear the news, the fatal business might be done; and ourselves suffering like the wretched Britons under the oppression of the Conqueror. Ye that oppose independance now, ye know not what ye do; ye are opening a door to eternal tyranny.

[1]Masaniello (Tommaso Aniello), leader of the Neapolitan revolt against Spain in 1647.]

[*The injuries done us by Britain have made reconciliation impossible:*]

The Almighty hath implanted in us these unextinguishable feelings for good and wise purposes. They are the guardians of his image in our hearts. They distinguish us from the herd of common animals. The social compact would dissolve, and justice be extirpated the earth, or have only a casual existence were we callous to the touches of affection. The robber and the murderer, would often escape unpunished, did not the injuries which our tempers sustain, provoke us into justice.

O ye that love mankind; Ye that dare oppose, not only the tyranny, stand forth; Every spot of the old world is overrun with oppression. Freedom hath been hunted round the globe. Asia and Africa, have long expelled her—Europe regards her like a stranger, and England hath given her warning to depart. O! receive the fugitive, and prepare in time an asylum for mankind.

OF THE PRESENT ABILITY OF AMERICA, WITH SOME MISCELLANEOUS REFLECTIONS

I have never met with a man, either in England or America, who hath not confessed his opinion, that a separation between the countries, would take place one time or other: And there is no instance, in which we have shewn less judgment, than in endeavouring to describe, what we call the ripeness or fitness of the Continent for independance.

As all men allow the measure, and vary only in their opinion of the time, let us, in order to remove mistakes, take a general survey of things, and endeavour, if possible, to find out the *very* time. But we need not go far, the inquiry ceases at once, for the *time hath found us*. The general concurrence, the glorious union of all things prove the fact.

It is not in numbers, but in unity, that our great strength lies; yet our present numbers are sufficient to repel the force of all the world. The Continent hath, at this time, the largest body of armed and disciplined men of any power under Heaven; and is just arrived at that pitch of strength, in which no single colony is able to support itself, and the whole when united, can accomplish the matter; and either more, or less than this, might be fatal in its effects. Our land force is already sufficient; and as to naval affairs, we cannot be insensible, that Britain would never suffer an American man of war to be built, while the continent remained in her hands. Wherefore, we should be no forwarder an hundred years hence in that branch, than we are now; but the truth is, we should be less so, because the timber of the country is every day diminishing, and that, which will remain at last, will be far off and difficult to procure.

[*Paine then expatiates for about five pages on the material advantages of America:*]

In almost every article of defence we abound. Hemp flourishes even to rankness; so that we need not want cordage. Our iron is superior to that of other countries. Our small arms equal to any in the world.

Cannon we can cast at pleasure. Saltpetre and gunpowder we are every day producing. Our knowledge is hourly improving. Resolution is our inherent character, and courage hath never yet forsaken us. Wherefore, what is it that we want? Why is it that we hesitate? From Britain we expect nothing but ruin. If she is once admitted to the government of America again, this Continent will not be worth living in. Jealousies will be always arising; insurrections will be constantly happening; and who will go forth to quell them? Who will venture his life to reduce his own countrymen to a foreign obedience? The difference between Pennsylvania and Connecticut, respecting some unlocated lands, shews the insignificance of a British government; and fully proves, that nothing but Continental authority can regulate Continental matters.

Another reason why the present time is preferable to all others, is, that the fewer our numbers are, the more land there is yet unoccupied, which instead of being lavished by the king on his worthless dependants, may be hereafter applied, not only to the discharge of the present debt, but to the constant support of government. No nation under heaven hath such an advantage as this.

The infant state of the Colonies, as it is called, so far from being against, is an argument in favour of independance. We are sufficiently numerous, and were we more so, we might be less united. It is a matter worthy of observation, that the more a country is peopled, the smaller their armies are. In military numbers, the ancients far exceeded the moderns, and the reason is evident, for trade being the consequence of population, men become too much absorbed thereby to attend to any thing else. Commerce diminishes the spirit both of patriotism and military defence. And history sufficiently informs us, that the bravest achievements were always accomplished in the non-age of a nation. With the increase of commerce, England hath lost its spirit. The city of London, notwithstanding its numbers, submits to continued insults with the patience of a coward. The more men have to lose, the less willing are they to venture. The rich are in general slaves to fear, and submit to courtly power with the trembling duplicity of a spaniel.

Youth is the seed time of good habits, as well in nations as in individuals. It might be difficult, if not impossible, to form the continent into one government half a century hence. The vast variety of interests, occasioned by an increase of trade and population, would create confusion. Colony would be against colony. Each being able might scorn each other's assistance: and while the proud and foolish gloried in their little distinctions, the wise would lament, that the union had not been formed before. Wherefore, the *present time* is the *true time* for establishing it. The intimacy which is contracted in infancy, and the friendship which is formed in misfortune, are of all others the most lasting and unalterable. Our present union is marked with both these characters: we are young and we have been distressed; but our concord hath withstood our troubles, and fixes a memorable aera for posterity to glory in.

The present time likewise is that peculiar time, which never happens to a nation but once, viz. the time of forming itself into a government. Most nations have let slip the opportunity, and by that means have been compelled to receive laws from their conquerors, instead of making laws for themselves. First, they had a king, and then a form of government; whereas, the articles, or charter of government, should be formed first, and men delegated to execute them afterwards: but from the errors of other nations, let us learn wisdom, and lay hold of the present opportunity —*To begin government at the right end.*

When William the Conqueror subdued England, he gave her law at the point of the sword; and until we consent, that the seat of government, in America, be legally and authoritatively occupied, we shall be in danger of having it filled by some fortunate ruffian, who may treat us in the same manner; and then, where will be our freedom? where our property?

As to religion, I hold it to be the indispensible duty of every government, to protect all conscientious professors thereof, and I know of no other business which government hath to do therewith. Let a man throw aside that narrowness of soul, that selfishness of principle, which the niggards of all professions are so unwilling to part with; and he will be at once delivered of his fears on that head. Suspicion is the companion of mean souls, and the bane of all good society. For myself, I fully and conscientiously believe, that it is the will of the Almighty, that there should be a diversity of religious opinions among us: it affords a larger field for our Christian kindness. Were we all of one way of thinking, our religious dispositions would want matter for probation; and on this liberal principle, I look on the various denominations among us, to be like children of the same family, differing only, in what is called, their Christian names.

In page twenty-seven, I threw out a few thoughts on the propriety of a Continental Charter, (for I only presume to offer hints, not plans) and in this place, I take the liberty of re-mentioning the subject, by observing, that a charter is to be understood as a bond of solemn obligation, which the whole enters into, to support the right of every separate part, whether of religion, personal freedom, or property. A firm bargain and a right reckoning make long friends.

In a former page I likewise mentioned the necessity of a large and equal representation; and there is no political matter which more deserves our attention.

[*Paine shows some distrust of the colonies' own assemblies and urges that they should lose the power of electing delegates to the Continental Congress which should be vested in the whole people.*]

To CONCLUDE, however strange it may appear to some, or however unwilling they may be to think so, matters not, but many strong, and striking reasons may be given, to shew, that nothing can settle our affairs so expeditiously as an open, and determined declaration for independence. Some of which are,

First. It is the custom of nations, when any two are at war, for some other powers, not engaged in the quarrel, to step in as mediators, and bring about the preliminaries of a peace: but while America calls herself the subject of Great Britain, no power, however well disposed she may be, can offer her mediation. Wherefore, in our present state we may quarrel on for ever.

Secondly. It is unreasonable to suppose, that France or Spain will give us any kind of assistance, if we mean only to make use of that assistance for the purpose of repairing the breach, and strengthening the connexion between Britain, and America; because, those powers would be sufferers by the consequences.

Thirdly. While we profess ourselves the subjects of Britain, we must, in the eye of foreign nations, be considered as rebels. The precedent is somewhat dangerous to *their peace*, for men to be in arms under the name of subjects; we, on the spot, can solve the paradox: but to unite resistance, and subjection, requires an idea much too refined for common undertaking.

Fourthly. Were a manifesto to be published, and dispatched to foreign courts, setting forth the miseries we have endured, and the peaceable methods we have ineffectually used for redress; declaring at the same time, that not being able, any longer, to live happily or safely under the cruel disposition of the British court, we had been driven to the necessity of breaking off all connexion with her; at the same time assuring all such courts of our peaceable disposition towards them, and of our desire of entering into trade with them: such a memorial would produce more good effects to this Continent, than if a ship were freighted with petitions to Britain.

Under our present denomination of British subjects, we can neither be received nor heard abroad: The custom of all courts is against us, and will be so, until, by an independence, we take rank with other nations.

These proceedings may at first appear strange and difficult; but, like all other steps which we have already passed over, will in a little time become familiar, and agreeable; and, until an independence is declared, the Continent will feel itself like a man who continues putting off some unpleasant business from day to day, yet knows it must be done; hates to set about it, wishes it over, and is continually haunted with the thoughts of its necessity.

APPENDIX

[*This was added to the second edition to meet the " bloody mindedness " of an opposing pamphlet. The following is an extract from it.*]

I shall conclude these remarks, with the following timely and well intended hints. We cught to reflect, that there are three different ways, by which an independancy can hereafter be effected; and that *one* of those *three*, will one day or other, be the fate of America, viz. By the legal voice of the people in Congress; by a military power; or by a mob: It may not always happen that our soldiers are citizens, and the multitude a body of reasonable men; virtue, as I have already remarked, is not hereditary, neither is it perpetual. Should an independency be brought about by the first of those means, we have every opportunity, and every encouragement before us, to form the noblest, purest constitution on the face of the earth. A situation, similar to the present, hath not happened since the days of Noah. The birth-day of a new world is at hand, and a race of men perhaps as numerous as all Europe contains, are to receive their portion of freedom from the event of a few months. The reflexion is awful—and in this point of view, how trifling, how ridiculous, do the little paltry cavillings, of a few weak, or interested men appear, when weighed against the business of a world.

30: RICHARD PRICE. Observations on the Nature of Civil Liberty, and the Justice and Policy on the War with America

February 1776

Richard Price (1723–91) was a protégé of Shelburne's who had achieved considerable celebrity through pamphlets on economic subjects. The *Observations* were a defence of Shelburne's position arguing in favour of the abandonment of all claims to sóvereignty over the Americans except in so far as concerned what Shelburne called " that regulation of trade for the common good of the Empire, which forms our Palladium ". This repudiation of the Whig view as embodied in the Declaratory Act was unacceptable to Burke and his associates among the Rockingham Whigs, and the wide popularity which it received appeared especially alarming at a time when radicalism in England seemed to be advancing to more extreme demands, based, like those of the Americans, upon the idea of natural rights. In the same year, John Cartwright published his pamphlet *Take Your Choice*, the first blow in his campaign for radical Parliamentary reform in England.

A second tract, *Additional Observations*, followed from Price in 1777. The extracts here are from the one-volume reprint of the two together, published in 1778.

[After discussing the nature of Liberty generally, Price uses language particularly apposite to the case of the Americans. . . .]

IN general to be *free* is to be guided by one's own will; and to be guided by the will of another is char-

acteristic of *Servitude*. This is particularly applicable
to Political Liberty. That state, I have observed is
free, which is guided by its own will; or, (which comes
to the same) by the will of an assembly of representatives appointed by itself and accountable to itself. And
every State that is not so governed; or in which a body
of men representing the people make not an essential
part of the Legislature is in *slavery*.

Government, as has been before observed, is, in the
very nature of it, a Trust; and all its powers a Delegation for gaining particular ends. This *trust* may be misapplied and misused. . . . Nothing, therefore, can be
more absurd than the doctrine which some have taught
with respect to the omnipotence of parliaments. They
possess no power beyond the limits of the trust for the
execution of which they were formed. If they contradict this trust, they betray their constituents, and dissolve themselves. All delegated power must be sub-
ordinated and limited. If omnipotence can with any
sense be ascribed to a legislature, it must be lodged
where all legislative authority originates; that is, in the
People. For *their* sakes government is instituted; and
their's is the only real omnipotence.

[*In a subsequent section, Price examines the reasons for
which one country may claim authority over another. . . .*

*After showing that the imperial connection as the advocates
of the sovereignty of the existing British Parliament would*

have it, means a denial of freedom to the inhabitants of the colonies, he goes on . . .]

In a word. An *Empire* is a collection of states or communities united by some common bond or tye. If these states have each of them free constitutions of government, and, with respect to taxation and internal legislation, are independent of the other states, but united by compacts, or alliances, or subjection to a Great *Council*, representing the whole, or to one monarch entrusted with the supreme executive power: In these circumstances, the Empire will be an Empire of Freemen. If on the contrary, like the different provinces subject to that Grand Seignior, none of the states possess any independent legislative authority; but are all subject to an absolute monarch, whose will is their law; then is the Empire, an Empire of Slaves. If one of the states is free, but governs by its will all the other states, then is the Empire, like that of the Romans in the times of the republic, an Empire consisting of one state free and the rest in slavery: Nor does it make any more difference in this case, that the governing state is itself free, than it does, in the case of a kingdom subject to a *despot*, that this despot is himself free. I have before observed, that this only makes the slavery worse. There is, in the one case, a chance, that in the quick succession of despots, a good one will sometimes arise. But bodies of men continue the same; and have generally proved the most unrelenting of all tyrants.

[*After pointing out that injured pride is the cause of much of the opposition to the colonies claims, Price goes on . . .*]

Before I proceed, I beg it may be attended to, that I have chosen to try this question by the general principles of Civil Liberty; and not by the practice of former times or by the *Charters* granted the colonies. The arguments *for* them, drawn from these last topics, appear to me greatly to outweigh the arguments *against* them. But I wish to have this question brought to a higher test and surer issue. The question with all liberal enquirers ought to be, not what jurisdiction over them *Precedents*, *Statutes*, and *Charters* give, but what reason and equity, and the rights of humanity give. This is, in truth, a question which no kingdom has ever before had occasion to agitate. The case of a free country branching itself out in the manner *Britain* has done, and sending to a distant world colonies which have there, from small beginnings, and under free legislatures of their own, increased, and formed a body of powerful states, likely soon to become superior to the parent state. This is a case which is new in the history of mankind; and it is extremely improper to judge it by the rules of any narrow and partial policy; or to consider it on any other ground than the general one of reason and justice. . . .

[*After pointing out that the powers claimed for Parliament would enable it to abrogate the political rights of the colonies altogether and referring to the great area in which the King had already become a despot by the Quebec Act, Price argues that the powers claimed are inconsistent with the fundamental principle of the British constitution* "the right of a people to give and grant their own money", *that a better policy would have strengthened the attachment to Great Britain which the colonies professed in* 1760, *he declares in words very akin to those of Jefferson:*]

Mankind are naturally disposed to continue in subjection to that mode of government, be it what it will, under which they have been born and educated. Nothing rouses them to resistance but gross abuses, or some particular oppressions out of the roads to which they have been used. And he who will examine the history of the world will find there has generally been more reason for complaining that they have been too patient than that they have been turbulent and rebellious. . . . Our governors ever since I can remember have been jealous that the Colonies, some time or other, would throw off their dependence. This jealousy was not founded on any of their acts or declarations . . . (*it*) was however natural; and betrayed a secret opinion, that the subjection in which they were held was more than we could expect them always to endure. In such circumstances all possible care should have been taken to give them no reason for discontent, and to preserve them in subjection, by keeping in that line of conduct to which custom had reconciled them, or at least never deviating from it, except with great caution; and particularly, by avoiding all direct attacks on their property and legislations. . . .

Had we never deserted our old ground: Had we nourished and favoured *America*, with a view to commerce, instead of considering it as a country to be governed: Had we, like a liberal and wise people, rejoiced to see a multitude of free states branched forth from ourselves, all enjoying independent legislatures similar to our own: Had we aimed at binding them to us only by the tyes of affection and interest; and contented ourselves with a moderate power rendered durable by being lenient and friendly, an umpire in their differences, an aid to them in improving their own free governments, and their common bulwark against the assaults of foreign enemies . . . there is nothing so great and happy we might not have expected. . . . The Liberty of *America* might have preserved our Liberty; and under the direction of a patriot king or wise minister, proved the means of restoring to us our almost lost constitution. . . .

4 July 1776

Between January and June, 1776, the leaders in Congress were content to allow the growing movement in favour of independence in most of the colonies to have time to influence the waverers, but they were aware that if the foreign assistance which they required was to be obtained, it could only be on the basis of independence. A resolution in favour of independence was introduced on 7 June but the conservatives from the middle colonies managed to get the question postponed until July 1. On June 11, however, a committee of five was appointed to prepare a Declaration to be used if independence was eventually agreed to. The matter was debated on 1 and 2 July, and the resolution in favour of independence passed on the latter day. On the same date there began a debate on the draft Declaration which was the work of Jefferson, with some assistance from John Adams and Franklin. Congress made certain changes including the alteration of Jefferson's original reference to "inherent and inalienable rights" to "certain unalienable rights". It was passed on 4 July. See *The Papers of Thomas Jefferson*, Vol. I.

THE UNANIMOUS DECLARATION OF THE THIRTEEN UNITED STATES OF AMERICA

WHEN in the Course of human events, it becomes necessary for one people to dissolve the political bands which have connected them with another, and to assume among the powers of the earth, the separate and equal station to which the Laws of Nature and of Nature's God entitle them, a decent respect to the opinions of mankind requires that they should declare the causes which impel them to the separation.

We hold these truths to be self-evident, that all men are created equal, that they are endowed by their Creator with certain unalienable Rights, that among these are Life, Liberty, and the pursuit of Happiness. That to secure these rights, Governments are instituted among Men, deriving their just powers from the consent of the governed, That whenever any Form of Government becomes destructive of these ends, it is the Right of the People to alter or to abolish it, and to institute new Government, laying its foundation on such principles and organizing its powers in such form, as to them shall seem most likely to effect their Safety and Happiness. Prudence, indeed, will dictate that Governments long established should not be changed for light and transient causes; and accordingly all experience hath shown, that mankind are more disposed to suffer, while evils are sufferable, than to right themselves by abolishing the forms to which they are accustomed. But when a long train of abuses and usurpations, pursuing invariably the same Object evinces a design to reduce them under absolute Despotism, it is their right, it is their duty, to throw off such Government, and to provide new Guards for their future security. Such has been the patient sufferance of these Colonies; and such is now the necessity which constrains them to alter their former Systems of Government. The history of the present King of Great Britain is a history of repeated injuries and usurpations, all having in direct object the establishment of an absolute Tyranny over these States. To prove this, let Facts be submitted to a candid world.

He has refused his Assent to Laws, the most wholesome and necessary for the public good.

He has forbidden his Governors to pass Laws of

immediate and pressing importance, unless suspended in their operation till his Assent should be obtained; and when so suspended, he has utterly neglected to attend to them.

He has refused to pass other Laws for the accommodation of large districts of people, unless those people would relinquish the right of Representation in the Legislature, a right inestimable to them and formidable to tyrants only.

He has called together legislative bodies at places unusual, uncomfortable, and distant from the depository of their Public Records, for the sole purpose of fatiguing them into compliance with his measures.

He has dissolved Representative Houses repeatedly, for opposing with manly firmness his invasions on the rights of the people.

He has refused for a long time, after such dissolutions, to cause others to be elected; whereby the Legislative Powers, incapable of Annihilation, have returned to the People at large for their exercise; the State remaining in the mean time exposed to all the dangers of invasion from without, and convulsions within.

He has endeavoured to prevent the population of these States; for that purpose obstructing the Laws of Naturalization of Foreigners; refusing to pass others to encourage their migration hither, and raising the conditions of new Appropriations of Lands.

He has obstructed the Administration of Justice, by refusing his Assent to Laws for establishing Judiciary Powers.

He has made Judges dependent on his Will alone, for the tenure of their offices, and the amount and payment of their salaries.

He has erected a multitude of New Offices, and sent hither swarms of Officers to harass our People, and eat out their substance.

He has kept among us, in times of peace, Standing Armies without the Consent of our legislatures.

He has affected to render the Military independent of and superior to the Civil Power.

He has combined with others to subject us to a jurisdiction foreign to our constitution, and unacknowledged by our laws; giving his Assent to their acts of pretended legislation;

For quartering large bodies of armed troops among us:

For protecting them, by a mock Trial, from Punishment for any Murders which they should commit on the Inhabitants of these States:

For cutting off our Trade with all parts of the world:

For imposing Taxes on us without our Consent:

For depriving us in many cases, of the benefits of Trial by Jury:

For transporting us beyond Seas to be tried for pretended offences:

For abolishing the free System of English Laws in a neighbouring Province, establishing therein an Arbitrary government, and enlarging its Boundaries so as to render it at once an example and fit instrument for introducing the same absolute rule into these Colonies:

For taking away our Charters, abolishing our most valuable Laws, and altering fundamentally the Forms of our Governments:

For suspending our own Legislatures, and declaring themselves invested with Power to legislate for us in all cases whatsoever.

He has abdicated Government here, by declaring us out of his Protection and waging War against us.

He has plundered our seas, ravaged our Coasts, burnt our towns, and destroyed the Lives of our people.

He is at this time transporting large armies of foreign mercenaries to compleat the works of death, desolation and tyranny, already begun with circumstances of Cruelty & perfidy scarcely paralleled in the most barbarous ages, and totally unworthy the Head of a civilized nation.

He has constrained our fellow Citizens taken Captive on the high Seas to bear Arms against their Country, to become the executioners of their friends and Brethren, or to fall themselves by their Hands.

He has excited domestic insurrections amongst us, and had endeavoured to bring on the inhabitants of our frontiers, the merciless Indian Savages, whose known rule of warfare, is an undistinguished destruction of all ages, sexes and conditions.

In every stage of these Oppressions We have Petitioned for Redress in the most humble terms: Our repeated Petitions have been answered only by repeated injury. A Prince, whose character is thus marked by every act which may define a Tyrant, is unfit to be the ruler of a free People.

Nor have We been wanting in attention to our British brethren. We have warned them from time to time of attempts by their legislature to extend an unwarrantable jurisdiction over us. We have reminded them of the circumstances of our emigration and settlement here. We have appealed to their native justice and magnanimity, and we have conjured them by the ties of our common kindred to disavow these usurpations, which, would inevitably interrupt our connections and correspondence. They too have been deaf to the voice of justice and of consanguinity. We must, therefore, acquiesce in the necessity, which denounces our Separation, and hold them, as we hold the rest of mankind, Enemies in War, in Peace Friends.

We, therefore, the Representatives of the united States of America, in General Congress, Assembled, appealing to the Supreme Judge of the world for the rectitude of our intentions, do, in the Name, and by Authority of the good People of these Colonies, solemnly publish and declare, That these United Colonies are, and of Right ought to be Free and Independent States; that they are Absolved from all Allegiance to the British Crown, and that all political connection between them and the State of Great Britain, is and ought to be totally dissolved; and that as Free and Independent States, they have full Power to levy War, conclude Peace, contract Alliances, establish Commerce, and to do all other Acts and Things which Independent States may of right do. And for the support of this Declaration, with a firm reliance on the Protection of Divine Providence, we mutually pledge to each other our Lives, our Fortunes and our sacred Honor.

32: EDMUND BURKE: Letter to the Sheriffs of Bristol

3 April 1777

In November, 1776, the Rockingham Whigs staged a " secession " from Parliament as a final protest against ministerial policy. They were still absent in mid-February when the Government brought forward a motion to suspend the Habeas Corpus Act in cases of high treason. Some Whigs returned to oppose it, but Rockingham and Burke stayed away. Burke's attitude was criticized by his constituents and the *Letter to the Sheriffs of Bristol* was intended to justify his party's proceedings. In doing so, he defended its attitude to the whole American question, and reiterated the doctrine of Parliamentary supremacy. For this he was attacked by the radicals, and in particular by Lord Abingdon, along the lines which Richard Price had made familiar.

The *Letter to the Sheriffs of Bristol* is in *Works*, III, pp. 133 ff.

[After discussing recent events, Burke goes on:]

WHEN any community is subordinately connected with another, the great danger of the connection is the extreme pride and self-complacency of the superiour, which in all matters of controversy will probably decide in its own favour. It is a powerful corrective to such a very rational cause of fear, if the inferiour body can be made to believe, that the party inclination or political views of several in the principle state, will induce them in some degree to counteract this blind and tyrannical partiality. There is no danger that any one acquiring consideration or power in the presiding state should carry this leaning to the inferiour too far. The fault of human nature is not of that sort. Power in whatever hands is rarely guilty of too strict limitations on itself. But one great advantage to the support of authority attends such an amicable and protecting connection, that those who have conferred favours obtain influence; and from the foresight of future events can persuade men, who have received obligations, sometimes to return them. Thus by the mediation of those healing principles, (call them good or evil) troublesome discussions are brought to some sort of adjustment; and every hot controversy is not a civil war.

But, if the colonies (to bring the general matter home to us) could see, that in Great Britain the mass of the people is melted into its government, and that every dispute with the ministry, must of necessity be always a quarrel with the nation; they can stand no longer in the equal and friendly relation of fellow-citizens to the subjects of this kingdom. Humble as this relation may appear to some, when it is once broken, a strong tie is dissolved. Other sort of connections will be sought. For, there are very few in the world, who will not prefer an useful ally to an insolent master.

Such discord has been the effect of the unanimity into which so many have of late been seduced or bullied, or into the appearance of which they have sunk through mere despair. They have been told that their dissent from violent measures is an encouragement to rebellion. Men of great presumption and little knowledge will hold a language which is contradicted by the whole course of history. *General* rebellions and revolts of an whole people never were *encouraged*, now or any time. They are always *provoked*.

EDMUND BURKE

But if this unheard-of doctrine of the encouragement
of rebellion were true, if it were true that an assurance
of the friendship of numbers in this country towards
the colonies, could become an encouragement to them
to break off all connection with it, what is the inference ? Does any body seriously maintain, that
charged with my share of the publick councils, I am
obliged not to resist projects which I think mischievous
lest men who suffer should be encouraged to resist ?
The very tendency of such projects to produce rebellion is one of the chief reasons against them. Shall that
reason not be given ? Is it then a rule, that no man in
this nation shall open his mouth in favour of the
colonies, shall defend their rights, or complain of their
sufferings ? Or when war finally breaks out, no man
shall express his desires of peace ? Has this been the
law of our past, or is it to be the terms of our future
connection ? Even looking no further than ourselves,
can it be true loyalty to any government, or true
patriotism towards any country, to degrade their
solemn councils into servile drawing-rooms, to flatter
their pride and passions, rather than to enlighten their
reason, and to prevent them from being cautioned
against violence lest others should be encouraged to
resistance ? By such acquiescence great kings and
mighty nations have been undone; and if any are at
this day in a perilous situation from rejecting truth,
and listening to flattery, it would rather become them
to reform the errours under which they suffer, than to
reproach those who forewarned them of their danger.

But the rebels looked for assistance from this country. They did so in the beginning of this controversy
most certainly; and they sought it by earnest supplica-
tions to government, which dignity rejected, and by a

suspension of commerce, which the wealth of this nation enabled you to despise. When they found that neither prayers nor menaces had any sort of weight, but that a firm resolution was taken to reduce them to unconditional obedience by a military force, they came to the last extremity. Despairing of us, they trusted in themselves. Not strong enough themselves, they sought succour in France. In proportion as all encouragement here lessened, their distance from this country increased. The encouragement is over; the alienation is complete.

I have always wished, that as the dispute had its apparent origin from things done in parliament, and as the acts passed there had provoked the war, that the foundations of peace should be laid in parliament also. I have been astonished to find, that those whose zeal for the dignity of our body was so hot, as to light up the flames of civil war, should even publickly declare, that these delicate points ought to be wholly left to the crown. Poorly as I may be thought affected to the authority of parliament, I shall never admit that our constitutional rights can ever become a matter of ministerial negotiation.

I am charged with being an American. If warm affection towards those over whom I claim any share of authority, be a crime, I am guilty of this charge. But I do assure you (and they who know me publickly and privately will bear witness to me) that if ever one man lived more zealous than another, for the supremacy of parliament, and the rights of this imperial crown, it was myself. Many others indeed might be more knowing in the extent of the foundation of these rights. I do not pretend to an antiquary, a lawyer, or qualified for the chair of professor in metaphysicks. I never ventured to put your solid interests upon speculative grounds. My having constantly declined to do so has been attributed to my incapacity for such disquisitions; and I am inclined to believe it is partly the cause. I never shall be ashamed to confess, that where I am ignorant I am diffident. I am indeed not very solicitous to clear myself of this imputed incapacity; because men, even less conversant than I am, in this kind of subtleties, and placed in stations, to which I ought not to aspire, have by the mere force of civil discretion, often conducted the affairs of great nations with distinguished felicity and glory.

When I first came into a publick trust, I found your parliament in possession of an unlimited legislative power over the colonies. I could not open the statute book, without seeing the actual exercise of it, more or less, in all cases whatsoever. This possession passed with me for a title. It does so in all human affairs. No man examines into the defects of his title to his paternal estate, or to his established government. Indeed common sense taught me, that a legislative authority, not actually limited by the express terms of its foundation, or by its own subsequent acts, cannot have its powers parcelled out by argumentative distinctions, so as to enable us to say, that here they can, and there they cannot bind. Nobody was so obliging as to produce to me any record of such distinctions, by compact or otherwise, either at the successive formation of the several colonies, or during the existence of any of them. If any gentlemen were able to see, how one power could be given up, (merely on abstract reasoning) without giving up the rest, I can only say, that they saw further than I could; nor did I ever presume to condemn any one for being clear-sighted, when I was blind. I praise their penetration and learning; and hope that their practice has been correspondent to their theory.

I had indeed very earnest wishes to keep the whole body of this authority perfect and entire as I found it, and to keep it so, not for our advantage solely; but principally for the sake of those, on whose account all just authority exists; I mean the people to be governed. For I thought I saw, that many cases might well happen, in which the exercise of every power comprehended in the broadest idea of legislature, might become in its time and circumstances, not a little expedient for the peace and union of the colonies amongst themselves, as well as for their perfect harmony with Great Britain. Thinking So, (perhaps erroneously) but being honestly of that opinion, I was at the same time very sure, that the authority of which I was so jealous, could not under the actual circumstances of our plantations be at all preserved in any of its members, but by the greatest reserve in its application; particularly in those delicate points, in which the feelings of mankind are the most irritable. They who thought otherwise, have found a few more difficulties in their work, than (I hope) they were thoroughly aware of, when they undertook the present business. I must beg leave to observe, that it is not only the invidious branch of taxation that will be resisted, but that no other given part of legislative rights can be exercised, without regard to the general opinion of those who are to be governed. That general opinion is the vehicle, and organ of legislative omnipotence. Without this, it may be a theory to entertain the mind, but it is nothing in the direction of affairs. The completeness of the legislative authority of parliament *over this kingdom* is not questioned; and yet many things indubitably included in the abstract idea of that power, and which carry no absolute injustice in themselves, yet being contrary to the opinions and feelings of the people, can as little be exercised, as if parliament in that case had been possessed of no right at all. I see no abstract reason, which can be given, why the same power which made and repealed the high commission court and the star-chamber, might not revive them again; and these courts, warned by their former fate, might possibly exercise their powers with some degree of justice. But the madness would be as unquestionable, as the competence of that parliament, which should attempt such things. If any thing can be supposed out of the power of human legislature, it is religion; I admit, however, that the established religion of this country has been three or four times altered by act of parliament; and therefore that a statute binds even in that case. But we may very safely affirm, that notwithstanding this apparent omnipotence, it would be now found as impossible for king and parliament to alter the established religion of this country, as it was to King James alone, when he attempted to make such an alteration without a parliament. In effect, to follow, not to force the publick inclination; to give a direction, a form, a technical dress, and a specifick sanction, to the general sense of the community, is the true end of legislature.

[*Burke urges that there are cases of constitutional rights which it is inexpedient to exercise: e.g., the Crown's veto:*]

These were the considerations, gentlemen, which led me early to think, that, in the comprehensive dominion which the Divine Providence had put into our hands, instead of troubling our understandings with speculations concerning the unity of empire, and the identity or distinction of legislative powers, and inflaming our passions with the heat and pride of controversy, it was our duty, in all soberness, to conform our government to the character and circumstances of the several people who composed this mighty and strangely diversified mass. I never was wild enough to conceive, that one method would serve for the whole; that the natives of Hindostan and those of Virginia could be ordered in the same manner; or that the Cutchery court and the grand jury of Salem could be regulated on a similar plan. I was persuaded that government was a practical thing, made for the happiness of mankind, and not to furnish out a spectacle of uniformity, to gratify the schemes of visionary politicians. Our business was to rule, not to wrangle; and it would have been a poor compensation that we had triumphed in a dispute, whilst we lost an empire.

If there be one fact in the world perfectly clear, it is this: " That the disposition of the people of America is wholly averse to any other than a free government; " and this is indication enough to any honest statesman, how he ought to adapt whatever power he finds in his hands to their case. If any ask me what a free government is, I answer that, for any practical purpose, it is what the people think so; and that they, and not I, are the natural, lawful, and competent judges of this matter. If they practically allow me a greater degree of authority over them than is consistent with any correct ideas of perfect freedom, I ought to thank them for so great a trust, and not to endeavour to prove from thence, that they have reasoned amiss, and that having gone so far, by analogy, they must hereafter have no enjoyment but by my pleasure.

If we had seen this done by any others, we should have concluded them far gone in madness. It is melancholy as well as ridiculous, to observe the kind of reasoning with which the publick has been amused, in order to divert our minds from the common sense of our American policy. There are people, who have split and anatomised the doctrine of free government, as if it were an abstract question concerning metaphysical liberty and necessity; and not a matter of moral prudence and natural feeling. They have disputed, whether liberty be a positive or a negative idea; whether it does not consist in being governed by laws; without considering what are the laws, or who are the makers; whether man has any rights by nature; and whether all the property he enjoys, be not the alms of his government, and his life itself their favour and indulgence. Others corrupting religion, as these have perverted philosophy, contend, that Christians are redeemed into captivity; and the blood of the Saviour of mankind has been shed to make them the slaves of a few proud and insolent sinners. These shocking extremes, provoking to extremes of another kind, speculations are let loose as destructive to all authority, as the former are to all freedom; and every government is called tyranny and usurpation which is not formed on their fancies. In this manner the stirrers-up of this contention, not satisfied with distracting our dependencies and filling them with blood and slaughter, are corrupting our understandings: they are endeavouring to tear up, along with practical liberty, all the foundations of human society, all equity and justice, religion and order.

Civil freedom, gentlemen, is not, as many have endeavoured to persuade you, a thing that lies hid in the depth of abstruse science. It is a blessing and a benefit, not an abstract speculation; and all the just reasoning that can be upon it, is of so coarse a texture, as perfectly to suit the ordinary capacities of those who are to enjoy, and of those who are to defend it. Far from any resemblance to those propositions in geometry and metaphysicks, which admit no medium, but must be true or false in all their latitude; social and civil freedom, like all other things in common life, are variously mixed and modified, enjoyed in very different degrees, and shaped into an infinite diversity of forms, according to the temper and circumstances of every community. The *extreme* of liberty (which is its abstract perfection, but its real fault) obtains no where, nor ought to obtain any where. Because extremes, as we all know, in every point which relates either to our duties or satisfactions in life, are destructive both to virtue and enjoyment. Liberty too must be limited in order to be possessed. The degree of restraint it is impossible in any case to settle precisely. But it ought to be the constant aim of every wise publick counsel, to find out by cautious experiments, and rational, cool endeavours, with how little, not how much of this restraint, the community can subsist. For liberty is a good to be improved, and not an evil to be lessened. It is not only a private blessing of the first order, but the vital spring and energy of the state itself, which has just so much life and vigour as there is liberty in it. But whether liberty be advantageous or not, (for I know it is a fashion to decry the very principle) none will dispute that peace is a blessing; and peace must in the course of human affairs, be frequently bought by some indulgence and toleration at least to liberty. For as the sabbath, (though of divine institution) was made for man, not man for the sabbath, government, which can claim no higher origin or authority, in its exercise at least, ought to conform to the exigencies of the time, and the temper and character of the people, with whom it is concerned; and not always to attempt violently to bend the people to their theories of subjection. The bulk of mankind on their part are not excessively curious concerning any theories, whilst they are really happy; and one sure symptom of an ill-conducted state, is the propensity of the people to resort to them.

But when subjects, by a long course of such ill conduct, are once thoroughly inflamed, and the state itself violently distempered, the people must have some satisfaction to their feelings, more solid than a sophistical speculation on law and government. Such was our situation; and such a satisfaction was necessary to prevent recourse to arms; it was necessary towards laying them down; it will be necessary to prevent the taking them up again and again. Of what nature this satisfaction ought to be, I wish it had been the disposition of parliament seriously to consider. It was certainly a deliberation that called for the exertion of all their wisdom.

I am, and ever have been deeply sensible, of the difficulty of reconciling the strong presiding power, that is so useful towards the conservation of a vast, disconnected, infinitely diversified empire, with that liberty and safety of the provinces, which they must enjoy, (in opinion and practice at least) or they will not be provinces at all. I know, and have long felt the difficulty of reconciling the unwieldy haughtiness of a great ruling nation, habituated to command, pampered by enormous wealth, and confident from a long course of prosperity and victory, to the high spirit of free dependencies, animated with the first glow and activity of juvenile heat, and assuming to themselves as their birthright, some part of that very pride which oppresses them. They who perceive no difficulty in reconciling these tempers, (which however to make peace must some way or other be reconciled) are much above my capacity, or much below the magnitude of the business. Of one thing I am perfectly clear, that it is not by deciding the suit, but by compromising the difference, that peace can be restored or kept. They who would put an end to such quarrels, by declaring roundly in favour of the whole demands of either party, have mistaken, in my humble opinion, the office of a mediator.

[*Burke then reviews the course of the controversy and his own conduct toward it and concludes:*]

There never, gentlemen, was a period in which the stedfastness of some men has been put to so sore a trial. It is not very difficult for well-formed minds to abandon their interest; but the separation of fame and virtue is an harsh divorce. Liberty is in danger of being made unpopular to Englishmen. Contending for an imaginary power, we begin to acquire the spirit of domination, and to lose the relish of honest equality. The principles of our forefathers become suspected to us, because we see them animating the present opposition of our children. The faults which grow out of the luxuriance of freedom, appear much more shocking to us, than the base vices which are generated from the rankness of servitude. Accordingly the least resistance to power appears more inexcusable in our eyes than the greatest abuses of authority. All dread of a standing military force is looked upon as a superstitious panick. All shame of calling in foreigners and savages in a civil contest is worn off. We grow indifferent to the consequences inevitable to ourselves from the plan of ruling half the empire by a mercenary sword. We are taught to believe that a desire of domineering over our countrymen is love to our country; that those who hate civil war abet rebellion, and that the amiable and conciliatory virtues of lenity, moderation, and tenderness to the privileges of those who depend on this kingdom are a sort of treason to the state.

It is impossible that we should remain long in a situation, which breeds such notions and dispositions, without some great alteration in the national character. Those ingenuous and feeling minds who are so fortified against all other things, and so unarmed to whatever approaches in the shape of disgrace, finding these principles, which they considered as sure means of honour, to be grown into disrepute, will retire disheartened and disgusted. Those of a more robust make, the bold, able, ambitious men, who pay some of their court to power through the people, and substitute the voice of transient opinion in the place of true glory, will give into the general mode; and those superiour understandings which ought to correct vulgar prejudice, will confirm and aggravate its errours. Many things have been long operating towards a gradual change in our principles. But this American war has done more in a very few years than all the other causes could have effected in a century. It is therefore not on its own separate account, but because of its attendant circumstances, that I consider its continuance, or its ending in any way but that of an honourable and liberal accommodation, as the greatest evils which can befal us. For that reason I have troubled you with this long letter. For that reason I intreat you again and again, neither to be persuaded, shamed, or frightened out of the principles that have hitherto led so many of you to abhor the war, its cause, and its consequences. Let us not be amongst the first who renounce the maxims of our forefathers.

33: EARL OF CHATHAM. Speech in the House of Lords

20 November 1777

This speech was made by Chatham in the debate on the address at the opening of the new Parliamentary session. The military news was unfavourable although the surrender of Burgoyne at Saratoga in the previous month was not yet known in London. The text from which this extract is taken is that in *Chatham Anecdotes*, II, pp. 298–315.

MY Lords, no man wishes for the due dependence of America on this country more than I do. To preserve it, and not confirm that state of independence into which *your measures* hitherto have *driven* them, is the object which we ought to unite in attaining. The Americans, contending for their rights against the arbitrary exactions, I love and admire; it is the struggle of free and virtuous patriots: but contending for independency and total disconnection from England, as an Englishman, I cannot wish them success: for, in a due constitiona! dependency, including the ancient supremacy of this country in regulating their commerce and navigation, consists the mutual happiness and prosperity both of England and America. She derived assistance and protection from us; and we reaped from her the most important advantages:—She was, indeed, the fountain of our wealth, the nerve of our strength, the nursery and basis of our naval power. It is our duty, therefore, my Lords, if we wish to save our country, most seriously to endeavour the recovery of these most beneficial subjects: and in this perilous crisis, perhaps the present moment may be the only one in which we can hope for success: for in their negotiations with France, they have, or think they have, reason to complain: though it be notorious that they have received from that power important supplies and assistance of various kinds, yet it is certain they expected it in a more decisive and immediate degree. America is in ill humour with France, on some points that have not entirely answered her expectations: let us wisely take advantage of every possible moment of reconciliation. Besides, the natural disposition of America herself still leans towards England; to the old habits of connection and mutual interest that united both countries. This *was* the established sentiment of all the Continent; and still, my Lords, in the great and principal part, the sound part of America, this wise and affectionate disposition prevails; and there is a very considerable part of America yet sound—the middle and the southern provinces; some parts may be factious and blind to their true interests; but if we express a wise and benevolent disposition to communicate with them those immutable rights of nature, and those constitutional liberties, to which they are equally entitled with ourselves, by a conduct so just and humane, we shall confirm the favourable and conciliate the adverse. I say, my Lords, the rights and liberties to which they are equally entitled, with ourselves, but no more. I would participate to them every enjoyment and freedom which the colonizing subjects of a free state can possess, or wish to possess; and I do not see why they should not enjoy every fundamental right in their property, and every original substantial liberty, which Devonshire or Surrey, or the county I live in, or any other county in England, can claim; reserving always, as the sacred right of the mother country, the due constitutional dependency of the Colonies. The inherent supremacy of the state in regulating and protecting the navigation and commerce of all her subjects, is necessary for the mutual benefit and preservation of every part, to constitute and preserve the prosperous arrangement of the whole empire.

The sound parts of America, of which I have spoken, must be sensible of these great truths, and of their real interests. America is not in that state of desperate and contemptible rebellion, which this country has been deluded to believe. It is not a wild and lawless banditti, who having nothing to lose, might hope to snatch something from public convulsions; many of their leaders and great men have a great stake in this great contest:—the gentleman who conducts their armies, I am told, has an estate of four or five thousand pounds a year: and when I consider these things, I cannot but lament the inconsiderate violence of our penal acts, our declarations of treason and rebellion, with all the fatal effects of attainder and confiscation.

34: EARL OF CHATHAM. Speech in the House of Lords

7 April 1778

The news of Saratoga reached London at the beginning of December, and on the tenth, just before the Christmas adjourn ment, North announced that he would bring in a project of conciliation when the House met again. Speaking on the following day, Chatham again declared his belief that America could not be reduced by force and pointed to the probability of France entering the contest. On the other hand, he argued as strongly that the union of Britain and America should be maintained for their common benefit and that prompt measures of conciliation could still secure this result. (This speech is given in *Chatham Correspondence*, IV, pp. 478–83.)

North's bill of conciliation moved on 17 February " virtually conceded all that America had long been asking ". (Lecky, *History of England in the Eighteenth Century*, New Ed., 1892, IV, p. 449.) Not only were the main acts objected to, repealed, but Parliament formally undertook to impose no taxes on the colonies for the sake of revenue and to spend those imposed as a part of the regulation of trade, in the colonies where they were raised. A peace commission was to be sent at once to treat along these lines. But the prospects of success were very slender since the alliance between the United States and France had been signed on 6 February. In March the treaty was communicated to the British Government and Great Britain and France were at war. In this crisis the opposition to North was divided; the Rockingham party advised the immediate recognition of American independence, while many other leading political figures (like North himself) advocated a ministry under Chatham who was strongly opposed to the idea of independence, as most likely to secure a reconciliation if this were still possible and best fitted to lead the country in the war, if it were not. Chatham's last speech was thus made in opposition to a motion by the Rockingham Whig, the Duke of Richmond, calling for the immediate withdrawal of British forces from America.

The extracts are taken from the text given in *Chatham Anecdotes*, II, pp. 350 ff.

HE began by lamenting that his bodily infirmities had so long, and especially at so important a crisis, prevented his attendance on the duties of Parliament. He declared that he had made an effort almost beyond the powers of his constitution to come down to the House on this day (perhaps the last time he should ever be able to enter its walls) to express the indignation he felt at an idea which he understood was gone forth, of yielding up the sovereignty of America!

My Lords, continued he, I rejoice that the grave has not closed upon me; that I am still alive to lift up my voice against the dismemberment of this ancient and most noble monarchy! Pressed down as I am by the hand of infirmity, I am little able to assist my country in this most perilous conjuncture; but, my Lords, while I have sense and memory, I will never consent to deprive the royal offspring of the House of Brunswick, the heirs of the Princess Sophia, of their fairest inheritance. Where is the man that will dare to advise such a measure? My Lords, his Majesty succeeded to an empire as great in extent as its reputation was unsullied. Shall we tarnish the lustre of this nation by an ignominious surrender of its rights and fairest possessions? Shall this great kingdom, that has survived whole and entire the Danish depredations, the Scottish inroads, and the Norman conquest; that has stood the threatened invasion of the Spanish armada, now fall

295

prostrate before the House of Bourbon? Surely, my Lords, this nation is no longer what it was! Shall a people, that seventeen years ago was the terror of the world, now stoop so low as to tell its ancient inveterate enemy, take all we have, only give us peace? It is impossible!

35: JOSIAH TUCKER. Four Letters on Important National Subjects

1783

As has been seen in the introduction, Josiah Tucker (1713–99) held a view which set him apart from nearly all his contemporaries. He had advocated American independence as a part of a general conviction of the unprofitability of Empire; and, in spite of his fierce hostility to democracy and to the whole political philosophy of natural rights, there is a link between his thought on this subject and that of some nineteenth century radicals. The *Four Letters* were addressed to Lord Shelburne, then Prime Minister, under whom the preliminary articles of peace were signed in November 1782, and whose connection with the " Lockian fraternity ", Tucker condemned.

As to *America,* and the Resistance which this honourable *Fraternity* have so strenuously excited throughout that Country, I am as glad of the *general Event,* though *not of the particular Circumstances attending it,* as the most flaming Republicans.—I say, I am glad, that *America* had declared herself independent of us, though for Reasons very opposite to theirs. *America,* I have proved beyond the Possibility of a Confutation, ever was a Millstone hanging about the Neck of this Country, to weigh it down: And as we ourselves had not the Wisdom to cut the Rope, and to let the Burthen fall off, the Americans have kindly done it for us. The only Thing to be lamented, which never can be lamented enough, was, that as soon as this ungrateful People had refused to pass a public Vote for contributing *any Thing*, or in *any Mode*, towards the general Expence of the Empire, but on the contrary, had entered into Combinations to forbid the Importation of our Manufactures, we had not taken them at their Word, and totally cast them off. Had we done this, it would have been happy for us; nay, it would have been happy for *them* too: Because this would have saved both them and us that Blood and Treasure, which have been so profusely lavished for many Years, without answering any one End whatever:—Unless indeed the raising of a few *American* Upstarts to be *American* Princes,—the enriching of a few Cormorants, and Contractors here in Britain,—and the placing of some of the more distinguished Members of the aforementioned patriotic Fraternity on ministerial Thrones can be thought to have been Objects sufficient to compensate such portentous Losses. As to the Threats and Menaces of the *Americans*, that they would have no more commercial intercourse with us, your Lordship knows, I was always of the Opinion (and the event has proved the Truth of it) that they were vain and idle words. Indeed, common sense might have informed us, that Trade depends on Interest alone, and on no other Connection or Obligation. The Fact is, that the Colonies never did trade with the Mother-Country, with an intent merely to serve us, and not themselves: Nor was it in our Power, even when we were strongest, and they in the weakest Stage of their Existence (as appears from their whole History) to compel them to trade with us to their own Loss. Mutual Interest was the only Tie between America and Great Britain at all Times and Seasons, And this Principle will hold good, I will be bold to say, till the End of Time; whether they are dependent on, or independent of us. As to the Planting of Colonies for the sake of a monopolizing, or exclusive Trade, it is the arrantest Cheat and Self-Deception, which poor short-sighted Mortals ever put upon themselves;—at least in a *national* View:—For I am not here considering, and never will consider the Interests of Individuals, when they are sacrificing the Public Good to their own private Emolument; no, not even though they were popular Orators, or republican Patriots.

BOOKS FOR FURTHER READING

R. G. Adams: *Political Ideas of the American Revolution* (Durham, N.C., 1922.)

C. H. McIlwain: *The American Revolution. A Constitutional Interpretation.* (New York, 1923.)

R. L. Schuyler: *Parliament and the British Empire.* (New York, 1929.)

C. H. Van Tyne: *The Causes of the War of Independence.* (London, 1922.)

John C. Miller: *Origins of the American Revolution.* (London, 1945.)

L. B. Namier: *The Structure of Politics at the Accession of George III.* (London, 2 vols., 1929.)

L. B. Namier: *England in the Age of the American Revolution.* (London, 1930.)

G. H. Gutteridge: *English Whiggism and the American Revolution.* (Berkeley, Cal., 1942.)

D. M. Clarke: *British Opinion and the American Revolution.* (Cambridge, Mass., 1930.)

M. C. Tyler: *The Literary History of the American Revolution.* (2 vols., New York, 1897.)

C. F. Mullett: *Fundamental Law and the American Revolution. 1760–1776.* (New York, 1933.)

Alexander Hamilton, James Madison and John Jay: *The Federalist.* Ed. by Max Beloff. (Oxford, 1948.)

Carl Becker: *The Declaration of Independence.* (New York, 1922.)

Max Beloff: *Thomas Jefferson and American Democracy.* (London, 1948.)

R. Coupland: *The American Revolution and the British Empire.* (Oxford, 1930.)

V. Parrington: *Main Currents in American Thought.* Vol. I. The Colonial Mind. (New York, 1927.)

C. H. McILWAIN: *Constitutionalism, Ancient and Modern.* (Ithaca, N.Y., 1940.)

C. G. HAINES: *The Revival of Natural Law Concepts.* (Cambridge, Mass., 1930.)

B. F. WRIGHT: *American Interpretations of Natural Law.* (Cambridge, Mass., 1931.)

SIR LESLIE STEPHEN: *History of English Thought in the Eighteenth Century.* (London, 1881.)

C. RITCHESON: *British Politics and the American Revolution.* (Norman, Oklahoma, 1954).

V. T. HARLOW: *The Founding of the Second British Empire,* 1763–1793. (London, 1952.)

INDEX OF PERSONS

303